OUT OF ~~AFRICA~~ EASTERHOUSE

OUT OF ~~AFRICA~~ EASTERHOUSE

THE BOBBY WILLIAMSON STORY

With Lorne Gardner

pitch

First published by Pitch Publishing, 2026
1

Pitch Publishing
9 Donnington Park, 85 Birdham Road
Chichester, West Sussex, PO20 7AJ
www.pitchpublishing.co.uk
info@pitchpublishing.co.uk

Set in Adobe Caslon Pro

Typeset by Pitch Publishing

Cover design by Olner Design

Printed in Great Britain by TJ Books, Padstow, Cornwall

The authorised representative in the EEA is Easy Access System Europe OÜ, Mustamäe tee 50, 10621 Tallinn, Estonia gpsr.requests@easproject.com

A CIP catalogue record for this book is available from the British Library

ISBN 978-1-83680-473-4

Papers used by Pitch Publishing are from well-managed forests and other responsible sources

MIX
Paper | Supporting responsible forestry
FSC® C013056

To all the family and friends who have helped me on my journey – I thank you. And to all the friends who are mentioned in this book but have passed on – you are always in my thoughts.

CONTENTS

FOREWORD

WHEN I joined Clydebank in 1980, Bobby Williamson was just a young lad coming through the reserves and it was about a year before he trained with the first team. We knew he was this aggressive boy but he actually started pushing the older, more experienced and established players about. He was always getting stuck in among them and squaring up to them. As a young boy coming in, you would have thought he would, at first, have been a bit respectful and listened to what people were saying. But Bobby just wasn't like that.

I'd say to him: 'Bobby, watch what you're doing. I know you want to make an impression but you don't want to get on the wrong side of people.'

He would tell me that was just the way he was – an aggressive type of player who would fly into tackles.

'That's great,' I would say, 'but keep it for the game on a Saturday.'

It's fair to say he made quite an impression, although when he broke into the team it wasn't as a striker. He was a right-back with an incredible energy about him. He was a workhorse with such effort and endeavour.

He trained like he played but it wasn't until he became a striker that we realised just how sharp he was in and around the box. You would never have thought he would be a striker when he first came in but he had this wee injection of pace and started to read the game well. When he partnered Tommy Coyne, they complemented each other brilliantly. Tommy was wanting the ball into feet, wee turns and balls slipped through. Bobby was the one who would get in behind. It was great because we had two of the best strikers in the league.

Bobby just became a goalscoring machine. It was brilliant for us in the middle of the park; you knew they would get in behind and you would always have options up front. He and Tam scored 50-odd goals one season and I think I was involved in about 40 of them!

We were building a really good team at Kilbowie, having just missed out on promotion, and at the end of one season my contract was up. The Bankies chairman, Jack Steedman, told me to sign because we would be keeping the team together and we would get promotion to the top flight. So, I signed, then Tam went to Dundee United and Bobby was sold to Rangers! I was gutted and although we eventually did get promotion with Clydebank, I often wondered how good we would have been and how much better we would have done with Bobby and Tam still in the team.

Bobby got the move to Ibrox because he was a winner – maybe that is the reason we became such good pals. Yet it was a volatile relationship, with plenty of shouting at each other on the park.

'Can you not give me a pass?' I'd say and he'd fire back: 'Can you not win a tackle?'

I remember we were on a good run at Clydebank and were playing Hearts at Kilbowie. I went into a tackle with Andy Watson – there was no malice from either of us – but I knew

I had done something to my groin. I was hobbling and told Bobby I'd have to go off.

'What do you mean go off?' Bobby shouted. 'Just run about, you'll be fine.'

I told him there was no way I could play on. I was done. They took me off and I was out for ten weeks. The muscle had torn off the bone at my groin. Bobby said he'd have played through it!

But we were great pals and would always go out after games – even when he was at Rangers and he would insist on going out in his Rangers jacket and tie. We would go into a pub called The Ranch in Hamilton where my dad drank. We used to sit and play dominoes with my dad and all his pals – a game called Knock-Out, where if you're over ten you're out. Bobby couldn't work out why he was always first out after getting landed with the double six. Everybody else knew there was a wee mark on it! But he'd always be wondering why he was first man out. I told him that every guy around the table was a Celtic fan.

He made a career as a very good, reliable goalscorer – which he proved again at West Brom and then at Rotherham, where he is still regarded as a hero. And he did it once more when he came back to Scotland with Kilmarnock.

I was finishing off my career, having just left Arbroath, and took a call from junior club Shettleston, who offered me another year playing. I was 41 but still felt good, so I decided to give it another go. I'd only played three or four games when Bobby phoned me to say that Alex Totten had been sacked at Killie and he had been put in temporary charge. He wanted me to join him and that if we did well, he was confident we'd get the job full-time. The two of us had spoken about it in our playing days, that if one went into management, he'd give the other the chance to join them.

I told Bobby I couldn't do it, as I had signed for Shettleston.

'What!' he shouted. 'You're 41! How much longer do you think you can keep playing?'

And that was that. We were in management, with Jim Clark completing the trio. It was wonderful. I loved it at Kilmarnock. The board were so supportive and the players were brilliant. Clarky was a great – so laid-back and the middle man in the arrangement. Bobby and I would be arguing about this and that and Clarky would be keeping the peace.

'Honestly,' he would say. 'You're like an old married couple! Every day you're the best of pals, every day you fall out.'

But Bobby always stuck up for his coaching staff if anyone had a wee go back. Not that they did, because we had a really good squad of players at Killie. Mark Reilly, Gary Holt, Ally Mitchell, all great guys to have in your squad. There was Gordon Marshall, Gus MacPherson, Kevin McGowne, Jim Lauchlan. Some great pros.

And for Bobby, it was never about him. It was about the players, his coaches and the staff. When it came to contracts, he always wanted us sorted out first. Even the physio, the groundsman, everybody. He made sure they were all looked after.

We went from going in on a temporary basis with the team bottom of the league to keeping them up, winning the Scottish Cup and getting a permanent deal. That was down to Bobby. He knew how to get a team together. He knew what he wanted – bringing in the likes of Christophe Cocard, Ally McCoist and Ian Durrant. We wanted to build after we won the Scottish Cup and Bobby did that. We were in Europe five years in a row.

He had a great spirit in the dressing room. While other managers would distance themselves from their players, he would socialise with them. Don't get me wrong, he knew when he had to be tough on them and had to discipline them – he wouldn't shirk away from it. But they all loved his honesty. He would defend players and stick up for them and be tough when he had to be.

We had seven wonderful years at Killie, winning the cup, taking them to the League Cup Final in 2001 and into Europe year after year. But after a defeat away to Viking Stavanger, we got pelters. What many didn't appreciate was that the Norwegian league was good, with strong teams. The fans were angry in the airport afterwards and Bobby, who would never walk away from anything, went to them and said what he had to say.

Some weeks afterwards, Bobby phoned me to say he was going to Easter Road to look at the set-up. I didn't really know why but it was an international weekend, so we all trooped through. I couldn't work out why they were bringing someone through from Killie but Alex McLeish had recommended him at first and although they gave the job to Franck Sauzee it hadn't worked out for him.

Jim Clark and I were, by now, still wondering what was going on and Clarky said to me that he was not wanting to leave Rugby Park and go to Easter Road. Bobby got separated from us and went into a room with his agent and others. When he came out, he said: 'Cabey, that's me … I've resigned from Kilmarnock.'

So, this was what it was all about. He said there was no way we were going back, we had done everything we could at Killie and he had a point. After the Stavanger incident, it was clear the fans weren't happy but the board were still supportive of us.

He said that he had resigned and that it hadn't gone down well with Killie chairman Bill Costley. Clarky was a real Killie man and he was not for resigning. I didn't want to do it either. Killie had done nothing wrong and I was enjoying it. I felt we could be rejuvenated and we could go again with the same squad we had.

But Bobby admitted he didn't want to come in to Easter Road on the Monday by himself. His agent said to me: 'Who's your loyalty with? Bobby or Kilmarnock?'

I said that Bobby was my pal and my manager but that Killie had done nothing at all to make me want away from the place. But I resigned as well. I shouldn't have, because I just didn't have a good feeling.

Clarky went back to Rugby Park, as he was determined they would not be left without a manager – but he joined us within a few weeks when Jim Jefferies came into Killie with Billy Brown.

I can honestly say, it wasn't the best move. They had a good squad of players but we didn't realise the obstacles Rod Petrie would put in front of Bobby. After a week, we were told we couldn't play this player or that player and we needed to get rid of that one or this one. We sold Ulises de la Cruz for £2m and we were in Finland and took a call to say we couldn't play Ulrik Laursen because he was being sold to Celtic for £900,000. We couldn't play guys like John O'Neil because they were on big appearance money. Players like Freddy Arpinon and Paco Luna – we were told the club couldn't afford these guys but they had contracts, so the club would need to pay them up if they wanted them to go.

Then we were told it was up to us to get rid of them! Bobby was arguing over how could it be up to us if it had been the club who gave them the contracts? I just didn't know how we were going to manage it. We thought we had come into a bigger club but we hadn't. We knew they had been struggling in the league – and that was why they had come in to get Bobby, because he had been working so well with more or less no budget. Everything we were having to do was completely different to what we had been dealing with at Kilmarnock. We went in, in January or February, and they were cutting contracts by the summer. It wasn't right but Bobby fought our case and got it sorted.

We still had to get rid of players but the club had real talent coming through – boys like Scott Brown, who they didn't fancy. He was coming to the end of his YTS deal and Bobby brought him into training. He was just so lively, like a young Bobby coming in and squaring up to guys on the training ground. We loved him, he was full of life, so Bobby recommended giving him a two-year deal. The club wondered if he was worth it and Bobby told them: 'He'll be in my first team in the next three or four weeks.' And he was.

Bobby brought in Scott with Steven Whittaker, Derek Riordan, Garry O'Connor, Tam McManus, Steven Fletcher and Kevin Thomson. He'd done it at Killie with boys like Peter Canero, Paul Di Giacomo, Garry Hay, Gary McCutcheon, Mark Roberts, David Bagan and Alex Burke.

That's what always annoys me. Bobby has never got the credit for bringing in these players. It's brilliant the players he brought through and the players he gave a chance to. He knew when he had to change it and he wasn't frightened to change it. I think people should look at just how many players Bobby brought through in his career. People always say young boys aren't getting the chance but Bobby was brave enough to do it.

Maybe it was two different scenarios. At Kilmarnock, we had a good team and it was easier to bring the boys in and get them into the team and blood them that way. Whereas, at Hibs, we were struggling and *had* to bring them in – but it was still brave for Bobby to do that. Look where their careers went.

He took that Hibs team to the League Cup Final, which was some achievement. We beat Celtic in the quarter-final and Rangers in the semi-final. And they made us favourites for the final! But we got beat 2-0 by Livingston and the writing was on the wall. We went back to the party and it was flat. I knew we were out the door.

As much as I love Hibs as a club and the fans, we came into a situation which we had never seen and it was a disaster for us leaving Killie for Easter Road. Maybe Bobby couldn't turn down the job at Hibs after he had been recommended for it.

In a way, it was a relief when we left. But we didn't know we were going to Plymouth!

We were aware Bobby was away somewhere – it was ahead of our last game of the season against Livingston. We knew our contracts weren't being renewed and the Hibs boys were all asking us after training: 'Where's the gaffer? Where's the gaffer?'

Genuinely, we didn't know anything – until the Sky Sports ticker tape on the TV behind us burst into life and announced: 'Plymouth appoint Bobby Williamson as their new manager.'

I joined Bobby at Plymouth. Clarky didn't. When he got there, Bobby had been told to keep John Blackley on as first-team coach, so there was only room for one other coach. Clarky wanted to take a break from the game, so that made Bobby's decision easier.

I loved John Blackley, who is known as 'Sloop', and I shared digs with him but he soon left to join Paul Sturrock at Sheffield Wednesday. I told Bobby to phone Clarky and offer him the job, because we worked best as the three of us, but it was not to be.

Jocky Scott came in and it's fair to say he wasn't my cup of tea. Don't get me wrong, technically he was a very good coach but things started to change and before long going into training was becoming a bit of a chore. Aside from that, I had some family issues back in Scotland. I was in a catch-22 situation. I didn't want to leave Bobby but I wasn't happy. I suggested to Bobby that perhaps it was better if I left. To be honest, I missed Clarky; we spent a lot of time together, whereas Jocky did his own thing.

I so wanted Bobby to succeed. I had been there with the good times at Killie and the bad times at Hibs and had come to Plymouth with him but Jocky had become a big influence.

I felt rotten leaving Bobby. I felt I had let him down. I knew he wasn't happy with me and he was quite right not to be. I really worried that it had damaged our friendship. When I went in to say cheerio, he barely lifted his head.

One part of me wishes I had stayed there to watch Bobby's back but another knows I had to leave because I wasn't okay.

Sometime later, I was playing for the charity team Dukla Pumpherston at East Kilbride and Bobby was there. There were some press guys around and everyone assumed Bobby and I had a big falling-out. But that wasn't the case. They were putting two and two together and making five. I just hadn't seen Bobby or had a chance to catch up with him. That day, I came out of the dressing room and Bobby was standing there. He's not one for cuddling, so we shook hands and he said: 'Great to see you, pal.'

We went out for drinks afterwards and were there until closing time! It was emotional, because I hadn't seen him since I'd left Plymouth. The banter was flying – he was digging me out for leaving him and I was telling him I knew what was going to happen. He admitted he wished he had listened to me. I said I had hoped I was wrong.

One night he phoned me to say that there was a job coming up in India and he was thinking of going for it.

'Do you fancy it?' he asked.

I said: 'You're steaming! I'll talk to you tomorrow.'

The next day, I phoned him and reminded him of the conversation the night before. I'm not sure he remembered it!

'Oh aye!' he said. 'Do you fancy it?'

'Bobby,' I said. 'I love it when you come home to Scotland for a couple of weeks – spend a couple of days with you, it's great. But do you think I'm going to India with you for two years? We'd never survive!'

And I do love it when he comes home and we all meet up. I'll phone Clarky and say: 'You know who's on his way home, don't you?' We all meet in the Horseshoe Bar in Glasgow. When he's home, he's got a note in his diary to meet someone every day. Maybe it's the Killie boys or the Rangers boys. When you have a night out with him, you need two days to get over it!

When he first came into the Clydebank team, he was a cheeky sod – arrogant but in a nice way. He had this way about him and I took to him immediately – and perhaps took him under my wing a wee bit. He has such a dry, cheeky sense of humour. You have to get to know him but, once you do, he's great company.

He's one of the best I've ever met in the game – on and off the park. You'd never have thought that if you'd heard the two of us arguing in the dugout or in the dressing room. On the training ground, Clarky and I would set it all up and have it all planned, then Bobby would come out and say: 'Lift the cones. We're doing something else.'

Clarky would look over at me.

'Lift the cones!' I'd be shouting. 'If you want to change it, you lift the cones!'

'I'm no lifting the cones, I'm the manager,' he'd say.

Clarky would be trying to calm it all but I'd be shouting: 'I'm not putting another cone down!'

The players all knew it – they'd be laughing.

I'd say to him: 'If it wasn't for me, you'd never have got your move; you'd be playing Junior football.'

'Aye, you're probably right,' he'd say.

They were great days. Happy days. Friends forever … Bobby, me and Clarky.

Gerry McCabe
December 2025

CHAPTER 1

WILL I LOSE MY HAIR?

I WAS standing in front of the mirror in the toilet of a pub in Nairobi and I couldn't stop the blood from gushing from my nose. Before you start – no, it wasn't a punch.

I had been due to meet a pal, Chris Harley, and had stopped in for a pint because I was a bit early. Just as I had got up to leave, the drip, drip of the blood started. And now, standing in front of this mirror, I couldn't get it to stop. I had to do something, so I stuffed toilet paper up my nose, cleaned myself up as best I could and rushed out. When I got to Chris's hotel, I phoned his room to tell him I was coming up because I had to borrow a shirt.

The next day, I was driving my daughter, Saoirse, and a couple of her pals to school when the nose bleed started again. Desperate that the kids didn't see what was happening, I managed to stem the flow. Thankfully, the three of them didn't seem to notice my predicament but, for the next hour, the blood was flowing.

I had been having a problem with my nose for some time but was dismissing it, as middle-aged Scottish guys always do. I seemed to have a blockage in my left nostril, which was making it difficult to breathe. The nose bleeds happened again the following week and it was my wife, Michelle, who told me I should see someone at the city's Agha Khan Clinic, where they cauterised my nose to stop the bleeding and referred me to the Anderson Clinic, which is part of Nairobi Hospital. We booked in for a full check-up and spent the day there getting one test after another. I was sent to see Dr Caroline Muturi, the ear, nose and throat specialist, who suspected it was a polyp, although she quickly added that polyps don't bleed, so she was unsure. It was best, she said, to remove a piece of the suspected polyp and send it away to get analysed. Better safe than sorry. It was also decided that I should come back in for a colonoscopy and an endoscopy, so we had to arrange a date for the next appointment.

The biopsy for the suspected polyp came back inconclusive, so they wanted to do another one. Fine by me. Other than the problem with my nose, I felt healthy, so they suggested I get another biopsy done when I was back in for my colonoscopy and an endoscopy. By the time that appointment came around, the blockage or whatever it was in my nose had come loose and it was hindering my breathing, which was very uncomfortable. I was booked in for the following Friday for prep and the procedure would take place on Saturday morning, with the nose operation on the Monday. I just wanted the whole thing over and done with and to get back to normal.

The Thursday before I was due to go in, I had gone out for lunch and had a few beers. Later that evening, I was in and out of the toilet. When I checked into the hospital the next day, the nurse gave me two litres of a liquid to clean out my system ahead of the colonoscopy. I joked with her that I didn't think it would be required, as I had been in and out of the toilet all night. She said that was a sign of cholera and laughed.

Christ, that liquid she gave me didn't half do its job. There were a couple of times I didn't make the bathroom and had to get my sheets changed. I never slept much. They came to take me down to the theatre. The endoscopy went well but they discovered I had, indeed, contracted cholera, so my nose operation on the Monday had to be cancelled. Still, I wasn't going anywhere; with the cholera diagnosis, I was staying in the hospital. I suppose I was lucky they had caught it. I mean, there are worse places to be told you have cholera than when you are already in a hospital. Cholera is deeply unpleasant but I hadn't noticed any of the symptoms, because I was so drugged up and on medication anyway.

I was discharged the following Friday and we had already booked for a few days away down the coast. By the time I went in for the rearranged nose op, I felt brand new. The op itself was fine, apart from the bloody plaster I had to wear. Still, job done. I had to return a few weeks later for the results but I wasn't worried.

Professor Isaac Macharia is one of the most renowned surgeons in Kenya. He is a member of several prestigious organisations, including the Kenya Surgical Society, the European Academy of Allergy and Clinical Immunology, the New York Academy of Sciences, the European Rhinologic Society, the Kenya ENT Society (KENTS) and the Kenya Medical Association. He is one of only two Kenyan otologists currently performing cochlear implantation. His surgical expertise extends to head and neck cancer surgery, nasal and sinus conditions and vocal cord disorders. He has received international training and recognition through the College of Surgeons of East, Central and Southern Africa.

He was also the guy who had done my operation. Top bloke. When I sat in his office to give me the results, I knew I had been in very safe hands.

'I'm really surprised by your results,' he said. Now he had my undivided attention. 'The tumour was cancerous. I'm sure I removed every piece of it but you will have to do the chemo and radiation treatment to make sure it's gone.'

I sat there for a few seconds to let it sink in.

'Will I lose my hair,' I said.

Professor Macharia looked at my balding head. I'm not sure he got my Scottish sense of humour.

'Maybe a little,' he said.

I drove home that day wondering how I was going to tell Michelle the news but she was out that evening with friends, and when she got back in she was tired and went straight to bed without asking me how the appointment had gone, which was a little odd. Never mind, I didn't want her to have a sleepless night, so I decided to leave it until the morning.

When I told her she was very practical, asking what the next move was. From that moment on, she was with me every step of the way. I told her I had an appointment with the radiation oncologist, an appointment she attended with me. It was there that my entire treatment programme was laid out. When he finished, Michelle stood up, thanked him and informed him that we would be using her company health insurance to have the treatment carried out in India.

A lot of Kenyans get their treatment in India – there are a lot of Indians in Kenya – and it was through my wife's company health plan anyway, so going back to Britain wasn't an option. The wife assured me the hospitals would be top-notch. She was right.

It was only a matter of days later and we were in Delhi's Indraprastha Apollo Hospital, where renowned oncologist Dr Ganesh Jadhav had just given me the news that I had an undifferentiated nasopharyngeal carcinoma.

That was easy for him to say! But I had no fear. In fact, I felt perfectly healthy. I'm told a lot of cancer victims feel the same. I didn't have any feelings that this was life-threatening in any way at all and I wasn't afraid in the slightest.

Let's get the procedures done, do what you need to do and let's get home so we can all get on with our lives.

Michelle turned to Dr Jadhav and asked him what stage the cancer was at.

'Stage 3,' he said.

That's when I started working things out in my head. I never had a clue whether that was good or bad but when I looked at Michelle, I knew the answer. I could see the emotion in her face and the tears welling up in her eyes.

Fuck. This might be more serious than I thought.

CHAPTER 2

EASTERHOUSE

IT ALL began for me on 13 August 1961 in the Duke Street Maternity Hospital. My mum and dad, Betty and Tommy, had been trying for a family for some time. There had been heartache along the way and my mum had suffered miscarriages before, so they were both delighted when I arrived on the scene. A few years later, my sister, Donna, was born and the Williamson family was complete. Originally, the family home was in the Gallowgate area of Glasgow but my earliest recollections came after we moved to a bigger property in Shandwick Street in a leafy suburb called Easterhouse. I think we needed more room after Donna arrived, although I don't know why, because we shared a bedroom until I moved out when I was 18.

What can I say about Easterhouse? Well, it was certainly interesting growing up there. It was one of the housing projects built by the then Glasgow Corporation to ease the housing crisis in the city and take people out of the crowded tenements. It was supposed to offer them a better life. At its peak, there were 60,000 people living there but, while the houses were an improvement, there were no amenities, no shops, no sports facilities or anything like that. There was no community feel at all – there was not even a good bus service. It was an explosive mix of frustration. There was such high unemployment, and many teenagers were left with nothing to do and no prospect of a job. I don't know what the planners were thinking of and there was little surprise that gang culture began to fester. Territorial battles were fought on a daily basis and there were streets it was unsafe to walk down if one gang member made the mistake of drifting into another gang's territory. Names like Drummy, Aggro, Torran Toi and Bal Toi – the names of the gangs – were painted on the walls all over the place.

It was hard not to be aware of the gang culture growing up. You were either in a gang or you got beat up by a gang. Easterhouse was divided into about ten or 11 areas and every area had its own little cohort. It wasn't terribly heavy at my age group. You used to throw stones and chase each other back and forth – there wasn't much else to do with your time, to be honest – but if someone did find themselves in the wrong area, they could find themselves in a pretty severe position. I remember a couple of people being murdered through gang fights and things like that. They were just stupid kids, not realising the damage they were doing.

I was never really beaten up. Somehow, I was always able to avoid it and I was a fast runner, so I used to be able to read the signs and get myself out of trouble.

We used to hang about the street corner and chat and talk nonsense and the most violent we would get was to throw stones at each other, even though I know some of the gangs ran about with knives and things like that. I was very aware that there were gangs that did do that – maybe lads slightly older than me at the time are still carrying scars from back then.

A few of my mates had paper rounds or were delivering milk and had a little money in their pockets, so I got involved as well. I'm not sure what I did first – stealing milk and papers or delivering them. I delivered milk in the morning and the *Evening Citizen* in the late afternoon. I had to go to Easterhouse train station to collect the papers, which was not very close to my house or my round. The milk round was closer. Getting back to my area to deliver meant I had to come back through another gang's area. Going there empty-handed was okay but coming back with the papers or the milk was somewhat more difficult. I've no idea how much I got paid but some residents could afford to tip me when I was collecting on the Friday. To paint the picture for young people who have never lived in a tenement block, you may have three or four flights of stairs to get to the top and a corner at every flight. You never knew what could be waiting round a corner. I was never robbed but some kids were; it was always an anxious time and a nervous experience. I somehow managed to hang on to my hard-earned cash, although I'm sure I squandered it myself later.

I remember the entertainer Frankie Vaughan coming to Easterhouse to settle the natives. It was crazy as he addressed the crowd insisting, 'There's no more gangs, there's no more Drummy,' as the cheers rang out. He somehow arranged with the police to agree an amnesty so that gang members could hand in their weapons, getting the blades and things off the streets without fear of being arrested.

It took place in a big field next to where I lived and all these gang members turned up to hand in their cleavers, machetes and swords. By the end, there were three bins filled with these weapons! Some mums even complained that their kids had raided their kitchen drawers just to pick up something that would allow them to get close to Frankie.

Many people thought it no more than a publicity stunt but, to be fair to Vaughan, this was no one-hit wonder for him. He returned and met with the gang leaders to try to persuade them to stop the fighting. Youth clubs did get built, thanks to Vaughan's Easterhouse project, and there was the incongruous sight of gang members jet-washing their tribal names from the walls. In the long run, though, it didn't stop the fighting, which I'm sure goes on to this day.

I've looked back on old YouTube footage of those crazy days, with Frankie Vaughan in the field outside my house. I was only about five or six at the time but I remember it and I've tried to see if I could pick myself out in the old black and white footage but to no avail.

Much as I was aware of these gangs as I grew up, I was never involved, although I wouldn't say I was lucky to escape it because of anything my parents did. They weren't exactly strict. We had a certain time we had to be home by in the evening for food and then we would go back out for another couple of hours and when the streetlights were glowing orange, you knew they had been on for a while, so you had to get back home. That was about the level of discipline I lived under. We had to be back home so that we would be ready for school the next day. My parents had enough on their plate getting themselves sorted out for work. We ended up as latchkey kids. I would have a key and would see me and my sister in and out and then wait for my mum and dad to come home so we could have something to eat. And then we would go out and play again.

My mum and dad did their best with the little they had and Donna and I had a happy childhood. I wasn't the best at school – there was too much nonsense and mischief in me for that – but they were good times. My mum was a very proud woman; if she didn't have it, she didn't ask for it. Dad was different. Many a Friday night, I had to get myself over to my dad's sister, Auntie Agnes, in Queenslie to pick up the messages because dad had blown his wages at the bookies or in the pub. That was a common occurrence back then.

I never knew any better and everybody was in the same boat. We were never affluent people; my mum and dad were hand to mouth. But, as children, we never noticed or knew anything different. Our Christmases were good and we had good birthdays and stuff – we never really lacked for much and I don't believe we missed out on anything. While other boys might have been riding around on Chopper bikes, I had a bike ... just not a Chopper.

I believe I had a good childhood, a good upbringing and a good grounding in life, apart from my education, where I was hopeless. My parents were typical Glaswegians. It was tough love – they would rather slap you than kiss you, put it that way.

My dad was an asphalter at one time and I also recall him working on the buses as a conductor when his wee mate was the driver. Then he worked in a place called Mine Safety Appliances. Mum worked there as well, along with Derek and Barry Ferguson's mother. It was a place in Queenslie where gloves and helmets were made for people in the mining industry.

My mum would always somehow manage to put some money away so we could get a holiday to Blackpool each year.

I don't know how she did it but I do know it took her the entire year to pay it all back. They used to run a menage, putting money away each week and then one week they would have a draw and if it was your turn, you got the whole lot.

We used to stay in the same B&B every year, a place run by a lovely old woman called Mrs Jolly. She would look after Donna and I in the evening so that Mum and Dad could go out.

These were happy times. I used to love the trampolines at Stanley Park. I'd be on them for hours, shouting at my dad to watch me when I was doing somersaults. The famous Pleasure Beach was fantastic but we could only go once, as the rides were so expensive. Mum would play bingo and Dad would go to the pub – and I'd be back and forth, pestering my mum for coins for the puggy.

My dad just lived for the weekend. He loved a bet and he loved a whisky. He lived for Fridays and Saturdays – and he did his tank in on a Friday, mostly. My mother was 24/7; the most important thing in her world was the family. She made sure we always had food on the table and all sorts. During the week, she was the boss of the family but on a Friday, if my dad had been to the pub, he would always like to put his tuppence in. But my mum was really the one who kept it all together.

I had a very good relationship with my mother. I loved her to bits and she loved me equally in return. She used to play my sister against me when we were slightly older, especially when I moved away. My sister would always be complaining about my mum going on about me and what a good boy I was and all this crap.

I would say to her: 'Donna, she's like that with me as well. She'll be telling me how she couldn't do without you and how wonderful you are.' Mothers, eh? It was just the way she was.

It was a happy home and I couldn't say I had a bad childhood at all. I really enjoyed that period of my life; no pressure, just going to school, playing football and no cares at all. Not like kids nowadays, who seem to be stressed up to the eyeballs and under pressure to do well at exams. I didn't experience anything like that. Maybe it was because I didn't care about school – I don't even remember my mum and dad checking a report card. They must have done but I can't recall it and I don't remember them ever giving me any bother about my schoolwork. But I could read from an early age and always had my nose in a book if I wasn't out playing football. I loved fantasy adventures like J.R.R. Tolkien and stuff like that – *The Hobbit* and *The Lord of the Rings* – but they took me years to get through. There were 1,000 pages a book!

The class environment wasn't set up for anyone to learn anything in the schools I went to. This is no disrespect to the teachers but we weren't clever enough and we didn't have enough sense about us just to knuckle down and get on with it. It was always a laugh and a joke and always messing around. That's all my school days were about. But I regret that now – especially when I was coming to the end of my football career and wondering and worrying about what I was going to do. I wasn't qualified to do anything and it was the same when I left school. Manual labour was my only option. I had no qualifications when I left school – nothing!

School for me, you see, was a distraction. I was just a kid who wanted to be out playing football. The primary school was called Easthall and it always felt so far away for me, although I don't suppose it was.

Life as I knew it changed on 22 March 1969 with my first real football experience when I was taken to the Scottish Cup semi-final at Parkhead between Aberdeen and Rangers. I'll never forget it. I remember walking up the steep staircase at the Celtic end. It seemed to take forever but then I was hit by this explosion of noise and colour. I had never seen a pitch so green. We played on that horrible red ash that would cut your knee open in a flash were you to take a tumble. When the teams came out, Rangers were in their perfect blue shirts and Aberdeen in the brightest red I'd ever seen. My experience of football was on a black and white television set with only two channels and the Rangers strip was a dirty grey. Here, in the flesh, I was swept away in the atmosphere and the passion.

I remember reading the report in the paper the next day and it said that the Rangers players had hunted 'like a pack of lions' as they blew Aberdeen away 6-1. I couldn't take my eyes off them, the likes of John Greig, Willie Henderson and Colin Stein but it was Willie Johnston who was the star of the show, scoring a hat-trick.

I was hooked and, from that moment, football was all I wanted to do.

Growing up in Easterhouse wasn't easy but it's only later in life that you realise quite how tough it was. On a Sunday, at the St Scholastica's School, we used to play ten-a-side. It was a nice tight red ash pitch and the game would start at around 10am. It was a ten-21 game; ten was half-time, 21 was full time. Ages ranged from 12 upwards and guys in their late 20s would be involved and they had no issue with kicking 12-year-olds. If you were playing, you had to take it. The game would not stop, although if the ice cream van came, guys would run off to buy ginger (for my English friends, pop), the game would continue when the guys came back and the goodies were shared among their team-mates. When I think about it, everybody dressed differently but you knew who your team-mates were. If we had a five-a-side game in training as a professional, one team would have to wear bibs! Players would disappear at different times to go for lunch but come back as quick as they could to join back in. Sometimes, one team would be heavily depleted and had to defend till their players came back. When I joined Clydebank, I couldn't take part in these games any more, as I would have been risking injury and these guys would have taken great pleasure in kicking a professional. It was a great education, recognising when to tackle and when to think twice.

For all that I went on to achieve in my life, it is funny looking back to remember that it all came so close to not happening at all. Kids do silly things when they are young and sometimes your luck just runs out. My moment of good fortune came one day when I had got home from school, dumped my bag and decided to head down to the nearby canal to try and catch some sticklebacks and tadpoles. The Monklands Canal was used to take coal from the pits at Monklands into Townhead in the city centre but it had long been out of use. Still, it was a great place for kids to hang out. We used to call it The Nolly.

I was minding my own business, searching for any small fish or frog spawn, but could see this lad skimming stones on the opposite bank. I had walked down this section which jutted out into the middle of the canal where the barges used to come up on either side. Suddenly, this young lad decided he was bored of skimming stones and started using me for target practice. His aim was off but he was getting progressively closer and I decided that enough was enough. I began to chase him but I knew I would never catch him unless I jumped over a section of the canal which was diagonally to my right. I thought I would make it with something to spare but I totally misjudged it and crashed into the water. I was not a strong swimmer and found myself sinking below the surface before coming up again, grabbing a breath of air before sinking once more. This must have happened a couple of times as I desperately tried to reach out and grab hold of the ledge that was my only source of salvation. But it was agonisingly out of reach; no matter how hard I stretched, I had no chance of grabbing hold. By this time, I really was panicking and thrashing in the water but, as I sank below the surface once again, I became enveloped in a strange calmness. I don't know if I had resigned myself to drowning, that I had somehow come to terms with the fact that this was the end.

Suddenly, I was aware of two massive hands grabbing me and pulling me out of the water like a rag doll. My life had undoubtedly been saved by an eagle-eyed lady who spotted what had happened and had the presence of mind to shout to a nearby refuse collector, who came to my rescue. To this day, I have always regretted that I never found out who this pair were. I never got their names and never got the opportunity to thank them. Without them, I wouldn't be here to tell the story. Many people drowned in The Nolly. It was only thanks to good luck – and my two guardian angels – that I wasn't one of them.

As always on these occasions, the message had reached home that I had been involved in an accident and my mum was there before the ambulance had even arrived. I vividly remember the medics pumping my stomach to get as much of the dirty canal water out of me as possible. Amazingly, despite the drama and near-death experience, I was able to walk home with my mum. Can you imagine that these days? I'm sure you'd be in hospital and under observation for days.

But, as lucky as I had been to escape The Nolly, I didn't escape the impact of the sorry affair. And so began the weekly visits to the Belvidere Hospital on London Road, near to Celtic's training ground, for observation, X-rays and treatment for the damage the water had done to my lungs. These medical adventures went on for the best part of a year and, on one trip, the doctor informed my mum that my chest would never fully recover from the ordeal and that, in his opinion, sporting activity should be avoided from then on. Can you imagine hearing that as a young kid? No more football!

It was a bit like a dream sequence. The doctor was speaking to my mum as if I wasn't there. But I was listening to every word he said.

'His chest is going to be a problem, Mrs Williamson,' the doctor said. 'It will affect him throughout his adult life. He won't be able to take part in much sport, with his breathing, you see, and he won't be able to run around like other children.'

Even though I was only a kid, I knew he was talking nonsense and I never gave it a second's thought. I just carried on regardless, running around like a lunatic, as all children do, and flying in the face of medical opinion, because football was fast becoming the most important thing in my life.

The condition the doctor talked of, the breathing problems or chest issues, never materialised. Touch wood, that continues.

Coming from the East End of Glasgow, it was almost assumed that any self-respecting football fan would follow Celtic. My dad's brothers were all fans. My uncle, John, and my cousin of the same name were regularly among the congregation at Parkhead. Celtic had such a great team then. The famous Lisbon Lions, the first British team to lift the European Cup, in 1967, were still roaring but they had been joined by a group that were known as the Quality Street Gang. They were young kids coming through the Celtic ranks but they were to become household names: George Connelly, Davie Hay, Danny McGrain, Lou Macari and a certain Kenny Dalglish.

The experience of the cup semi-final had whetted my appetite for more and I would go along to games with my uncles. My dad would also take me at times but he was forever the last guy out of the pub as I sat there impatiently with my Coke and crisps. He always maintained there was method to his madness and that by arriving late, I would avoid the crush. I didn't believe him but I loved the fact he was doing it for me and I was able to spend time with him.

I still miss him.

I suppose my relationship with my father wasn't like that of most father and sons, because my dad wasn't really interested in football and, obviously, I was very keen. As I recall now, very seldom did my dad ever see me play football. There was one game he came to see me play which was actually in Easterhouse against Barlanark across the Edinburgh Road. He told me afterwards that he spoke to the referee and asked him why I was always offside. My dad never had a clue about football! The ref just told him I was too fast for my own good!

I think that is the only time my dad ever saw me play football. He came to Kilbowie once and he went to the nearest watering hole, which happened to be the Kilbowie club. We were playing Celtic Boys Club and I was substituted at half-time. I remember my dad walking up the touchline looking for me on the park and I was sitting in the stand behind him. Eventually, he turned round and saw me.

'Whit are ye doing?' he asked.

'I was subbed at half-time,' I told him.

You could see him thinking, the cogs turning in his head. 'I'm away back into the club. I'll see you after the game.'

He never watched me in a professional game and neither did my mum. It just wasn't their thing. Did it bother me then? Not a bit. Does it bother me now? Not at all. There was no pressure on me whatsoever. I know a lot of kids whose parents did put pressure on them and they would be at games, shouting from the touchline, but mine never came near. I was okay with that; I knew that was just the way it was and I got on with it.

When I was 18, I moved out of the family home and moved in with my girlfriend. I had been sharing a room with my sister for 18 years, so when I got the opportunity to get out of there, I took it. My dad was always one of those guys who would say, 'When you get old enough, get yourself out there and make a life for yourself.' My mother would have liked me to hang around a bit longer. My dad would want to see us go and do something.

Easthall Primary didn't have a football team and I was introduced to playing the game after a classmate called Dunky Murray took me to 211th Glasgow, Boys Brigade.

Then, when I was in primary seven, Easthall began their own team and I was made captain. I took it very seriously and, while the other boys were having a laugh, I was crying when we lost.

My strike partner was a lad called Alan Callaghan. He was super-fast and scored plenty of goals. I used to keep notes on how many points other schools had won, who was top scorer, that kind of thing. Alan was always top of the charts and I was always second but I never told him! I don't think he was that bothered – and, anyway, I had more assists! Alan packed it all in to concentrate on his schoolwork, which I'm sure was the right decision, given he would no doubt have gone on to be a success in whatever career he chose to follow. I, on the other hand, packed in the schoolwork to concentrate on the football.

At a local derby with near rivals Blairtummock, I realised that our teacher was in deep conversation with a man who had been avidly watching our game. I was called over and introduced to a Mr Wallace who explained he wanted to sign me for local side Auchingill Star. It was another step up the footballing ladder but he had to get clearance from my parents. That, of course, was a formality and soon I was playing three games at the weekend – the school and BB on a Saturday and Auchingill on a Sunday. I loved it – even though I was about to have a big wake-up call.

The secondary school at Westwood was just across the field from my house, so the early rises that haunted my primary school days were a thing of the past. But those carefree days when I put my schoolwork aside to focus on football were coming home to roost. The classes at Westwood were allocated 1A through to 1F, with the smartest kids in A and educational attainment plummeting as you went down the alphabet. I was in 1F. I kidded myself on that it was an alphabetical decision given the class was full of kids called Wallace, Wilson and, of course, Williamson. What a bunch of loveable rogues they were.

The teachers soon realised they were wasting their time with us and I don't blame them. We were a lost cause and we were dragging the rest of the class down with us. Things could get out of hand in a heartbeat and the new shopping centre that had been built across the road from the school was ripe for picking.

One of the lads realised that the car park at the back door led up to some unmanned tills at the Buywell store but it wasn't the tills they were after – it was the unmanned chocolate that was displayed beside them. Genuinely, I don't recall stealing anything. I'd have been too scared but I certainly gorged myself on the goodies that the boys generously shared around. It was all great fun until, back in the classroom after the dinner break, we all started throwing up. The place was covered.

Then 1F was followed by 2F, 3F and so on. By the time I left school at 15, I hadn't a qualification to my name. I wasn't even allowed to sit any O levels but I'm sure I would have failed them anyway.

Football was all I was interested in. By this time, my mates were all Rangers fans and I found myself switching allegiances. I had picked the perfect time, because the team were on the up, ably led by the likes of Willie Waddell and Jock Wallace. They had won the Cup Winners' Cup in 1972 with such legends as Willie Johnston, Colin Stein and their talismanic leader, John Greig.

At a somewhat lower level, I had made the school team in first year but was shocked to miss out on selection in second year. We had two PE teachers at the school – Jim Allan and Danny Reece. Mr Allan was the senior of the two and he had need to one day break up a fight between myself and a classmate who had come off the worse and was sporting quite a significant bump to his head. Mr Allan deduced, not too surprisingly, that I was the cause of the injury and that I had kicked the boy in the head. I had no idea if I had or not; I was caught up in the moment. In the playground, no quarter is asked nor given. Acting as both judge and jury, Mr Allan saw fit to give me the belt but let my sparring partner off scot-free! And it was he who was the coach for the second year team. Not for a second, though, did I think Mr Allan had judged me on that fight. He was a good man and a good teacher.

Danny Reece came to my rescue. PE with him was football, football and football – unless we had annoyed him and then it was basketball. He ran the first-year team and, aware of my age, informed me that I could drop down and play for them. That suited me fine. I knew most of them and they were a good team, so no problem. Danny and I kept in touch and when I was at Kilmarnock, he asked me to present prizes at a school prize giving. In the car, I had mentioned to Danny that it was strange the school never had awards nights when I had been there. He told me that they did, every year, it was just that I never had any chance of winning, so I was never invited.

In my final year at school, I was granted an audience with a housemaster or, in modern parlance, a guidance teacher. It was a waste of time; same question, same answer.

'What do you want to be when you leave school?'

'A footballer.'

'Right, next!'

Perhaps he was right. No club had shown any interest in me. I had a trial at East Stirling under Billy Lamont but I think I was just there to make up the numbers. I never heard anything from them.

I did have trials for Glasgow Schools, though, alongside a few of my mates from Auchingill. Tommy McGarvey, whose son, Scott, would go on to play for Manchester United, was one of our managers at Auchingill alongside another lad, Joe Forbes, who helped us all tremendously. My team-mates were all from the Roman Catholic school, St Leonard's, who had a great team. They had Jamie Doyle, who went on to play for Motherwell, John Gillen, who would play for Falkirk, and Jimmy Anderson, who would go on to play for a short spell with me at Clydebank. They also had a tenacious little full-back called Paul Lister. He really helped me to toughen up. At each training session, I would make sure I was close enough to him to hit him.

He never liked it and would fire back: 'Hey, Williamson, you've got to work harder cos you've got nae ability.'

He was right. These guys had more ability than me but they couldn't match me for desire. Still, they had clubs falling over themselves to get them on what were, in those days, called S-forms and I was still failing to grab any club's attention.

The school taught everyone how to fill out job applications and I took the advice on board, diligently filling out letter after letter and sending them to construction companies as I prepared for a life on the building site. I would get excited waiting for the postman, even though some of the companies didn't even bother with a reply.

Eventually, my luck turned and I got a job with a firm run by a guy called Frank Lafferty, so it was out of school and on to the tools. Glasgow was going through a full-on renovation spree and it was a case of 'all hands on deck'. I had originally wanted to be a painter and decorator but we were told the firm wasn't taking any on, so I had to decide what apprenticeship I wanted to do. I could have selected joiner, electrician or plumber but, as it turned out, I put down bricklayer.

Once I had started the apprenticeship, I decided to stop playing football, because I was getting paid overtime at weekends, which was too good to turn down. But I never got to lay a brick for about two years! Instead, I was more or less a dogsbody for a stonemason but I didn't complain; actually, I quite enjoyed it, as we were sent from site to site as the boss saw fit. As a youngster, I was small and not very strong but I started to fill out, volunteering to carry bricks or whatever up the stairs as a way of bulking up with muscle. Pretty soon, football was a distant memory. But I was worried that, with just a year of the apprenticeship to go, I had learned almost nothing. One of the bosses, a guy called Jimmy McColm, used to drive around the sites in his big Mercedes and had the power to hire or fire who he wanted. He certainly kept everyone on their toes; just knowing he was there meant you kept your head down. He used to fire people on the spot if he thought they weren't pulling their weight. He once caught three guys coming out of the lunch shop and sacked them for taking their lunch early – but they didn't actually work for Lafferty's and told him to fuck off!

For weeks, I had been working up the nerve to talk to him and finally got my big chance. I plucked up my courage and told him that I had been a bricklayer apprentice for two years and hadn't laid a brick. I didn't know what was going to happen next but he was brilliant with me. The very next week, I was transferred to a squad of brickies in Royston – or The Garngad, as we called it. It was a father and son team, with the dad, Wullie Grant, the boss. They were great guys and I really enjoyed their company. We were building bin shelters one day and, once they had finished the brickwork, I was responsible for the pointing, making sure the mortar was smoothed off, then brushed to a finish. They had all moved on to the next shelter when I noticed a huge spider climbing up the wall. I went over and flattened it with the sole of my boot but the cement hadn't yet set properly and it all collapsed. The lads, hearing the noise, were all staring, mouths open, as I stood there, my foot still hanging in thin air as the bricks crashed down around me. I'll never forget the look on their faces – it was hilarious. I thought I would get a roasting but the good thing was I had to build it all back up, so, in the end, I learned something.

The Grants were great guys. I still miss the banter.

Everything was to change for me one Friday night with a knock at the door. It was a guy called Jim Weir and he said he wanted me back at Auchingill. They had a game that weekend and were short of players. I told him I had plans to go and watch Rangers play Hearts at Tynecastle. Given how my playing career would turn out, it was kind of eerie when he said: 'Do you want to watch Rangers or *play* for them?' I knew he was spinning me a line but the guy had made the effort to seek me out on a Friday night, so it was back on with the football boots and turning out for my old team.

I found, to my surprise, that I was a different boy from a few years before. Perhaps it was all that time on the building site but I was stronger, bigger and with a fair amount of testosterone coursing through my veins. I enjoyed the battle and loved getting stuck back in.

We played in Drumchapel one Sunday. I remember there were quite a few of us who had been to a party on the Saturday night – one of those all-night jobs – and when we got our stuff together to go to the game, the prospect threatened to be too much for some of us. We discussed whether we should go or not but we all recognised that we couldn't let the others down – especially Jim Weir, who was running the team. I still felt I owed him something. So, we went. It was in Drumchapel and on a grass park. We didn't have many grass parks and generally had to play on that dreaded red ash. The other teams, who were more used to playing on grass, always found it tricky to switch to the ash and that meant we would normally beat all these teams when they came to our place.

I managed to score a few goals in the first half, before asking to come off because I wasn't feeling great. I was laying down behind the goals, hardly paying attention to the game, when a gentleman in a hat approached me and asked why I had been subbed. I told him I had caught some bug going around but he and I both probably knew I was hungover.

He introduced himself as Jack Steedman, chairman of Clydebank, and said that he had been impressed watching me and wanted to sign me. At last, a club had shown an interest and I was told to be at Kilbowie, their home ground, which sadly doesn't even exist any more, at 6.30 the next day to sign my forms – no agent, no negotiations, nothing. I remember speaking to my parents about it but for this momentous moment in my life, I travelled to the big signing along with Jimmy Anderson, who they wanted to sign as well.

That evening – 2 July 1979 and just short of my 18th birthday – I put pen to paper on my first senior contract. My signing-on fee was the princely sum of £100 … not Lionel Messi level, I grant you, but everyone has to start somewhere.

CHAPTER 3

THE BANKIES

WHEN I signed for Clydebank, the club had been struggling in the First Division but I didn't care. I felt I was, at last, on my way to properly pursuing a career in the game. It was a great club for youth players. It was also a family club – well, a Steedman family club, to be more exact. They were everywhere. Our youth coaches were all Steedmans and, although I don't think any of them had played at any great level, they all convinced us they knew what they were doing. There was Iain, Colin and Graeme – all Steedmans. Jack, or Mr Jack as we called him, was the figurehead and there was also his brother, Charles.

Mr Jack was always on the lookout for young talent to nurture and sell on for a healthy profit. The professional youth league system had only just started and he had put together a right good team, with the likes of Mark Treanor, who would go on to be inducted into the club's Hall of Fame, Billy 'Budgie' McGhie and Martin Hughes.

There were only nine teams in the league and you only played each other once. Our opening game was against Partick Thistle at Firhill. It was the first game of the new set-up and I scored the only goal, the first in the new league. I was as proud as punch to see my name in the *Sunday Post* the next day. We would go on to win all of our subsequent games, only for Celtic to beat us at Kilbowie in our last one. That was so hard to take but our success was an indication that we had a good bunch of kids coming through and Mr Jack was always keen to open the door for us to train with the first team. Mark Treanor and I both took up the offer and it played a huge part in developing us as players, working with the senior pros, guys who knew the game inside out.

Clydebank were a part-time team and I found balancing my work and football commitments arduous, to say the least, but there was no way I was going to let this opportunity slip by. It might, after all, have been my one and only chance. I was determined to give it my best shot and if I didn't make the grade, then I could still look myself in the mirror and say I could have done no more.

I'd be up by 6.30am and it would be off for a day on the site in whichever part of Glasgow I was working. That usually meant two buses, so I had to buy a weekly pass that ate up a huge chunk of my massive £16-a-week wage! Thankfully, my mum never asked for digs money – although I don't think my dad was too pleased with that. I'm sure he would have wanted me to make a contribution because I was earning.

My working day would start at 8am and it would be hard graft until we finished at about 4.30pm. Then I would hop on a train to Singer station in Clydebank and walk up to the ground for training at 6.30pm and this would finish at about 8pm. This would be twice a week – and then I would join the first team for an extra night. After training, it was a train back into Glasgow and then another to Easterhouse for the half-hour walk from the station to my house and straight to bed.

It was tough but I loved it – being coached by Iain, Colin and especially Graeme Steedman – and it instilled in me a strong work ethic, something I retain to this day.

One night, we all pitched up to be told we were to jump in the minibus as we were to be training on an AstroTurf pitch in Erskine, which was about 15 minutes' drive away. We motored down the road and over the Erskine Bridge, which straddles the River Clyde at the village of Old Kilpatrick. I really enjoyed training on the Astro, which was pretty new back in the early 80s, and was looking forward to it.

On arriving, we piled out of the minibus and started to put our boots on, only to hear Iain, who was driving, shouting that there was no training and we were, instead, to run back to Kilbowie. I can still hear him laughing as he drove off – he was killing himself.

We were fuming and it was worse for me because I had to psyche myself up for the longer runs and, mentally, I wasn't prepared for this. We set off and within minutes it was no surprise that I was in the group that was already lagging behind. We were well off the pace and were just getting over the bridge when one of us saw a train rolling into Old Kilpatrick station. I'm pretty sure we all had the same thought, knowing fine well that just one stop down the line would get us back to Singer. We picked up the pace and hurtled straight past the guard. Within minutes, we were nearly home but knew that we would probably be back even before Iain and the minibus, so we hid up a tenement close and waited. Ten minutes later, the minibus drove past but it was a good 45 minutes before the first players were spotted. We let them go past us, joining in with the stragglers at the back and even had the presence of mind to work up some kind of a sweat.

We were never found out but I remember at the time that I wasn't pleased because I knew the only person I was cheating was myself. Then again, I wasn't happy they had sprung it on us.

With me finishing my work at 4.30 in the afternoon, I would always be the first into the ground for training and would have to sit waiting for the rest to turn up. There was an old guy, Alec, who was the groundsman at Kilbowie and he had a bulldog with a long snout which would always come up and jump on me. Alec thought this was really funny but I was terrified.

As I was waiting one day, the phone rang just outside the dressing room. Alec was miles away at the other side of the pitch, so I answered it.

'Get me Alec,' this brusque voice said at the other end of the line. Well, it immediately got my back up – no pleasantries, nothing.

'Excuse me?' I said.

'Get me Alec!', the voice even louder this time.

I wasn't taking it, so I replied: 'Nah, fuck off!'

'What did you say?' the caller replied. 'Do you know who this is?'

I knew fine well who it was and said as much before asking: 'And do you know who this is?'

'No,' the caller replied.

'Well, fuck off then,' I said and slammed down the phone.

The phone began ringing off the hook after that but there was no way I was going to answer it. By the time Mr Jack reached the ground, the dressing room had filled up nicely. He was demanding to know who had answered the phone. Of course, the other players had no idea what he was talking about and I certainly wasn't going to put my hand up.

I was loving my time at Clydebank, and living life as a footballer, but I have to talk about one incident on the park when I committed the worst sin imaginable. Even now, when I think about it, I cringe.

We were playing Celtic in an under-18s game at Kilbowie and I was up against Mark Reid, a full-back who would go on to play more than 100 games for the Celtic first team before he moved down south for a good career with Charlton. He was a really talented player and I always struggled against him – and this day was no different.

Anyway, this ball gets played to me and Mark has feinted to go in for a tackle. I bought his dummy completely and he was away with the ball. I felt so stupid and the frustration got the better of me. I couldn't get close enough to punch him or tackle him, so I did the worst thing possible – I spat at him. I don't know if it landed on him or even if Mark was aware of what had happened but it is the worst thing you can do on a football field.

To this day, all those years later, I've regretted it and am ashamed by it. I couldn't even put it down to inexperience or being so young, because everybody knows how wrong it is, no matter how old you are.

Years later, Danny Crainie, who had been playing in the game, mentioned it when he joined me at Kilmarnock. I found myself apologising to him! I wanted the ground to swallow me up.

It was totally out of character. I mean, I've made some bad tackles in my day and have thrown a few elbows, but back then I thought the football field was a war zone – and it was. I came up against some really hard players who made their presence felt and you had to give some back. But, to this day, I feel ashamed to talk about that incident with Mark.

Pretty soon, we had forced ourselves into the reserve team, where I began to get to know Gerry McCabe, who would go on to have such an important role to play in my later career. We now had a van, which meant no more miserable train journeys, and Gerry would drop me off in Easterhouse and then take Mark Treanor on to Baillieston. I was giving my all in training and any of the matches we played in as I pushed to get a chance in the first team.

Training was now being taken by Tommy Callaghan and Gerry O'Brien. Tommy was a legend of a player and holds the distinction of twice being signed by the great Jock Stein – once for Dunfermline and once for Celtic. I don't know how many titles he won while at Parkhead but he had come to Clydebank at the end of his career and was now a key part of the coaching team. They were great guys with a wealth of experience, which was just what we all needed. The youth stuff with the Steedmans was all well and good and I enjoyed it – but this was a proper lesson in football from guys who had played the game at the top level. The grounding they gave us was crucial as we climbed the pro ranks.

But I was desperate to progress and was getting increasingly frustrated that those around me were getting a chance while I felt I was being ignored. It is harder when you are a striker, of course, but I felt I was ready.

The thing was, although Bill Munro was the manager and Sammy Henderson his assistant, there was no doubt who was in charge, and that was Mr Jack. I reckon he told Bill and Sammy who should be playing or that this young player or that young player was ready to get his shot. I don't think he actually picked the team, that would be unfair, but he definitely had his say on who was to get pushed forward. Bill and Sammy complemented each other well. Bill was a real gentleman and I don't think I ever saw him angry. Sammy, on the other hand, had a fiery temperament. When the occasion arose, he used to play in the games and could more than handle himself. I never really got the opportunity to thank Sammy for helping me develop as a player. At that age, you do tend to believe you did it all yourself, which is wrong. Many a coach or manager or senior player helped me develop. Indeed, there are far too many to mention but it doesn't mean I ever forgot what they did for me.

Mr Jack would be taking in games all around Glasgow, watching young boys playing football and searching for the next gem. I would imagine he saw it as money. He was going to give you the opportunity but you had to grab it and then he would cash you in.

And he did cash you in! When I left to go to Rangers, the club got £100,000 for me and I didn't see a penny. That really annoyed me at the time and still does now. Ted McMinn, who joined Rangers around the same time as me from Queen of the South, got £10,000 from Queens, along with what he got from Rangers to sign, while Jack never gave me a penny. I found that very disappointing.

At training one night, messages were being sent down from Mr Jack's office that he wanted to speak to one player, then another, then another. There was a steady stream heading for his office but I wasn't one of them. My hackles were up as player after player came back and instructed another to head in to see Mr Jack.

I couldn't take it any more and when the last player came back, I asked if Mr Jack wanted to see me, only to be told that my presence was not required. I turned to big Tommy and asked if I could go and speak to the chairman. My adrenaline was pumping now, partly through putting my all into the training session but also because I felt I was getting a raw deal. I was playing well for the reserves and not getting a look-in and here I was being ignored again.

I was still raging by the time I got to the top of the steps outside Mr Jack's office, which was a good thing, because it gave me the courage to state my case. I knocked and went in.

'I didn't ask to see you,' Mr Jack said.

'I know but I want to see you,' I replied, steeling myself not to back down, although I don't know where I found the nerve to speak to the chairman in the way I did. 'I'm noticing some of the reserve players are getting opportunities in the first team and I'm not getting a sniff. I'm doing well in the reserves but others are getting in ahead of me.'

Mark Treanor and Budgie had both got into the first team before me but when Mr Jack asked for an example, I, for some reason, blurted out: 'Davie Jones!'

Now, Davie was a great guy, everyone enjoyed his company. He had signed for the club not long after me. We came through the youth system together and in no way was I trying to undermine him or diminish him. He had great technical ability but I reckoned my work rate was better. But Davie was now round and about the first team, starting the odd game or getting a place on the bench, and I was getting nowhere.

'Davie Jones will be a star and you will never be a player, even if you live to be 100,' Mr Jack bellowed.

His response floored me. I was in shock as I descended back down the stairs and my head was all over the place. Was he right? Was I just wasting my time, with no chance of ever making it? His words haunted me for days and I spoke to Tommy Callaghan about it. He told me to keep working hard and if my future wasn't with Clydebank, I'd get my chance somewhere else.

Looking back on it, I still don't know if Mr Jack was playing mind games with me or if he actually meant it. I certainly didn't feel I needed a kick up the backside. As for Davie, we lost touch and I really don't know how his football career panned out after he left Kilbowie. He was a good guy, intelligent and I'm sure he would have been successful in whatever he chose to do.

It's always tough for a striker to force his way into the team and we also had some talented players leading the line. Blair Miller was an excellent striker and then there were the likes of Tam McGorm and Willie Connell, two local lads, Mike Larnach, an experienced pro who had played at Newcastle and was back at the club, and big Joe Sweeny. Then, on New Year's Day 1981, Mr Jack brought Tommy Coyne to Kilbowie.

Credit to Mr Jack because I don't know where he discovered Tommy, who had been balancing his fledgling career with life as a joiner. He really was a gem of a player and would go on to become my regular strike partner. We were a strong double act who complemented each other well; we were both happy to do the hard graft and we never gave defenders time on the ball. But Tommy was an intelligent player and also a great finisher who would often beat me in the scoring charts – but, then again, he did take the penalties!

I actually made my debut in the October before Tommy arrived. I came on as a sub in a 2-1 win over Berwick Rangers at Kilbowie but I have to admit I can't remember anything about it. It's funny the way old pros struggle to recall so many things from their careers.

I should have made my debut before that. However, I had blotted my copybook. I had met up with the reserve team at Queen Street Station, only to be informed that I was to make my way to Kilbowie for the first-team game. I didn't really have time to be nervous and, when I got to the ground, I was told I was to be on the bench. I was out warming up and the boss, Bill Munro, emerged on to the pitch. He was immaculate; smart red tracksuit, not a silver hair on his head out of place. Bill would always jog about the pitch with us or ping balls about and, just as he was running across the pitch, he jogged straight into the path of one of my wayward passes. There wasn't a lot of pace on the ball – it was one of those chipped passes – but such was the shock that Bill was knocked off his feet. There weren't many fans in at the time but the few who were there – and some of the players as well – were laughing and I don't think Bill could take that. He got to his feet and started looking for a culprit. My sheepish expression gave me away and Bill sidled up to me, put his arm around me and said: 'I know it was you, Williamson, you'll not be going on today.'

My debut was going to have to wait a little longer.

In fact, it was to be on 11 October 1980 when I came off the bench for Blair Millar in that win over Berwick in front of a passionate crowd of 831 people. I only know this after consulting the Clydebank FC archive. I don't even remember my first goal, which, incidentally, and thanks again to the archive, was against Dumbarton on 21 January 1982 in a 2-1 defeat in a Stirlingshire Cup semi-final. It was on a Thursday night – and 123 turned up to watch my moment of history.

The first game I truly remember was again against Dumbarton, about a month or so later. My big mate Mark Treanor had been sent off the week before against Queen's Park and the suspension meant there was a vacancy at right-back. I wasn't expecting to get the tap on the shoulder, as I'd never played there before, but the gaffer adjudged I was the only right-sided option he had and, so, I was in. I was so desperate to play that I didn't mind what position it was.

The game was so different at right-back and I found the pitch opened up for me. As a striker, you are usually playing with your back to goal and for much of the time your passing options are limited. You may have a strike partner to hit or a winger or a supporting midfield player if you were lucky. At full-back, you had a winger, options in midfield, a centre-back or even a striker if you went long. If you were deep, there was also the option of using the keeper. It was a whole different ball game.

We won 2-0 and I must have done all right, as, with Mark still out, I started the next game, which was at home against Hearts and we won 2-1. I loved it and I played really well.

Back then, I was really fit and I would bomb forward at every chance I got. I gave their poor winger a hell of a time, because I recognised early in the game that he couldn't match me for fitness. His head would be shaking every time he had to match my run and because he was tiring, he was unable to offer up anything on the offensive side.

I played at right-back for the next couple of games – a draw at Kilmarnock and a win away to East Stirling. Then Mark was straight back in, although I didn't drop out of the team, as I was moved up front. We lost 5-1 to Hearts at Kilbowie, with Willie Pettigrew scoring four of them.

I do wonder what would have happened had I been allowed to stick it out at full-back. Could I have made a career as an attacking defender? I wonder just how far in the game I could have got.

I really enjoyed Clydebank. We had the makings of a really decent team and were nearer the top of the division than the bottom.

We had a smashing big keeper in Jim Gallacher, an ever-present who would go on to play nearly 750 games for the club. My big mate Mark Treanor was at right-back, Tony Gervaise at left-back, with our skipper, Jim Fallon, and big Gerry McLauchlan in central defence.

Fallon, or Faldo as we called him, was a great player, and there was no way Mr Jack would ever sell him, even though he could have played with the best in the land. He was hugely important in helping to develop the young players.

One day after training, I was in the big communal bath with Faldo. I never brought a toilet bag with me – I just used the soap that was there – but I noticed Faldo had one of those wee bottles of shampoo you usually get in hotels. I politely asked him if I could use it but he told me: 'Fuck off!' Now, Faldo was bald across the top but had hair on the sides and I cheekily asked if the bottle would last him all season. Christ, he nearly drowned me!

Of all the highlights of my time at Clydebank, one game sticks out – a hat-trick at Hampden towards the end of the 1982/83 season. It was a soaking wet day in May and, with only a few hundred inside the vast stadium, it had an odd atmosphere, but I always loved playing there.

Faldo was our usual free-kick taker and, with the ground and ball being so wet, I told him that, if he got a chance, he should hit it low at the keeper, because I reckoned he would not be able to hold the ball, which was like a bar of soap. This happened not once but twice. Faldo rattled in a free kick, the keeper spilled it and I was there to pick up the pieces. I got two like that – and my pal Tommy Coyne set me up with the other. Happy times!

That 82/83 season, we had been pushing at the top of the league and ran eventual winners St Johnstone close. We lost our last game of the campaign, 2-1 at home to Partick Thistle, with Maurice Johnston among the Jags' scorers. We would eventually finish third, with Hearts joining St Johnstone in going up and Morton and Kilmarnock coming down.

But we knew we had the makings of a right good team.

We had Gerry Ronald on the right and Jimmy Given on the left, with Gerry McCabe and Dave Houston in the middle.

I always thought guys like Gerry McCabe and Gerry Ronald should have had a chance at a higher level with one of the bigger teams. There were always rumours that Celtic were interested in Gerry McCabe – but I think he started them himself!

Tommy Coyne was arguably the best striker I ever played with. We had a great partnership, we linked up well and we worked hard for each other, which is all you ever want. We were the perfect double act. Sometimes, one would sacrifice a run or a shot because the other had a better option and then vice versa.

But the man who really made us as players was Gerry McCabe. He played off the front and was a good midfield player who was always able to find one of us with a telling pass. We would do cross-over runs, working at it with coach Sammy Henderson in training, and Gerry would play one of the two of us through and we would finish with a shot at goal. So, we would take that into the game on a Saturday.

Sammy always made sure that if a team was breaking up our right-hand side with their left-back, I had to track him and go all the way with him. If he never crossed that ball, I had to keep going and keep going.

We used to terrorise defenders. We wouldn't give them a moment's peace. The two of us were really fit and we worked really hard. We were good for each other and we scored a lot of goals.

The problem with building a successful partnership is that envious eyes were watching us and it was clear that Tommy was destined for bigger and better things. It was no surprise when Dundee United came calling and my partner was soon away to Tannadice. He would go on to play for Celtic and the Republic of Ireland, through an Irish family connection, and even played at the World Cup in the States in 1994.

Tommy certainly deserved his move; it meant he would be going full-time and was off the building sites, while I was still having to work on just to make ends meet. But with every silver lining, there is a cloud ... well, two in fact. The first was that I was worried that, without Tommy, things would drop off for me and I wouldn't get the move I craved. The second was that Tommy was a key part of the team we were building at Kilbowie and that, without him, we would be less of a threat. I suppose we shouldn't have been surprised, though. Mr Jack never hid from the fact that he was always looking to sell the talent.

I went in to see him soon after Tommy left. 'You told me you were building a team that was good enough for promotion,' I said. 'But you've let one of our best players go.'

He just looked at me and said: 'Don't you worry, I'll be selling you soon as well.'

At the time, I didn't believe him, although I knew there were scouts from a couple of clubs south of the border who were watching me and had spoken to me. I just had to keep on plugging away. I was never going to let my efforts drop – it was all about the team and I certainly wasn't going to let anyone down.

The season drifted on into December. I was still scoring goals. I had got a couple against Alloa and had scored the opener in a 3-0 win away to Meadowbank Thistle. Off the field, things were changing as well and I was about to buy my first house in Riddrie with my girlfriend.

We were at her parents' house one night when the phone rang. She answered and said it was Jack Steedman.

I took the phone from her and he immediately asked: 'Have you bought that house in Riddrie yet?'

I told him that, while we were close to tying up loose ends, nothing had been signed and sealed.

'Well, don't,' he said. 'I'm selling you to Berwick Rangers.'

I'm sure Mr Jack could feel my stunned silence from the other end of the line. I didn't know what to say. I mean absolutely no disrespect to Berwick but there was no way I was going there.

'Stand by the phone,' Mr Jack said. 'I'll call you back in an hour with the details.'

I think I probably still had the phone in my hand with my mouth hanging open when I turned to my girlfriend and told her I was being sold to Berwick.

'It's not happening,' I said. 'I'm not going to Berwick.'

I mean, apart from anything else, I still had my job on the site. There was no way I could move away from Glasgow. So, the next hour was spent in tense conversation with my girlfriend and her family, planning what I was going to say when Mr Jack phoned back. I was ready for him. I wasn't going to back down.

True to his word, the phone rang almost exactly an hour later. Before I could say anything, Mr Jack spoke.

'Right, it's Glasgow Rangers you're going to,' he said. 'You've to meet Mr Wallace at Ibrox tomorrow morning at 9am. Do the deal and all the best!'

Bang! The phone was put down. There was no 'thanks for your time with us' or 'thanks for the 37 goals you scored in 88 appearances'. I didn't even have the chance to thank him for giving me the opportunity. Still, not that I knew it at the time, but the club were to become £100,000 richer and I was to see none of it.

I didn't sleep a wink. I was a Rangers player.

The next day, after the formalities of my transfer were completed, I returned to Lafferty's to say my thank yous and goodbyes and to pick up my tools.

Lafferty's was a curious place in that it was full of current and ex-players. Marty Hughes, who broke through from the Clydebank youth team with me, was a quantity surveyor. Tommy Coyne had been a joiner. Alan Logan, known to everyone as Inchie, was a plumber when he wasn't turning out for St Mirren. Christ, Jimmy Johnstone would be driving the van on some occasions. Jimmy Johnstone! The finest player ever to pull on a Celtic jersey. He was the best I ever saw and a true gentleman into the bargain.

But the star of the show was my site manager, Bobby Shearer. He had made more than 400 appearances for Rangers, was a true legend and had captained the club to the treble in 1964.

As I was leaving, with everyone wishing me good luck, Mr Shearer took me to one side.

'Now, you know what you're joining here,' he said. 'This is more than a football club. It's an institution. These people will expect a lot from you.'

I thanked him and he wished me all the best. I got my tools and left. There was a story that I threw them in a skip but that's nonsense. My trowel alone was worth about 20 quid!

Anyway, I didn't know if I would be needing them again if it all went wrong.

CHAPTER 4
TO IBROX

TODAY, IF Rangers are making a new signing, there is a press conference and a large media presence. Photographers are flashing away, usually with the new arrival pitch side or sitting in a prime seat in the stand, perhaps with the blue Rangers strip on, their name on the back, but most certainly with the obligatory scarf raised over his head. Agents and the club may have been talking for some time to hammer out the deal, with specific terms haggled over in the prospective player's contract. When I wandered along Edmiston Drive on 7 December 1983 in the shadow of the Bill Struth Main Stand, I was on my own. There was no press pack awaiting my arrival.

Entering the main door, into the hallowed inner sanctum of the club, always feels special. The stand itself was designed by the famed architect Archibald Leitch in the 1920s and it reeks of history. Great wood panel walls surround you, paintings of legends of the past stare down at you and a vast marble staircase bends out in front of you as it climbs up to the next level. To the right, in those days, was a little window, where Stan the commissionaire was stationed, resplendent in his uniform – all brass buckles and sharp crease in his trousers. I had got to know Stan over the years but I still felt a little awkward.

'I've been told to report here to meet the manager,' I told him. Stan's expression hardly changed as he directed me towards a bench at the bottom of the stairs and invited me to take a seat and wait.

The nerves were kicking in now and the time seemed to pass forever before Stan returned and invited me to climb the marble staircase to the manager's office. I walked up, past the bust of legendary manager Bill Struth, which is strategically positioned so that he can keep an eye on everybody who goes in and out of the stadium. At the top of the stairs is a life-size painting of Alan Morton, all 5ft 4in of him, the Wee Blue Devil who played more than 400 times for the club. At this point, I was hoping I would be able to play more than one.

I knocked on the manager's door, which is just to the left at the top of the stairs. A gruff, booming voice came back and Mr Wallace told me to come in.

Jock Wallace had returned to the club only a matter of weeks before and I was to be his first signing. In his first spell at the club, he had been Willie Waddell's right-hand man, helping to lead the team to perhaps their greatest hour – the victory over Dynamo Moscow in the European Cup Winners' Cup in 1972. He also had a key role to play in one of the darkest episodes of the club's history. Jock was in goal for Berwick when they beat Rangers 1-0 in 1967 in the Scottish Cup. John Greig, who played that day, was to describe it as 'probably the worst result in the history of our club'.

Taking over the manager's job when Waddell moved upstairs, Wallace led Rangers to two successive trebles and had halted Celtic's run of nine consecutive titles. Despite this obvious success, he had left the club to try his hand south of the border with Leicester City but was at Motherwell when the SOS came from Ibrox once again. Things had not been going well at all under Greig, who was a legend at Ibrox as a player but who was toiling as manager. By October of the 82/83 season, Rangers were sixth in the table and angry fans had been gathering outside the main door on Edmiston Drive to demand change. How fickle fans are. This was the man who had lifted the Cup Winners' Cup on that magical night in Barcelona. In 1999, they were to vote Greig 'the greatest ever Ranger'. There's a statue of him outside the stadium.

As it happened, the Rangers board had first approached Alex Ferguson and then Jim McLean, both of whom rejected their advances.

The McLean move had looked a done deal. Dundee United had given Rangers permission to speak to him and he would have brought Walter Smith with him as his assistant. Walter would get there eventually and become a legend at the club but he would have to wait, because Wee Jim knocked back Rangers, even though he would have become one of the best paid managers in British football! He was quoted in the papers as saying that he 'felt a big regret for letting Rangers down but it would have been a bigger regret leaving Dundee United'.

If Wallace had any qualms about returning as third choice, he didn't show it. Rangers needed him and that was all that mattered.

Jock stood up behind his desk and held out a massive shovel-like hand. He was, let me tell you, a huge, intimidating figure. And, my God, did he have a presence about him. You certainly didn't have to turn around to know Jock had entered the room.

I sat down and Jock buzzed through for the club secretary, Campbell Ogilvie, to join him and bring the contract.

As we were waiting, Jock asked me: 'Is you dad a Blue Nose?'

I don't know if this was some sort of test. Jock was very close to James Mortimer, a well-known Glasgow pub owner, who I knew and who shared an aunt with my mother. He would certainly have known that Mum was a Protestant and Dad was a Catholic, although neither had much interest in religion.

I chose my words carefully, although I was being honest, and said: 'Dad's not interested in football. I just know that he'll be pleased for me.'

Campbell duly arrived and handed the contract to Jock, who flicked through it before sliding it under my nose. He offered me a pen and I signed where I was instructed.

'Nothing to discuss?' Jock asked me. 'Do you not want to read it?'

In all my time, first as a player then as a manager, I have never been any good with contracts and all I wanted to do was to sign it to officially become a Rangers player.

'No, it's fine,' I replied. Jock would later say it was the easiest contract negotiation he ever had.

As I was putting my name to a contract that would earn me £300 a week over the next three years, Jock turned to Ogilvie, who was standing beside his desk.

'I want this place checked for bugs,' Wallace said. News of my signing had appeared in the paper the night before and Jock was fuming. I certainly hadn't leaked anything and I have often wondered if it was Jack Steedman who tipped off the press but I couldn't be sure.

They talked about it for a few moments – and I was wondering what kind of place I was joining.

Jock then turned to me. He laid it on the line in no uncertain terms what it meant to be a Rangers player and the standards the club demanded of anyone who signed for them. Such strict rules fitted Jock's character perfectly. This was a guy who had served his country in both Northern Ireland and the Malaya jungle. He would tell tales of his times in the army – and rumour has it he arranged for a radio mast to be constructed in the jungle just so he could find out the Rangers score. But his military background certainly shaped his managerial style – and he ruled with an iron fist.

Bill Struth, whose bust I had passed as I climbed the marble staircase earlier, had started it all when he took over managing the club in the 1920s, insisting from the outset that all players wore a suit, shirt and tie – in those days, even a bowler hat – and were all clean-shaven. Herein was my first problem as a Rangers player.

I had arrived that day in a collar and tie but, as was the fashion, was sporting a fair chin full of what I suppose would later become known as designer stubble.

'Get that off,' Jock instructed me, pointing at my beard.

So, my first act as a Rangers player was to head off to the nearest barber's for a clean shave. Somewhat fortuitously, although I always believed Jock had arranged it, a photographer was waiting in the Ibrox foyer to join me. The first pictures of me as a Rangers player were in a barber's chair getting a shave.

I arrived at Ibrox the next day for my first time training with my new team-mates. Football is a small world and already I knew most of the boys. The Clydebank connection was there with Davie Cooper – an absolute legend of a player.

There were guys like Ally Dawson, Colin McAdam and Bobby Russell, who were to become great mates. Peter McCloy was an iconic Ibrox keeper. There was Ian Redford and Robert Prytz.

Despite the poor run of form, Greig had been given money to spend. John McClelland, an Irish international, had arrived, as had Jim Bett, but most of the cash at the club was being ploughed into the redevelopment of Ibrox, so every penny was a prisoner. I suppose that was why they bought me! The talk was Jock had been trying to get Ian Wallace from Nottingham Forest but the price tag was too much.

Among the strikers who I was to challenge for a starting place, there was a young lad who had come up in the summer for £200,000 after a tricky spell at Sunderland. His name was Ally McCoist.

He's people-friendly, Coisty. He's always been like that and is great company. We never had a problem. And he's never changed. He was a character from day one. The only thing he changed was his ability to put the ball in the back of the net but that came from experience and he had that desire and that willingness to go in again and again. Even though he was missing chances, he would still go back in and try and score. He never ran away or tried to hide from anything. He's never changed over the years. Everybody still likes him, has still got time for him.

It wasn't a problem going into the dressing room and meeting up with the Rangers guys. They were all very welcoming. We used to go and play snooker after training.

Four or five of us would go out for some lunch. We used to socialise, alcohol-free obviously, because everybody recognised you and you weren't supposed to be drinking during the week.

But the one guy I was nervous about seeing was the centre-back, Craig Paterson. Earlier that season, when I was still at Clydebank, we had played Rangers at Ibrox in the League Cup. Don't let the 4-0 scoreline fool you – we gave as good as we got that night. McCoist opened the scoring with what was his first goal at Ibrox but, after that, we were in control and Gerry McCabe came close to levelling when he rifled in a shot from all of 30 yards, only for it to cannon off the bar with Peter McCloy well beaten. Shortly after that, Gerry had another great chance but McCloy pulled off a decent save. Ten minutes into the second half, a mazy Davie Cooper run set up Bobby Russell for their second. McCoist added a third and Robert Prytz completed the scoring late on.

The game had been a bit of a feisty affair and Tommy Coyne had caught Craig Paterson with a flying elbow that had bust open his lip. Craig was raging and he was hunting for bodies. He didn't care if it was Tommy or whoever he got, he just wanted to get someone! He tried to get me but I was too fast for him and, so, the verbals started flying. These things happen in the heat of battle and I've always been able to leave them on the pitch when the final whistle sounds. I hoped Craig was of a similar mind because, as I was heading for training that morning, I suddenly remembered that I had shouted to Craig: 'Ach, you're not fit to wear the jersey!' I felt sick to my stomach, hoping to God that big Craig had a short memory!

Craig lived in Edinburgh but, being the true pro he was, he always made sure he was one of the first in for training.

Being super-keen on my first day, I made sure I was in sharp as well – and it meant Craig was one of the first people I met. I braced myself for what was to come but the big man held out his hand, had a big beaming smile and welcomed me to Rangers.

I couldn't have been more wrong about him and have always regretted what I shouted at him. Craig was a gentleman off the pitch and a class act on it.

I thought that training full-time would be easy. Turn up in the morning, do a bit of ball work, some fitness stuff, maybe work on some tactics and then home after lunch. And I was no longer having to get up at the crack of dawn to do my shift on the building site. But it took me time to adjust. We would all gather in the morning for some warm-up and fitness work at Ibrox and then go over to the Albion training ground, which was just across the road from the stadium. It was the site of an old greyhound track that the club had taken over.

Jock was very much a hands-on manager. I liked working with him. Coaching-wise, I didn't learn much, because it was all about desire. He knew how to deal with players, though, and get the best out of you. He would always be drilling you in training, with his assistant, Alex Totten. I could pretty much cope with all of that – although it was a jump up in standard from what I was used to – but it was when we would return to Ibrox and do some circuit training in a makeshift gym under one of the stands that I struggled. I'd never done much in the way of weight work and I would often find myself feeling nauseous.

But I got my head down and worked and worked. That first week was a bit of an eye-opener but there was a game approaching that weekend, away at Motherwell, and, while I didn't expect to be in the starting XI, I was confident I would make the matchday squad, which I duly did. Matchday itself with Rangers, on an away day, meant a pre-match meal at the stadium before the bus trip to wherever we were going. Jock always kept his starting line-up close to his chest, so it was pretty close to kick-off before I discovered I was going to be starting in the No.8 jersey.

Jock's wise words to me before we went out was just to go out and 'do what you do!' But for 45 minutes, the game passed me by. The week before, I had been playing in front of a handful of fans at Clydebank against Meadowbank. Now there were nearly 14,000 in Fir Park and it seemed most of them were there just to scream and shout at Jock. After his spell managing Leicester, he had returned north to take the manager's job at Fir Park. It was from there that he left to take the job at Ibrox. This was his return to Motherwell for the first time – and the frustrated Fir Park fans were letting him know, in no uncertain terms, what they thought of him.

The report in the paper the next day read: 'Rangers' new £100,000 signing Bobby Williamson must have been wishing he had stayed at his old job of sandblasting. It certainly was safer than some of the flak flying around Fir Park as Motherwell sought to put one over former boss Jock Wallace.'

Somehow, we went into half-time a goal up after Colin McAdam headed home a pinpoint Davie Cooper free kick. But there had been two penalties missed, one for each side, and it was a tight, tousy affair. Not that I had done much to help proceedings. No matter how hard I tried, I couldn't get on the ball and, when I did, my second touch was a tackle.

When we got into the tight away dressing room, before I could even sit down, Jock had me by the throat.

'What the hell are you doing?' he shouted. 'You were a crabbit wee bastard at Clydebank and that's why I bought you. Now go out there and do it.'

Talk about having to hit the ground running! There was no gently easing yourself into the role. This was Rangers. Mr Shearer had been right with the advice he had given me just the week before when I picked up my tools from Lafferty's. A lot was expected of me and I had to show it from the very start. Christ, Rangers at the time must have had about eight strikers to pick from – guys like Coisty, Sandy Clark, Big Colin McAdam, Davie Mitchell from Australia, John MacDonald, Andy Kennedy, Iain Ferguson and a young Robert Fleck breaking through. It wasn't like my time at Clydebank where, if the goals dried up, you could play your way through until you hit the back of the net again. Not at Ibrox. If you weren't scoring, you were out and it could be weeks before you got your chance again.

We eventually won the game 3-0, with second-half goals from Davie Cooper and Davie Mitchell, but it was a tough learning experience for me. I tell you, Rangers played with ten men that day – I was just a fan who happened to be on the pitch.

One interesting side note from that game came just a week later. If the Motherwell fans had been angry that Jock had left them to go to manage Rangers, they were fuming when he went back and bought their goalkeeper Nicky Walker!

Big Jock was great at getting the lads to bond. Team spirit within the squad was so important to him. Perhaps it was his background in the army and seeing action on the other side of the world. I suppose that, in that scenario, if you're not part of a team, all pulling for one and other, you're dead. You can't compare a football team with life in combat but that all-for-one one-for-all attitude does exist in both worlds. To Jock, it was the beginning, middle and end. He was always looking to get the lads away and I had only been there a week when we were up in the Highlands for a testimonial at Ross County, with an overnight stay so the guys could have a few beers together. It didn't take me long to realise that when you're with either side of the Old Firm, your team-mates became your social buddies. I had already begun to drift away from my old social scene and was spending more and more time with my new team-mates – guys like Ally Dawson, John MacDonald and Bobby Russell. We would go out after games with our girlfriends – a close-knit group. We were all aware that you had to be careful if people who weren't players joined our company. You had to watch what you were saying and were always fearful that something, some little bit of idle gossip, could end up in the press. Ally McCoist's mates, a lad called Knoxy and another named Cliffy, were an exception and were trusted members of the group. There was another lad, Billy Jones, and the Scottish comedian Mr Abie, whose real name was Robert Abraham, who would often join us. There were others but we kept it pretty tight, although I have to say that in all my time as a player at Rangers, I never had one bit of bother from fans of any club – Celtic included.

I realised against County that, while it was a non-competitive game, Rangers don't really play friendlies. County were a Highland League side at the time but Jock insisted we kept our foot on the pedal and we ran out 6-0 winners. To cap it all, I scored a hat-trick. Two games for Rangers and I had scored three goals. I felt I was off and running.

We got back to the hotel and Big Jock let us loose with a few beers and a singsong before allowing us out, under strict orders that we had to be back by midnight – and there were to be no women brought back to the hotel. The night was uneventful and I was back in the room, sharing with Sandy Clark. We were chatting away when we heard young women laughing and giggling. Sandy poked his head out of the door, only to met by the boss, whose face was like thunder.

'What ye doing, Clark?' he bellowed.

Thinking quickly, Sandy said he was off to the loo – there was no en suite. 'Hurry up then,' the boss ordered.

We found out the next day that the young writer from the club magazine, *Rangers News*, had been unaware of Jock's order about women and had brought them back. Peter McCloy had found him screaming outside the room because Big Jock had floored him with a punch. He had been about to follow through when Peter, brave man that he was, got between them to break it up.

My scoring touch continued in the next two games as I netted against Dundee in a 2-1 win and then against Hibs in a 2-0 victory at Easter Road.

One of the best goals I ever scored for Rangers came in January 1984 but, no matter how hard I have tried in this YouTube age, I have never been able to find any footage of it.

We were to play in a one-off match against Feyenoord for something called the KLM Challenge Cup. For the life of me, I don't know why the game was arranged or what it was all for but I do remember the kind of night it was. It was bloody freezing, the icy rain sweeping in across the park and the wind so cold it chilled you to the bone. I'm sure a couple of the players had hypothermia after it! Ibrox was virtually empty. Few fans could be persuaded to leave their warm homes and I can't say I blamed them. But Feyenoord had two nuggets of gold in their team – Johan Cruyff, who was coming to the end of his sparkling playing career, and a young guy called Ruud Gullit, who was being tipped as the new kid on the block.

The game kicked off and the two Feyenoord centre-halves were letting themselves into things gently. They passed it from one to another and I reckoned I could intercept the ball if they were going to do it again. Sure enough, that's exactly what they did and one of them, a guy by the name of Bernie Wijnstekers, took a bad touch. I was already on the move, nicked the ball and rattled it past the keeper to score. There were 18 seconds on the clock. When I turned to celebrate, my team-mates were still standing in the positions they had been in at kick-off. Big Jock had been late getting into the dugout and arrived just as Feyenoord were restarting the game. He was totally oblivious to my goal and assumed what he was watching was the game kicking off for the first time. He watched the Dutch players skilfully pass the ball about and turned to Alex Totten beside him to voice his concern that we could be up against it. Only then did Totts tell him we were 1-0 up!

After ten minutes, Ian Redford put us 2-0 up. All good. Then the class began to tell. Two minutes later, Gullit rattled one in from 25 yards. Then Cruyff, who was 36 but still a genius of a player, carved open our defence with a sublime pass that Willy Carbo finished off. Midway through the second half, Cruyff tapped his side into a 3-2 lead. Robert Prytz got us level with a penalty but we were to lose 7-6 in a shoot-out.

It was a memorable experience to be on the field with these players. Cruyff coasted through the game, until he limped off, but Gullit had such power and pace that few of us were surprised he went on to have the career he had. That night at Ibrox, however, had a major impact on him. It was the first time he had come across our genius on the left wing, Davie Cooper. Years later, Gullit was to proclaim Coops as one of the best players he had ever seen and included him in his all-time top XI of players he had played with or against. 'He had incredible skill and a command of the ball,' Gullit said. 'There was something about his play that made him stand out. When I saw him play, I was flabbergasted. I remember thinking to myself "Who is this guy?" I fell completely in love with his play. It surprised me a lot he didn't become a big international name. It's incredible that a player with his skills did not make it to the international top flight. I don't know if it was because he stayed in Scotland but he had the talent to be one of the greats. He was a unique player, not comparable to any other. No, Davie Cooper was one of a kind.'

I don't know why he hadn't included me in his top team. I mean, I scored before anyone else had touched the ball! Honest, I did! But he was right about Coops. He just always seemed to be on the same wavelength as McCoist. I just couldn't time my runs correctly with Davie. I'd always be in too early, because I thought he was crossing it but he would then jink back out and beat the full-back again. So, I had to recycle my run, clear the space and Coisty would arrive to score. Time and again.

Jock had been able to work his magic with the team and, after the poor start to the season that had cost John Greig his job, we went on an unbeaten run of 19 matches, if you take into account cup competitions. As way of a reward, Jock arranged for a few days away in Palma. Much as there was to be some downtime and we would get some time to relax, we did train most days. I shared with Nicky Walker. At the time, we hardly knew each other. Nicky had not long arrived at the club from Motherwell and I'm sure it made sense to put the two new boys together. Nicky and I couldn't have come from more different backgrounds. He was part of the famous Walker's Shortbread dynasty – he runs the company now – and I was a lad from Easterhouse. But we hit it off immediately. We had to. Our room only had one double bed, which we had to share. I remember waking up one morning, wondering what the time was. Instead of getting out of bed and walking round to the bedside cabinet where Nicky's watch was, I instead tried to reach over him. I didn't have a top on and the look on Nicky's face as he opened his eyes as I put my bare arm over him is one I will take to my grave. The utter fear and confusion in his eyes. I was in tears laughing.

Jock also took us on a trip to Malta for a couple of friendlies and some R&R. He included a number of the young boys who were forcing their way into the team. Guys like Hugh Burns, Derek Ferguson, Iain Durrant, Scott Nisbet and Stuart Beattie. All would go on to have good careers but poor Stuart had to pack it all in in his early 20s after a back injury.

They were all full of mischief and when the gaffer let us go out one night, we made the mistake of letting the young team out of our sight. Sometime later, the older boys, me included, were hanging around the reception of the hotel when we spied this local with a policeman standing at the desk. They came over and asked to speak to the manager. Jock wasn't around, so, when Peter McCloy asked what the matter was, we were told that some damage had been caused to parked cars when a group of boys had detached a trailer and let it roll down a hill. The crew had scarpered but the obvious insinuation was that this was our young team-mates up to high jinks. We knew how Jock would react to this blatant disregard of orders, so Peter asked how much it would cost to fix the damage and we all had a whip-round to keep the lads out of trouble. The boss would never have to know; problem solved, end of story.

We were still hanging around when the gaffer and Totts came back into the hotel, followed by another policeman, who went straight up to a different receptionist, demanded to see the gaffer and proceeded, much to our horror, to recount the same sorry tale.

Big Jock listened and then asked: 'How do you know it was our players?'

The policeman was silent.

'You've got no evidence,' Jock said. 'Now, fuck off!'

And he did! We could have saved ourselves a whip-round had we taken the Jock Wallace approach to international relations!

Our great run came to a crashing halt when Dundee beat us 3-2 at Ibrox in a Scottish Cup replay. But the team had a chance to make amends just a week later when we faced

Celtic in the League Cup Final at Hampden. I was to play no part in the game. After playing for Clydebank earlier in the competition, I was cup-tied. But I had a front-row seat for the day Ally McCoist rescued his Rangers career.

I always thought that I had been brought in to replace Coisty. He had done well at his first club, St Johnstone, and earned a move south to Sunderland but he struggled at Roker Park. He had arrived at Ibrox the summer before me but these were tough times at Rangers and the fans, who had already seen John Greig out of the manager's office, were turning on Coisty, who had become a target for their frustrations. He never gave up trying, though. He always made the runs, always made himself available, always wanted the ball. His resilience and determination were something to behold. A lesser player, a weaker character would have struggled, would have hidden. Not McCoist.

For all that, though, I reckoned Big Jock was losing faith in him. Perhaps time was running out. That all changed on 25 March 1984. True to form, Jock had the team ready to run through brick walls. In a TV interview before the game, he said: 'I fancy us very strongly. We've got the battle fever on today.'

He was right. Rangers 3 Celtic 2. McCoist hat-trick. That was the game in which McCoist convinced Big Jock of what he could be and the player he would become. Even though I didn't play, I couldn't have been more delighted for the team and for McCoist. As he was to prove over the years, each time he was written off, he came bouncing back. Look at the time when Mark Hateley and Mo Johnston were ahead of him in the Graeme Souness era. Ally had to spend a lot of time sitting on the bench. He could have left but he didn't and came back to be a key starting figure. It's about character and McCoist had that in spades.

The League Cup win had given the whole place a much-needed feelgood factor and I was thoroughly enjoying being part of the Rangers family. For a massive club, a sporting institution, I always felt there was a close-knit feel to the whole place.

There was Davie Marshall, the head groundsman, and his team, who were responsible for the upkeep of the pitches and that kind of thing, and in the kitchen, there was Irene, old Lizzie and Tiny. There were real characters. Lizzie's eyesight was failing her and she would ask you what you would like on your roll in the morning – link, square or bacon. If you asked Lizzie for a link sausage, she would put her hand in the pan to find it!

There was a great lad, Dougal, who ran around doing odd jobs, and Stan, the well-groomed commissioner at the front door, was a gentleman. Upstairs, we had Campbell Ogilvie, the club secretary, who was in with the bricks of the place, and legends of the past like Willie Thornton were always about. The women in the offices, the people who kept the place running were all great and you felt part of a big team all pushing in the same direction.

We also had the ladies in the laundry room who had great patter and liked to tease the younger players. At Rangers at that time, your training kit only got washed at the weekend and you hung up your kit in the drying cupboard in the dressing room. You can imagine the smell when you opened the door near the end of the week. The socks were not numbered, so, if you got in early, you could swap your socks with a softer pair. Otherwise, the socks you were left with, you had to break up to put on after a few days!

When I became a manager, I let the players know in no uncertain terms that it's not just about the team in the dressing room, it's everyone at the club. We were representing THEM. We needed to win for THEM. They were all doing their bit off the park, unseen and without any recognition from the fans in the stand. Everything they were doing, all the hours they were putting in was focused on making sure the team on the park had the best chance of success, and when you lost or didn't play well, you really did feel as if you had let them down.

I was back in the team for the next game after the cup triumph, a 3-0 win away to Motherwell. Although I didn't score that day, I had my chances. One, in particular, fell to me just beyond the penalty spot. I made good contact but got just too much on it and the ball clipped the bar on the way over. I should have scored but didn't think too much about it, as the team had won quite convincingly. But Jock was not happy and instructed assistant Alex Totten to schedule individual shooting practice for me that week at the Albion training ground. Totts did exactly that but he didn't schedule any goalkeeper to be there with us, so we ended up shooting into an empty net. It was boring, so, to keep myself interested, I started trying to put the ball in top corners – left and right – but without much success. The Albion had a large wall surrounding it to keep the local kids out and, because everybody just lived for football, if you kicked the ball over the wall, you had to race out and get it smartish or some wee devil would be away with it. With it just being me and Totts at the session, it was yours truly who had to race out to get the ball each time I put it over the wall. The third time I did it, Totts was so fed up and frustrated he abandoned the session.

Celtic got their revenge for our League Cup win just a couple of weeks after the final when they beat us 3-0 at Parkhead, with the McStay brothers, Paul and Willie, getting a goal each and Davie Provan a late third. The feelgood factor from that Hampden success had well and truly disappeared. We had given the fans something to shout about with the cup win – and our long unbeaten run – but the league season was threatening to peter out once again.

I remember one game at St Mirren. Big John 'Cowboy' McCormack was playing in midfield for the Buddies. He was a great guy who I had got to know at Clydebank when I was breaking through. We were part-time but I had no doubt that Cowboy was a real pro! Back then, after training, Cowboy would drag some players on to the park to work on throw-ins! He was a manager even back then.

We both scored that day and, with the game level, we won a corner. I wasn't even marking Cowboy but they got a breakaway and he took off up the middle. I thought I had the pace to catch him but, as we reached the halfway line, I was struggling to keep up. The ball was in the wide area and I knew that if they got a decent enough cross into the box, Cowboy was sure to get on the end of it. I had to stop him, so I tugged at him. He just stopped running, turned round and grabbed me by the throat and gave me some proper verbals. I could have reacted but I didn't, I just took it. I was always good at not responding to anything anyone said to me on the pitch. Vinnie Jones once had a go at me, calling me, among other things, 'a Sweaty', which I knew was rhyming slang (Sweaty Sock – Jock), but I let that go, just as I was not responding to Cowboy on this occasion. I never understood why other players reacted to it or why players today go squealing to the newspapers complaining about what someone called them. That's just sad. I could never be offended on the park if an opponent decided to mouth off. I knew it was heat of the moment stuff and I left it out on the park.

I would never shy away from the physical stuff, though. I never tried to deliberately hurt an opponent – that was a definite no-no – but I would never pull out of anything. My biggest victims were goalkeepers. If I was running through, my last touch to set up a shot was more often than not over-hit but, as I had put a lot of effort in, I would try and retrieve the situation. If a goalkeeper was stupid enough to slide out and take the ball, then I was equally stupid enough to try and slide in and kick it through him. I remember catching St Mirren keeper Billy Thomson as he slid out and gathered it. I was sliding in too and caught him in his back. I couldn't complain when I was booked.

With the team having had such a terrible start to the campaign, we were always playing catch-up but it was tough because, as well as our great rivals Celtic, we had to put up with a resurgent Aberdeen and Dundee United. This was the finest Dons team in their history, with the likes of Willie Miller, Alex McLeish and Mark McGhee. Christ, the year before they had beaten Real Madrid to win the Cup Winners' Cup! United were just as strong. They had Richard Gough, Paul Hegarty, Eamonn Bannon and Ralphie Milne, with Paul Sturrock and Davie Dodds up front. United had won the league the season before and Aberdeen would win it this time. We would finish fourth but we knew the final Old Firm game of the season would be important for bragging rights.

The game was at Ibrox and, other than our win in the League Cup Final, we had lost each time we faced them. I played up front alongside Ally McCoist while, in the Celtic team that day, a very young Peter Grant was making his debut. The only other notable mention before kick-off was Jimmy Nicholl being made captain, as he was playing his last game for Rangers after his loan spell for Toronto Blizzard. It wasn't a great game. Both sides huffed and puffed but neither looked as if they would score had the game gone on for a week. At half-time, Jock had drilled it into us just how important it was for us to get the win, how the momentum could carry us into the next season and how vital it was for McCoist or I to try and get on the end of something.

Midway through the second half, Ian Redford pounced on a loose ball on the edge of the box and fired in a shot which Pat Bonner, in the Celtic goal, did well to turn past the post. Davie Cooper flighted in the corner with that wand of a left foot of his and the ball was missed by John McClelland and Danny McGrain as they challenged for it in the air. It came through to me as I was loitering around the penalty spot but I had my back to goal. I could hear McCoist shouting, 'Take a touch!', but it sat up so nicely for me. With one swing of my right boot, I arced the ball over my head with an acrobatic bicycle kick that flew past Bonner into the net. It was my first goal against Celtic, although I'm pleased to say it wasn't my last. You would think that scoring in front of a packed Copland Road Stand, I would celebrate with some gusto. But

I've never been one for overdoing it and I simply raised my hand in the air as first McCoist, then Coops, then the rest of the team mobbed me. It was a fantastic moment – one I'm happy to say I've watched back on many occasions!

Celtic got on top after that but we held firm, and when I was subbed with about 15 minutes to go, I was too nervous to sit in the dugout – choosing instead to head down to the dressing room, hoping the lads could hang on. Time seemed to pass so slowly and then, all of a sudden, the dressing-room door flew open and in walked Jimmy Nicholl.

'Have we won?' I asked him.

'Nah, I've been sent off,' Nicholl replied. He had been booked early on and then had a late kick at Brian McClair. It wasn't the best way to say his farewell to the Rangers fans – although Jimmy would be back in blue before too long.

We did hang on that day. The win was important for morale and it meant Ally Dawson, John MacDonald, Bobby Russell and I were in an even better mood for our trip away, having booked caravans in Port Seton with our families. I was waiting for my girlfriend to pick me up when I got a tap on the shoulder to say I was wanted on the phone. My blood ran cold when I was told it was the police. They asked me what car I drove and when I told them it was a silver Fiesta they replied: 'Aye, it *is* you.'

They told me that Lorraine had been involved in a crash on the motorway. By now, my stomach was doing somersaults and the high of scoring the winning goal was miles away from my thoughts. Thankfully, despite the car being hit and facing the wrong way on the motorway, Lorraine was unhurt and our trip away went on as planned.

We had six games left of that season and, other than a 2-1 win at Dundee United in the very last one, we drew them all. Things had fizzled out and the fourth-place finish in the table was not what anyone wanted. But I had played in 23 games and scored 12 goals, so felt I had made a contribution. I wanted to build on that for the next season and Jock, always keen on a global adventure, had arranged for a tour Down Under. We were to play a series of games and, despite these being friendlies, I knew they were important. I had a feeling that the summer was going to be a big one for me and my career.

I was right – but for all the wrong reasons.

CHAPTER 5

A BROKEN LEG ... THE REAL STORY

JOCK WALLACE loved travelling and promoting Rangers around the world. There are few teams anywhere who can rival the club's global reach. The sprawling diaspora of Rangers fans in places like North America and the Far East means there is always a desperate desire among fans thousands of miles from Scotland to see their team. There cannot be many places on the globe that do not have a Rangers supporters' club somewhere. Apparently, there are more than 600 Rangers supporters' clubs in 35 countries worldwide. That's quite a statistic. In America, there are such clubs as the Texas True Blue, the Big Apple Bears and, in Houston, Texas, the Bayou City Loyal. In Canada, there are the Niagara True Blues, the RSC of Calgary and, in Toronto alone, there are three clubs. From Florida to Vancouver, they fall under the umbrella of the North America Rangers Supporters' Association. They are also in Hong Kong, Thailand, Luxembourg, Spain, Israel, Germany, Sweden, Canada, USA, Dubai, Hong Kong, Bahrain, Thailand, New Zealand and Australia. And it was to those last two that Jock had arranged our tour for the end of the 1983/84 season.

Games were to be played in Melbourne, Sydney, Adelaide, Brisbane, Newcastle and Auckland. But I had a problem. Two days before we were to leave, I still had an issue with my pubic symphysis, which is a joint sandwiched between the left and right sides of your pelvic bone. The doc suggested I take an injection to speed up the recovery but he would have to shave my pubic hair. Little did I know that decision was to come back to haunt me later.

On the day of departure, we all assembled at Ibrox. I had packed four suitcases. Peter McCloy just looked at me, shaking his head.

'What's all that for?' he asked.

'We're going to be away for a while. I thought I'd better bring as much stuff as possible. We're going to need a lot of clothes,' I told him.

Before I had joined Rangers, I hadn't been much of a world traveller. The furthest I went was a trip to Torquay with my mates.

Peter looked at me as if I was mad and told me that the hotels we were to be staying at would have laundry services where our clothes could be washed and ironed. So, on his advice, I left half my gear behind. Big Peter was a great guy and I really enjoyed his company, even though I didn't play golf, which was his true passion. For many years after retiring from football, you could find Peter as the official starter at the prestigious Turnberry golf course in Ayrshire. He also kept McCoist in check – which I loved. If ever Coisty overstepped the mark, there was Big Peter to administer a swift punch to the shoulder.

True to form, Coisty was late getting to Ibrox and he was met by one of Big Jock's steely glares. There was no need for words. The flight to Heathrow was uneventful. When we got there, the only incident of note was the laugh we had while watching this older woman trying to go up the down escalator. I know we shouldn't have been laughing but she was knocking her pan in as we cheered and clapped her every effort to get to the top, only to be met with a resigned sigh when she was back at the bottom again. She must have tried it about five times before we pointed out where the up escalator was.

As we checked in for our flight to Melbourne, Coisty was late again! The boss was waiting for him, the steam coming out of his ears, when he eventually ambled up to the check-in desk. He grabbed Coisty and told him, in no uncertain terms, that if he was late again for anything, he was on the first flight home. Honestly, I've never met anyone like him for poor timekeeping. He gets so much stick for turning up late when he's arranged to meet people but there's just not enough hours in the day for the guy. He might, for instance, arrange to meet someone at five o'clock, then someone else at seven o'clock, thinking he would have plenty of time to make it. But once he's in company, he can't rush away, so his later meeting gets pushed back. The secret is to agree for seven o'clock but don't turn up until eight.

The flight to Melbourne was the longest I've ever been on. I thought we were never getting there and the gaffer had us wearing flannels, blazer and club ties, as was Rangers' tradition. We weren't even allowed to take them off during the flight! When we eventually arrived, we looked like a bag of washing. The boss? He was immaculate, not a hair out of place.

We were all knackered, stumbling through the terminal, desperately wanting to get our heads down, but, as we made for the exit, we were met by this fan waiting for us with his young son. He had a massive Union Jack with Papua New Guinea

Rangers Supporters' Branch in big letters over it. There was no way we could walk past him and Big Jock made sure we all signed this lad's flag. It took a while, because the guy only had one marker pen! But he had travelled over 2,000km just to see us walk through an airport on the off chance we might stop and sign something. What did I tell you about Rangers fans? They're all over the world!

Before we left the airport, Big Jock told us that, when we got to the hotel, we should check in, go to our rooms, drop our luggage and come straight back down for breakfast. Under no circumstances, he said, were we to lie down. We had to push through with the jet lag. I was sharing with Coisty, which we had done on a few trips, and when we got in our room, we threw down our bags and immediately emptied the minibar of the beer, just before the guy knocked on the door to come in and empty the alcohol out of it! We made the mistake of lying down on the beds, just for a few minutes. I don't know how we woke up, or when, but we both knew we were late.

We raced back downstairs and Coisty was really worried. He was well aware we had only just got here but he was on his final warning. Jock had said he would be put on the next plane home and he was not a guy to back down. As this was my first misdemeanour, I was pretty sure I was all right. When we got to the restaurant, there were only three seats left. We sat down and waited for the boss to go mental. Just then, the door flies open and in races Jock's trusted assistant, Alex Totten, all dishevelled, his hair all over the place and full of apologies for being late. There was no way Jock could discipline Coisty without also giving Totts a dressing-down. So, he had to leave it. Coisty was in the clear again!

The breakfast in the hotel was a buffet, so we helped ourselves. I remember eating something in batter – a little round ball. I would eat anything in batter, so I tried it and it was nice but there was an aftertaste that I wasn't sure about, so went back for more. The chef was dishing it out, so I asked him what it was. When he told me it was sheep's brains, I passed.

If we thought that this was a holiday, we were wrong. We trained most days but we did get the odd evening off, with a midnight curfew to be back in the hotel. We were out one night and as it got to about 11.45pm, I turned to Peter McCloy to tell him it was probably time to head back.

'Nonsense,' he said. 'Don't worry about Big Jock. Just relax. I know him, he won't be that strict.'

Fair enough, I thought. Peter had worked with the boss before and obviously knew him better than I did. Who was I, a Rangers player for all of six months, to argue any differently? So, we went to the bar, Peter wanted a gin and I got myself a pint. Before I've even got my drink, Peter's downed his gin and is heading for the door. I just threw some money down on the bar and raced after him. By the time I got outside, Peter was legging it up the road, with me desperately trying to catch up with him. I learned a lesson that night – when it came to Big Jock's curfews, it was every man for himself.

Our Scottish accents were always an attraction when we were out and often made us the centre of attention. When we got back to the hotel, Coisty got into the habit of throwing the crumpled bits of papers with the women's numbers on the table between our beds. We never had any intention of following up on them – as I recall, both of us were in serious relationships back home – but there was a small mountain of numbers, that's for sure. One evening, sitting bored in the room, I decided to give some of the numbers a phone, stringing them along to think I was Coisty. Long story short, one of the women suggested we meet up for a drink. In order for my plan to work, I had to persuade Coisty to join us, which, as you can imagine, was not the toughest job in the world. For moral support, I also roped in Ally Dawson.

When we arrived, I went straight to the bar. Not recognising any of the Aussie beers, I looked at the taps and asked the barman for three pints of X-X-X-X lager.

'You mean four-X?' the barman replied.

I was so embarrassed and, as the barman and I laughed about it, glad my two mates hadn't heard me.

On meeting the woman, who had brought along a pal of her own, it didn't take long for McCoist to realise he had been set up and, more importantly, who the culprit was. I knew he would try to get me back, so I had to be on guard. After a few hours, Dawson and I were back in the hotel well before curfew when Ally appeared. He told us to get our gear back on, as there was a party to go to. I quickly got dressed and raced down to the front door of the hotel, only to be met by Coisty and this woman hanging out of a taxi window laughing at me as they roared off into the night. I'd been had and slunk back to my room. Coisty arrived back not long after, still laughing about it.

The next morning, Ally was up first and he was at the hotel-room door bending down to pick up the newspapers that had been left outside. I spotted my opportunity for revenge and rushed at him, both of us now out in the corridor desperately trying to get back in the room, as we are both completely naked. Just then, the lift door opens and out walks Totts. God knows what scene met him but he would recall it in glorious detail for the newspapers many years later in the build-up to the 1997 cup final between Kilmarnock and Falkirk. And the papers had us mocked up like Oliver Reed and Alan Bates in *Women in Love*. I had a hell of a time explaining to my mum that it wasn't me!

Our first game of the tour was played at the famous Melbourne Cricket Ground against an Australia B side. Other than the absence of Davie Cooper, who would join the tour later after international duty, Jock put out a really strong team and I had to make do with a place on the bench. Iain Ferguson had joined the club from Dundee and he had a couple of good chances to score on his debut. But the match was to finish goalless – the most notable thing being an eye injury sustained by Bobby Russell in an accidental head clash. Such was the concern that Jock was forced to phone Bobby's family back home after the match to assure them everything was okay. He was to spend a good few days in the hospital and got rather excited when one of the nurses said she was away to fetch 'some Durex'. Little did he know that Durex was a brand of tape in Australia at that time.

Bobby would get out of the hospital and rejoin the tour but, sadly, injuries were to become a recurring theme of our trip. And I was to be next.

Our next stop was Brisbane, where we were due to play the same Aussie B side we had drawn 0-0 with in Melbourne. On arrival, we discovered that Manchester United were also touring and Big Jock and the United boss, Ron Atkinson, who I would later work under at West Brom, got talking.

It turned out United were staying in a place called Surfers Paradise. It sounded brilliant and, if it was good enough for United, it was good enough for us. We checked into the new hotel, dumped our cases and were off out again.

There are moments in your life that are of such importance and make such an impact that, no matter how much time passes, the memories never fade. This was one of those nights. Forty years have passed – but only now will I tell the real story. To be honest, ever since the idea of writing my autobiography came about, I've been dreading this aspect of it. But it has been 40 years since the incident and I'm pretty sure that enough time has passed for the truth to be told. The true story of how I broke my leg.

There was some story going about that I did it jumping out of a woman's window. Bollocks! And the official line was that I did it trying to jump over a fence. Also bollocks!

The truth is that it was a drunken altercation with Ally McCoist that did it – and it was all my fault.

We had been given an evening pass from the boss and everybody was up for a night out. Surfers Paradise on the Gold Coast is packed with restaurants and bars, boasting a great nightlife and golden beaches that run along its shorefront. It has grown a bit since we were there but it very much felt like the place to be. As the night progressed, we started getting separated – one group going one way and another group, probably the younger lads, off somewhere else. I found myself with Craig Paterson, Ally Dawson and Coisty. We had left one pub and were looking for our next watering hole. As strangers to the place, we obviously didn't have a clue where we were going and found ourselves walking down this really wide road, which wasn't particularly well lit. In the darkness, we couldn't see any sign of the bright lights of a pub – nor any clue as to how we could get back to where we were staying, the Beachcomber Hotel. As we discussed our next move, we thought we would take advantage of a grassy area to have a comfort break against one of the trees. Before you say anything, there was nobody else around, just the four of us. As we were standing there, I began to joke with Coisty that I was going to 'wash his shoes', if you know what I mean. I never did it but one thing led to another and, before long, it was East Kilbride versus Easterhouse! Perhaps, if we had been boxers, it would have been fists up but we both kicked out with our feet, which resulted in an almighty clash of shins. As I went down and landed on my backside, I wasn't in any pain ... but I immediately knew something was wrong. The other lads, Craig and Ally Dawson, were telling the two of us to get a move on. I was lying on my back, my legs bent above me and I was thinking about getting up but I noticed there was something protruding from just below my knee. I put my hand down – and that was when I realised that the thing sticking out was my bone, which had pierced through my skin. The lads' patience was, by now, wearing a bit thin, but as soon as they came over and saw the situation with their own eyes, they immediately knew the only place I was going was to the hospital. As I say, I don't remember being in too much pain and quickly we discussed what was to happen next. One of the lads went to phone an ambulance – the other had the dubious pleasure of going to inform Jock Wallace. When Jock demanded an explanation, which he was sure to do, we agreed they were to say they hadn't seen anything.

This left me and Coisty alone, in the dark. He was a bit tearful as the full realisation of what had occurred began to register. There might have been tears from me, too. I knew that this was a potentially career-threatening injury.

'It wasn't your fault,' I said to him. 'It was basically down to me.'

But Ally was distraught.

I then looked over and saw a nearby fence. And I knew exactly what I had to do.

'Right,' I said. 'See that fence, I tried to jump it and I never made it. That's what we're going to say.'

But Ally was having none of it. He was adamant that, no matter the repercussions, he was going to tell the truth. I knew that wasn't a good idea. Ally was on his last warning and Jock's patience with him was wearing thin. Any breach of rules and he was to be on the next plane home and, believe me, Jock would have done it. Imagine if that had happened. Who knows what future Ally would have had at Rangers – if any? Look what he went on to achieve at the club, the goals he scored, the trophies he won, the legend he became. Was that really going to be put at risk because of some daft incident? The way I looked at it, my career could have been over but there was no way he should pay such a high price for what was my stupidity. I knew then, just as I know now, that what had happened was no fault of Ally McCoist's. It was all down to me. It was my fault we had squared up but still he wanted to tell the truth.

So, I said to Ally: 'You don't want to be doing that. You were on your last warning before we left London and Big Jock's not really got a lot of time for you. No, you can't do that. We'll just say I tried to jump the fence and didn't make it. That's what happened. I'm sure Craig and Ally will back that up.'

He took some convincing but, eventually, Ally came round to my way of thinking and Ally Dawson and Big Craig stuck to the line that they didn't see anything. It was a story that would hold firm for four decades!

Big Jock caught up with us in the hospital and we were taken into a room where I was put on a trolley and two nurses began trying to take off my trousers. They were going to cut them off but I persuaded them not to. They were leather – Robert Prytz had introduced me to the tailor – and I had waited ages to get them. It was then that I remembered that I wasn't wearing any underwear and, even worse, I remembered that I had been shaved downstairs before we left for the trip so the club doc could administer those injections. Both nurses started giggling and then 'Wham!' ... Big Jock whacked me on the back of the head.

That was the first bit of pain I felt. The leg break wasn't painful. I don't know if it was shock or the nerve endings had all died or maybe the booze was doing its job but I wasn't in any discomfort. But even the nurses were wincing when they tried to get my trousers over my leg. It had swollen to twice the size and the bones were making a horrible grinding noise each time they hit.

Then, remarkably, Jock told me what happened, how my leg break had come about. He said Coisty had told him everything – and, to my relief, he recounted the tale of me trying to jump the fence. Then he paused.

'Did Coisty top you?' he asked.

How the fuck did he know that, I thought. But my brain was working overtime. I was going to stick to our story no matter what.

'No, I tried to jump a fence,' I said. 'It was further away than I thought. I landed on top of the thing and snapped my leg.'

Over the years, I've come to the conclusion that Big Jock knew the truth. I think he felt there was some kind of undercurrent between me and Coisty but I never felt it and I'm sure Ally didn't either. But, at the time, I was laying there wondering how he could possibly know what had actually happened?

Jock looked at me. 'Well,' he said. 'If that's the story you're telling, you'd better stick to it. I don't want to hear anything else.'

I was taken to a room, given a Walkman personal stereo and told to get some sleep, as the operation would be going ahead the next morning. I did manage to nod off. In fact, they had to wake me up just to put me to sleep again for the surgery!

The surgeon came to see me after the operation, talking me through the procedure and what he had done. He was confident he had done a good job, putting in a plate and some screws to hold everything in place. But at the end of it, he couldn't say with any confidence what effect the injury would have on my career. He said he didn't know if I'd be able to continue with football, saying only that it was very much down to me and how the recovery developed. But I had no idea just how it would impact on my career. I never really dwelt on it and always believed I could get through it. I had to – there was no way I was going back on the tools. I was determined not to let my career finish like that.

The incident was making all the headlines once word filtered home about what had happened. It even made the front page of the *Glasgow Herald*. The article, which I include in full here, read: 'Rangers' striker Bobby Williamson who broke his leg in "horseplay" with team-mates after a night out in an Australian surfing resort, was well enough today after an operation, to receive visitors.

'They included manager Jock Wallace and some slightly sheepish Rangers players queueing to autograph the plaster cast on his right leg.

'Williamson, 22, snapped a shin bone trying to hurdle a fence at the Beachcomber Hotel in Surfers Paradise. The striker, signed from Clydebank for £100,000, was taken to Southport Hospital, five miles from the hotel.

'Mr Wallace said "Williamson went out with some of the other players for a couple of drinks. Nobody was drunk. I saw them all sitting here when they came back. There was a bit of horseplay and Williamson did not quite make it over the fence, caught his ankle, broke his leg."

'Mr Wallace warned that no more should be made of the incident than what it was – a simple accident.

'Mr Wallace, who described Williamson as a bit groggy after an operation to pin his leg, said that otherwise he was in good spirits.'

I was transferred on to a ward that seemed to be full of bikers and surfers who had suffered mishaps. Most of them were younger but much bigger than me – the sun does make everything grow! The nurses used to wake us up early in the morning for medication and then I used to try to get back to sleep. But these guys would be up talking and playing music, which annoyed me. If I did catch some sleep, I used to wake up again about nine-ish when they would all be sleeping. That was when I used to put my music on and head to the toilet but I could hear them all cursing behind me.

In my absence, the team managed to get a 2-1 win over Australia B in front of 10,000 fans – many of them ex-pat Rangers fans – at the Lang Park Stadium in Brisbane. Iain Ferguson got his first goal as a Rangers player, netting the winner, adding to Sandy Clark's first-half equaliser.

The players and the boss all came to see me before they moved on to Sydney for the next leg of the tour. Being a former soldier, Jock wasn't wanting to leave a man behind but there was very little option, as I needed follow-up procedures with the surgeon and additional ongoing treatment that would keep me in Australia for weeks. I was amazed that my leg wasn't encased in plaster. Instead, there was just one heavily stitched scar where the surgeon had put in the plate and screws.

So, with the team all away, there I was alone – a total stranger, with a broken leg, in an Aussie hospital. Some of the younger players had lined me up with visitors they had met clubbing. Not that I wasn't grateful but, to my dismay, they turned up. They were teenagers and I was so embarrassed. After a couple of days of them visiting, I had to go to the bathroom just to get away from them. I left them sitting there on the end of my bed. By the time I came back, they were gone – much to my relief. One of the nurses came over and said she had noticed that I wasn't looking too comfortable, so she had kicked them out.

The days in the hospital dragged on and on, so you were happy for any kind of distraction. One day, I was told there was a phone call for me and the nurses wheeled me through to the desk where the phone was. A voice at the end of the phone gave me his name and told me what newspaper he worked for. At this point, I'm still totally out of it on morphine but if I had known it was a journalist, I'd have told the nurse I didn't want to speak to him. He then starts telling me there was a story that I broke my leg climbing out of a woman's bedroom window and would I care to comment or put the record straight. Even in my weakened state, I started saying that's not what happened, sticking to the party line. I then hear giggling at the other end of the phone. It was Coisty and a few of the others, crowded round the phone and having a laugh at my expense! I put the phone down and went back to the ward. That's footballers for you – always looking at new ways of having a laugh. Still, at least they were thinking about me, even if not one of them actually asked how I was getting on!

There were a few Rangers fans who would pop in and, even though I've forgotten their names over the years, I will always appreciate the time they gave me. Once I was up and about and on crutches, it was a bit easier and I managed to get a number for my mate, Colin McAdam, after word reached me that he, too, had broken his leg in the 3-2 defeat to Australia at the Sydney Cricket Ground. He'd actually done it tackling another Rangers player! In fact, Davie Mitchell was playing for Australia and, with the match getting a bit tousy, Big Jock had sent Colin on to sort out a few. He went into a tackle on Davie and came off worse! Fortunately for him, it was a hairline fracture, so he could head back to Scotland almost immediately. We would eventually do our recovery work together.

For now, though, I was in hospital for three long weeks. When I eventually got out, the club had fixed me up with a lovely apartment to stay in while I waited for the injury to heal. My girlfriend, Lorraine, even came out to help me. The guy running the apartment looked after us really well. His name was Barry and he loved his football. I even went to see him play in an amateur game, which was a great social occasion, and he invited us to his house for Sunday lunch. It was a massive place where his in-laws stayed downstairs in their own self-contained unit. Over lunch, Barry asked if everything was all right with the accommodation. When I told him that the only problem I had was the cockroaches I kept finding, he said that he sympathised but they were very difficult to keep out. That was true. I recalled that even in the hospital, which was always sparkling clean, I'd find them in my locker. That night, when we got home, there were dead cockroaches all over the flat. While he was entertaining us, Barry had also been on to the fumigators to come in and get the flat sorted. They couldn't do enough for you.

My story was also getting well known locally and I was even invited on to TV to answer the phones on one of those charity, fund-raising programmes. The trouble was that not many of the people who phoned in could understand my accent. I even heard one guy shouting to his wife: 'Oh, no! I've got that Scottish guy!'

One old lady came on and asked for me, personally. She was Scottish as well and we had a good wee blether. I asked if she wanted to make a donation, say a tenner?

She shouted: 'A cannae afford a tenner, son!'

I just laughed. 'Look missus,' I said. 'I'll pay your donation and put it in your name. It's been lovely speaking to you.'

I was supposed to be working in the gym on a daily basis but, with my injury, it was just too much hardship getting to and from the place. My thinking was that this is a long-term injury, so I'll knock my pan in when I get back. I was always fighting the weight every pre-season anyway. I would always come back overweight but my view was that in close season you rested up and pre-season was payback time. You had to get back in shape quickly and, as I got older and wiser, I kept my weight in check.

The flight back home was not too uncomfortable, just incredibly long, and when I arrived back in Glasgow, I was met by a welcoming committee. There was Rangers chairman John Paton, Big Jock and an assembled media army. As we stood in line for a few photos, Big Jock let me know he wasn't happy that I hadn't worn the club blazer. I did have the club tracksuit on, arguing that was more comfortable to travel in. Plus, I had put on a few pounds.

Jock said: 'Aye, I've noticed that, too!'

As I couldn't drive, Coisty volunteered to act as my chauffeur once I was home. It was kind of him, because it took him well out of his way, but, typically, we were always late. I knew Laura Tarbet from the club lived quite close to me in Lenzie. Being the lovely lady that she is, she offered to step in.

Bob Findlay was our physio, a great lad who had to put me and Colin McAdam through our paces – running up and down every step in the four stands at Ibrox. I was a lot younger than Colin, so I was always way ahead of him. When it came to endurance stuff, I never let anyone hold me back. At Clydebank, I remember a few senior players telling me to slow down as we lapped the park but I always refused – it was my fitness I was working on, not theirs!

As we were both injured, the club decided to send us to a Rangers supporters' function in Larne, which meant a drive down to Stranraer for the ferry across. When we arrived, a car was there to pick us up and take us to the event. When we entered Larne, I noticed all the kerbs were painted red, white and blue and, when we got into the club, it was all Union Jacks, with Rangers flags everywhere. We went into the committee room, had a few drinks and exchanged pleasantries – only to be told that later in the evening we were both expected to say a few words. That was okay for Colin, as he was used to that kind of thing, but for me it was all new and that's when the sweats started. The place was packed and Colin could see I was nervous. He told me that when I get to my feet I should just look over everyone's heads to the clock at the back of the hall – don't make eye contact. Colin spoke first and then it was my turn. I found myself just repeating what Colin had said – only jumbling up the order a bit. Honestly, the sweat was lashing off me. Once the meal and event was coming to an end, I found myself in the hall playing a fruit machine and having a beer. The night was nearing a conclusion and they started playing 'God Save the Queen'. I was just dropping another coin into the machine when I realised the two guys either side of me were standing to attention! I thought it best to do the same. These were always good nights, though – good people and good hospitality.

Spending so much time together, it was only natural that Colin and I socialised together. He lived in Torrance and I was in Stepps, so we were not too far apart. The big man never touched alcohol – something which, thankfully, didn't rub off on me! He didn't need a drink to be good company, unlike me, who can't string a sentence together without a few. I'm not one for chit-chat or small talk. We would eventually go on holiday to Portugal together, the wives and families. It's funny; as players you drift apart, what with moving from club to club, but some friendships remain and you know you can lift the phone and catch up. Colin was one of those and I was devastated when he passed away in 2013. He was far too young. I still miss the big man.

My leg was still giving me a problem. As the weeks went on, I was finding it difficult to move without a limp. The flexibility of my ankle was the issue and when I started trying to run, the plate was interfering with my ankle joint. The Aussie surgeon, who did an excellent job, had erred on the side of caution to protect my leg and the plate was too long. The initial plan was to keep the plate in there but that wasn't going to be possible if I wanted to play again. Another operation was scheduled to remove it and I was booked into the Bon Secours Hospital in Langside. It was one of Glasgow's first private hospitals but I had no idea it was run by nuns called the Sisters of Bon Secours. Not that I was bothered. This was going to be routine stuff and I reckoned if the plate didn't hurt going in, then it certainly wouldn't hurt coming out. How wrong was I? It was agony. When I woke up after the operation, it felt as if someone had taken a hammer and chisel to my leg. I'm pretty sure there would have been some industrial tools that had to be used to get the nuts or screws out of the plate! When I saw the plate later, it was about a quarter of an inch thick with six or seven holes where the nuts or screws went through into my bone. One of the lads on the ground staff at Ibrox later asked me for the plate, because he wanted to get it mounted and displayed. You never know, he might still have it.

I certainly wasn't refusing any painkillers afterwards. After a couple of days, Big Colin McAdam came and picked me up. The doctors had given me a whole load of instructions for the best recovery and stressed how important it was to keep the leg raised. I didn't listen and Colin and I went straight to Ibrox to see the reserve team playing Celtic that night. When I got home, I was in agony and piled the painkillers into my system. I found out the next day that the wound was now infected – so it was back to Bon Secours to get the bad blood out! It was agony as well, the nurse ignoring my cries of pain to squeeze the infected blood out and then restitch the wound.

I was back a few days later to get the stitches out. It was quite funny. The old nun who was removing them didn't have the best eyesight and was plucking out more hairs than stitches!

Once the plate was removed, I had more flexibility in my ankle but, although I didn't notice it and thought I was moving okay, I was told I was still noticeably limping. Plus, I realised that the break had robbed me of some of my pace. I had always been fast but I noticed I had lost a bit.

I kept on being positive and did all the gym work. Big Jock even told me to park my car as soon as I came over the bridge and then walk into the stadium. I did this a couple of times but I wasn't comfortable leaving my car unguarded.

The toughest thing about the injury was that I couldn't do anything to help the team. I really felt I had let them down, that this was my fault, because it had been my stupidity out in

Surfers Paradise that had caused the injury. In saying that, as a player and later as a manager, I always felt these trips away with the team were important for bonding and ensuring you have the right 'all-for-one' attitude in the dressing room. But there has to be control, there has to be discipline. In this day and age, players need to be extremely careful when out and about, with mobile phones and cameras everywhere. People out there know that if players are recognised, it's game on for anyone trying to make a few bob. A few years back, Leicester City had problems at La Manga, which was a great place to take a team – great pitches, golf course, tennis courts, so recreationally very good. After a night out, nine of the players were taken for questioning after claims made by three German women staying at the resort. Three of them were arrested and charged but three months later all charges were dropped. DNA evidence proved that they had done nothing. But I felt for manager Micky Adams – who is on record as saying the 2004 incident still haunts him – and I think a lot of managers have learned from Micky's experience. One player letting his small head rule his big head can mess it up for everyone and tarnish a club's name. It happened with me at Kilmarnock. I had taken the players to Largs – not La Manga – and a player's wife had phoned his room. His roommate had a woman in who answered the phone and the wife went berserk. The player had to go home. This all went on unbeknown to me. I found out much later. But it was undoubtedly my fault for being too lax and trusting them too much.

With my broken leg, I just felt sick that I had let everybody down – especially Jock. I watched most, if not all, of the games with frustration, desperate to get back to action.

In fact, I gave an interview to *Rangers News* predicting that the injury would make me a better player.

'If I'm not a better player when I get back into the first team, then I'll give up the game,' I said in the club magazine. 'All the time I have been nursing my leg back to full fitness I have been watching every first-team game and as many reserve matches as I can.

'While I much rather would have been playing all season, I have learnt so much from just watching the other lads in action that I am certain it is going to make me a much better player on my return.'

Laura was still acting as my personal chauffeur, taking me here, there and everywhere. I'll always be indebted to her for her kindness and patience. But that season, 1984/1985, was a write-off for me, the team and for everybody at Ibrox. I ended up playing as a sub in a single league game and made four appearances in friendlies. I do remember a reserve game up in Aberdeen, with Neale Cooper playing for the Dons – long before he wore the blue of Rangers. He was known as Tattie and was infuriating to play against. He always had that bit of chat, which was fine, and came across as a bit of a hardman. They were winning and taking the piss, passing the ball around at the back. As usual, I'm running back and forth desperate to get a look-in. I thought to myself that if they passed it back to Tattie, I'm getting something. Well, they did and I certainly got something, although it wasn't the ball, it was Tattie. I was very late, although, much to my annoyance, he was a bit of a screamer. I had actually been booked for a tackle on him earlier in the game, so I knew the next colour I was seeing was red. Actually, fast forward a few years and I was on a coaching course with Tattie down at Largs. He was a great lad, likeable and funny. It just goes to show you can be wrong about people. Sadly, Tattie was another one who was taken from us far too early.

The one game I do recall was right at the end of the season – a fundraiser at Stamford Bridge against Chelsea to raise money for the victims of the Bradford disaster. I came on as sub, as did former Aberdeen player Doug Rougvie, who, by then, had moved south to London. At one point in the game, Doug and I contested a bounce ball – something you never see in the game any more. Doug was a brute of a man but it's not in my nature to shy away. I felt it was good for my mental strength and I was thinking, if the leg breaks again, then it breaks. Whatever happens, I'll deal with it. I don't recall who won the ball but we both came out of it unscathed. I knew then that the bone was fine – and I was ready to make up for lost time.

Next season was going to be different.

CHAPTER 6

SOUNESS AND OFFSKI

THE BIGGEST disappointment for me at Rangers was the manager getting sacked. I'd never experienced it before. At Clydebank, when Bill Munro left, I wasn't really part of the first-team picture. With Jock Wallace's departure, I really felt it. I owed the man so much and loved him as a manager. With Jock, if you always gave him 100 per cent, he would always have your back. Big Jock had brought me into Rangers, the club I had supported, and I had let him down with my stupidity in Australia and the broken leg that had kept me out for the best part of a season. I'm sure, or should I say I hope, that my team-mates were of a similar mind but I know that not all of them felt the same way I did about the gaffer. There were a few who were right out of the picture and couldn't stand him. But I definitely felt I had let down the manager and everybody, especially when the team had been struggling the previous season. It is frustrating when you can't help but there were plenty of players at Rangers at the time who could have made things happen but, for one reason or another, it just didn't.

The strange thing was that we started the season well. We won our opening game of the campaign, 1-0 at home to Dundee United, then followed it up with a 3-1 win over Hibs at Easter Road, a game in which I opened my scoring account for the season. We then thumped Clyde 5-0 in a League Cup tie and I scored a hat-trick. And I got a double in a 3-1 win over Hearts, a match which was equally notable for the number of cards referee Dougie Hope dished out. Three of them were red – to Ally McCoist, Sandy Clark and Walter Kidd.

Despite the good results, warning signs were there. I had to score a late equaliser in a League Cup game with Forfar just to take it to extra time and we eventually scraped through on penalties. In the next round, against Hamilton, we went behind inside three minutes when John Brogan netted but I scored two in as many minutes right on the stroke of half-time – both headers from corners – to see us through. It would have been a hat-trick had Rikki Ferguson in the Accies goal not pulled off a stunning stop from close range. Still, I won player of the round for that and was photographed days later with the customary big cheque.

In between the two League Cup ties, we had stumbled to a 1-1 draw with Celtic that had probably flattered us but a 3-0 win over St Mirren kept us up near the top of the league. A press report of that day reflected the upward trajectory we all felt we were on. It read: 'The Jock Wallace roadshow rollercoasters on and more and more Rangers fans leave their hiding places to lend vocal support. On an afternoon when you wouldn't send the wife out with the dog, 27,707 fans saw growing confidence in an Ibrox side which now has allied patience to sheer physical strength.'

We also claimed our first piece of silverware. It was only the Glasgow Cup and a 5-0 win over Queen's Park with what was virtually our reserve team but they all count!

At the end of September 1985, we made the short trip to my old stomping ground, Kilbowie Park, Clydebank. The tight wee place was rammed but we struggled to put away our stubborn hosts. With the clock ticking into the final minute, I found myself at the back post awaiting a set piece and being marked by my old mate, Mark Treanor. Just as it was being delivered, I got myself on the move, ran across Mark and met the ball with a diving header for the only goal of the game. It put us top of the league. Considering the struggles we had had the previous season, there was a buoyant mood in the squad, which Jock had reshaped ever so slightly in the summer. Only Robert Prytz and Ian Redford left – to Gothenburg and Dundee United respectively – while we had really only brought in Dougie Bell from Aberdeen.

There was a spring in everyone's step when we faced Spanish side Osasuna in the UEFA Cup. For the Spaniards – and myself – this was to be a European debut. I was so excited to be playing continental opposition for the first time, but the night turned into a game of attrition. A monsoon fell upon Ibrox before and during the game and the pitch was a quagmire. Had it been a bog-standard league game, I genuinely don't think it would have been played. The Czech referee may have been put under pressure to let the game go ahead. We took the lead early in the second half when Craig Paterson knocked in Hugh Burns's cross. We knew we needed to get another to take with us on the return trip to Spain but their keeper, a guy called Vicente Biurrun, pulled off a number of decent stops.

Just as everyone was beginning to think we had turned a corner, we tripped up in Dundee when we lost 1-0 at Dens.

Then our grip on the League Cup we had won the season before was loosened when we lost the first leg of the semi-final, 2-0 away to Hibs – our misery all the more painful given that Alan Rough saved a penalty from Coisty.

Then came what the press labelled in big headlines 'the Shame Game'. Aberdeen were the top side in Scotland and the defending league champions when they travelled to Ibrox that day. They were packed with talent, with guys like Jim Leighton in goal and Willie Miller and Alex McLeish the rocks at the heart of their defence. There was Neil Simpson, Billy Stark, John Hewitt, Eric Black and Frank McDougall – and my old mate, Neale 'Tattie' Cooper. But for all the talent on display that day, the game can only be remembered as a battle. The half-time whistle hadn't even sounded before we had seen Hugh Burns and Craig Paterson sent off. Tattie was booked for a late lunge on me and there were yellow cards and tackles flying all over the place. With everything going wrong on the pitch, it began to go pear-shaped off it when the crowd in the packed enclosure at the front of the Main Stand began spilling out on to the pitch. Objects were being thrown. I think a linesman and the referee, George Smith, were both hit but I know Craig Paterson was. By this time, the police were getting involved and the players were taken off the pitch. We waited in the bowels of the stand, wondering if the game was going to restart. Big Jock was out on the touchline telling the fans to get back into the enclosure. TV pictures would later show at least one fan being carried away on a stretcher. The whole atmosphere was really unpleasant and – down to just nine men – there was little surprise that, when the game resumed, we slumped to a 3-0 defeat.

Days later, we had to put the Aberdeen defeat behind us as we travelled to the El Sadar Stadium in Pamplona for the second leg of the UEFA Cup tie with Osasuna. We were defending the 1-0 lead we had earned in the rain at Ibrox and I was excited at the prospect of my first competitive game on European shores. But I was gutted when Big Jock named the team and I was on the bench, with Ally McCoist and Derek Johnstone starting up front. Curiously, Osasuna players had applauded the Rangers team on to the pitch in front of a capacity crowd but it was to be the last bit of hospitality shown to us that evening. In the 12th minute, Patxi Rípodas cancelled out our one-goal advantage and, with half-time approaching, striker Enrique Martín nosed the hosts into the lead. Still, with away goals counting at the time, we still only needed the one and we would be through. Craig Paterson had an effort cleared off the line but, no matter how hard we tried, we couldn't breach the Osasuna defence. My old mate, Ted McMinn, and I were introduced. He replaced Bobby Russell and I came for Davie Cooper but it didn't make much of a difference. Our European dream was over almost as soon as it had started.

We raised ourselves to win 3-0 at Motherwell in our first game back from that disappointment in Spain but any confidence in the camp all but disappeared when we lost our hold of the League Cup. We were 2-0 down from the first leg at Easter Road and although we beat Hibs 1-0 at Ibrox, it wasn't enough. I hit the bar shortly before Davie Cooper scored a worldie of a free kick. But the one meaningful bit of silverware we had in the cabinet was gone. What's more, with the hot streak with which I had started the season now a distant memory, I dropped out of the starting line-up – either to the bench or out of the matchday squad altogether. I returned for the N'eerday game with Celtic – only to bring down Danny McGrain and give away the free kick from which they scored their first goal. Brian McClair got Celtic's second in a 2-0 win. But the nadir of the season was to come with a 3-2 defeat to Hearts in the Scottish Cup at the end of January. The agony was that we were fuming, because John Robertson's late winner should have been chalked off for a push on keeper Nicky Walker, who dropped the ball, leaving Robbo with a tap-in. But the referee ignored our complaints and that was it – game over, season over. We had nothing left to play for.

Little did we know, however, that the real action was taking place thousands of miles away in Nevada, where club director Lawrence Marlborough, who had a long family connection with the club, was battling to transform the club and had put in place his representative on the board – a real mover and shaker called David Holmes. Clearly unhappy with the way things were going on the pitch, David was making grand plans for a revolution at Ibrox. The thing was, as players, we were totally oblivious to it. We were still trying to rescue what was turning out to be another dismal season. But, apart from a high of a 3-0 win over Celtic at Ibrox, there were only a series of lows. That was one of only two wins we would have before the end of the campaign, finishing a dismal fifth in the table.

In order to drum up some revenue, a friendly with Spurs was arranged but, as a perfect illustration of how far the fans had fallen out of love with the team, only 12,665 turned up. I didn't play in the game but it was terrible and Jock didn't spare the players afterwards. At the post-match press conference, he said: 'I don't understand the attitude of players at times.

For me, our performance was a disgrace. We didn't play at all. We let ourselves down and we let the fans down.'

Perhaps he knew what was heading his way. The very next day, Jock was sacked.

I never saw it coming – I don't think any of the players did – and I truly believed they would give him until the end of the season. One minute he was there, the next he was off. We never saw him again and there was no address to the players or the squad, no emotional farewell. The first we knew of his departure was when the club announced it. He did have one parting message, telling a journalist: 'Rangers will be back, there is no fear of that.'

I was gutted. I felt I had let him down. But all the time, moves were being made in the background by chief executive David Holmes. He had already identified who he wanted as the new manager at Rangers – Scotland captain Graeme Souness. The club had held meetings with him in Italy – where he was playing with Sampdoria – and in London. Amazingly, none of this leaked out. This was in an era with no social media, no internet, no keyboard warriors watching your every move. So, when Souness was announced as our new player-boss, we were as stunned as anyone. Nobody expected that. There were no whispers at all. None of the players were aware of what was going on behind the scenes. It was not the talk in the dressing room until it happened.

Everybody knew that, in Souness, we were getting a quality player – one of the best midfielders in the game – but we didn't know if we were getting a quality manager. He had not been tried as a manager, so it was new to everybody to see how he would develop or how he would handle it. As it turned out, he handled it very well. He would go on to revolutionise Scottish football, bringing in top talent from south of the border and consigning to the bin the club policy of never signing Catholics. He inherited a club that was broken and transformed it from top to bottom.

But in those early days, he was still a Sampdoria player and the captain of the Scotland team that would soon be heading to Mexico for the World Cup. That meant the first two games after Jock was sacked were taken by Alex Totten – a 2-1 defeat at Clydebank and another 2-1 defeat to St Mirren. It was hardly the most auspicious start to the new era and the reports being sent back to Souness must have been quite a read. In the game in Paisley, he even had his former Liverpool boss, Joe Fagan, in the stand to run his eye over the team.

As a player, when a new manager comes in, it's an uncertain time and you wonder if you will be part of the new man's plans. But, with Souness still in Italy, you really didn't know where you stood. The best call he made was to bring in Walter Smith from Dundee United as his assistant. History now shows us what an astute decision that was!

Walter came in and was quick to get his feet under the table. He immediately impressed the players on the training pitch with his routines and we quickly realised here was a guy who knew the game and, more importantly, knew people. Even then, you knew Walter would go on to greatness.

With Big Jock, shooting practice consisted of the gaffer standing at the edge of the box facing away from the goal and the players ten yards in front of him in single file. There were 20 or so players lining up to take a shot at goal and the player at the front would chip the ball into the gaffer's hands and the gaffer would catch and decide whether it was a right-footed shot or left-footed, full volley or half volley, by dropping the ball on whatever side he decided. The player would then shoot, go and fetch his ball and go to the end of the queue. If they were brave enough to try and chip the keeper, you took a risk if he caught the ball, because he would launch it as far away as he could. You then had to go and get it and it would take a while to get to the front of the queue, where the players would take the opportunity to punch your ball away, if you were naïve enough to hold it under your arm, and then skip the queue. There was a lot of standing around and misbehaving. Walter's sessions were sharp. His shooting practice was more stimulating and had more players involved, with very little standing around. About 20 yards from goal, there would be a marker on the right side of goal, and the left, at the angle, there would be three further cones with men stationed on them. The man at the front of the queue would pass to the first man, who would lay it back and then he would pass to the second man and so on and so on and it would finish with the second man having a shot at goal. Then they would all move up a station and the left side would go. There would be a man stationed behind the goal and he would fetch the ball and go to the end of the queue. You were using both feet and there was not much waiting around and you were more involved. Walter was clearly a young, knowledgeable coach with great enthusiasm and his training was fresh and different. You could instantly see, with his demeanour, the way he carried himself and the way he walked about and the way he conducted himself, that Walter was extremely capable and knew what he was doing and he certainly showed that on the training ground. His training schedules and routines were top-notch and we all respected that.

With the whole place in a state of flux, Walter held a meeting with all the players in the home dressing room. He explained that Graeme would not be coming in until the end of the season but that regular reports would be sent to him in Italy, assessing performances, both individually and as a team. I just thought it was a fresh start for everybody. Most players were hoping that, when the new manager came in, everybody would get a clean slate but that wasn't the case. Graeme came with his own ideas and he knew the players he wanted to bring in. He wasn't too bothered about the players he had at his disposal. I reckoned Davie Cooper was assured of a place in the team and that Coisty would have to prove himself, which he did, obviously. But I never got an opportunity. I played in only one of the games under Walter, a 2-0 win over Motherwell, which at least secured us a place in Europe for the new season. As the campaign stuttered to an end, we did at least retain the Glasgow Cup with a 3-2 win over Celtic, with Coisty scoring a hat-trick.

The first training session I remember with the new gaffer was across the road at the Albion. He both took the warm-up and participated in it. The gaffer was still trying to get to know our names but even then, right from the start, I felt my days were numbered. I thought Derek Johnstone would be okay, as he knew the gaffer from international duty, but the big man was out of the door. The gaffer had asked DJ to give us an exercise Scotland had used when playing England at Wembley just prior. During the game, the gaffer had an altercation with Ray Wilkins – someone he would later bring to Ibrox. The gaffer was holding him off and started throwing his elbows back, left and right. Not one to miss an opportunity, DJ tried to copy it and proceeded to swing his elbows back while twisting and turning. A few of the lads had a giggle. The gaffer didn't see the funny side.

I was lucky enough to make the pre-season trip to Germany. As we had all expected, the gaffer hadn't been too slow in the transfer market. Colin West, Avi Cohen and Chris Woods had all joined the club. Souness had been taking advantage of English clubs being banned from Europe following the Heysel disaster by attracting big names with the lure of continental competition and more stars were to follow.

I don't recall being involved much but we played a game on what was little more than a public park against some amateur outfit. In the first half, Chris Woods had not had a save to make, so Souness arranged to swap him into the opposition goal. He also told me that I was going to get a chance at half-time. But when the game restarted, I had not been given the nod, so I waited, kicking my heels on the touchline. Again, we were very much on top and I was waiting for my big chance to impress. I thought, 'Fuck, he must have changed his mind.' Five minutes in, the gaffer turns round, sees me and almost does a double take.

'I thought I told you to go on at half-time,' he shouted, as if it was my fault.

What was I supposed to do? He was the manager – that was his job. Was I supposed to take someone off so that I could get on?

Still, this was my chance and I soon found myself clean through, racing down on Chris Woods, who was now in the opposition goal. He was exposed around the penalty spot and, quickly weighing up my options, I lifted the ball over him and chipped it into the goal. He wasn't happy! No keeper likes to be chipped, so there was a bit of banter flying.

Afterwards, he insisted there was no way I would have tried to chip him if it had been a proper game. Maybe he was right but I had a good chuckle about it.

One night, the gaffer took us out to the house of a German agent he seemed to know well. It was a massive place, really impressive, but I had no idea why we were there. We were just sitting around talking, trying to kill time, when I spotted the gaffer zeroing in on Hugh Burns. He blew his top because Shuggie was sitting with his feet up on the guy's table. He came over and slapped Shuggie's feet on to the floor, telling him to show some respect. It was the first time we had seen that side of him, that discipline. Respect and standards were vital to his make-up. It was one thing improving standards on the park but he was going to do it off the park as well. He seemed to have taken an instant dislike to Shug for whatever reason – I suppose it saved time! I'm joking, of course. Shug's a great lad and was a decent footballer. My problem was his ten-yard pass had the same weight as his 40-yard pass! He used to fire balls up to me – good balls that a decent striker would have controlled – but my first touch was not the best and my second was usually a tackle. When Shug blasted the ball up to me, there was a good chance it would end up behind him!

Like so many of us, Shug's days at Rangers were numbered, and one afternoon I got a call from the gaffer telling me that West Bromwich Albion were looking for a striker and that I should drive down for a couple of days to see how things go.

Drive down! I didn't even know where West Brom played. By that time, Lorraine and I were married and our wee girl, Emma, was just four months old. When I got off the phone, I told Lorraine the plan and she said I'd better make other arrangements, because we only had the one car and she needed it. I phoned Laura Tarbet at Ibrox and she booked me on a train to Birmingham New Street that evening. Before I left, Lorraine told me not to sign anything until we had talked things through.

I headed down to Birmingham with mixed feelings. I had a nagging feeling in my stomach that I couldn't shake off, a feeling that I hadn't done anything at Rangers. The only thing I had won was the Tennent's Sixes, where we each won six crystal glasses, which have all been broken over time. I had nothing to show for my three years at Ibrox other than the scar on my shin and a signed match ball for my hat-trick against Clyde. Truth be told, that ended up in Hogganfield Loch thanks to one kick from little Emma! I never had a conversation with Souness. He never spoke to me all the time I was there, never spoke to me in training or when playing a game. You know you're out the picture and all you can do is work hard and hope that you get an opportunity. But I never got that opportunity. All I got was a phone call saying that West Brom were looking for a striker and I should go down.

I was met at the train station and taken to a hotel not far from West Brom's stadium, The Hawthorns, and was told I would be picked up in the morning and taken to their training ground. On arriving the next day, I changed into my training gear and headed in to meet the manager, Ron Saunders, for the first time. Saunders was a bit of a legend in the area and, as far as I know, he's the only manager who has been in charge of all the big three in the city – Birmingham, Aston Villa and West Brom. He told me he was glad I had come down and that he needed a striker and would have a look at me over a couple of days. If he liked me, he would make me an offer.

He informed me that the first team had a friendly match that evening, so it was only the surplus players who were training. He had enough players to set up a defence and we had six players to attack them – four across the middle and two strikers. Training over, it was back to the hotel and the wait to be picked up to watch the game that night.

I must have done okay, because, after a couple of days, the manager offered me a two-year contract with the same signing-on fee I got at Rangers, £100 more than Rangers were paying me and £100 in appearance money. As I've said before, I've never really been good at contracts and, although Lorraine wanted us to discuss things before reaching a decision, I never really thought about it for long. I signed and my Rangers days were over.

I knew that if I had turned it down and returned to Ibrox, Souness would not have been pleased and I would have been bumped into the reserve dressing room, where I would stagnate and be forgotten about. I could easily have taken that option, waited for the season to start and hope for injuries or bad form from the strikers. But I knew I wasn't wanted at Ibrox and that the welcome mat was being rolled out for me at West Brom. But I was so naïve. I didn't even realise that West Brom had been relegated to the Second Division the previous season.

I phoned Lorraine and she was not happy. It was a wrench for the wife, because we had just had Emma – she was only four months old. Football can be quite brutal. Now, having been a manager, it is easy to understand that, as a player, you are actually walking a tightrope. You could pick up a bad injury or, as happened to me, the manager might not fancy you and you are out of the door. It is only when you become a manager that you understand you have the future of players in your hands and if you really don't want them, you move them on.

You try to do it for their benefit and to make their career better. If they are not going to play for you or you don't fancy them, they are better playing somewhere else where they can play football for somebody who really wants them. As a manager, it's all about kidology, trying to convince bad players they are good players, giving pats on the back when what you really want to do is slap them in the face. As a manager, you've got to be able to handle that and try to treat them fairly. If they are doing the business, they'll get an opportunity. If they are not, they'll have to drop out of the team and somebody else will get a chance. As a player, you don't realise that – you always think you've got a chance. It is a precarious life.

But back then, I knew I had to back myself and I believed I was capable of getting through this difficult period and would prove myself. As far as my career was concerned, I made the decisions when it came to actually playing football. I was the one who had to go and train and perform. It was very selfish but that was the way it was.

I was looking forward to meeting up with Jimmy Nicholl again. I had played with him at Rangers and he was now at West Brom. I planned to travel back up to Glasgow on the Friday, clear out my locker at Ibrox and say goodbye to people who had made me welcome at Ibrox.

The manager was not on my agenda of people to see.

I got a phone call to my room that evening. It was none other than Jimmy Nick. It was good to hear from him but I was surprised when he asked me if I would bring his boots up the road with me. Only then did I realise that it was a swap deal – me heading south, Jimmy heading north. I was stunned, thinking that Rangers had paid a hundred grand for me and were swapping me for a player who was in his 30s. Swap deal or not, I had signed and that was that. I travelled up to Ibrox with Jimmy's boots under my arm and went in to say my goodbyes and clear out my locker. One pair of sandals – that was it. After wishing everybody well, I was heading out of the door, that door I had walked through three years earlier when all my dreams were coming true. Suddenly, I heard the gaffer's voice shouting my name as he was coming down that marble staircase.

I stopped and he came over to speak to me. He told me that I would do well at West Brom, that there were a lot of good teams in the area and that I could make myself a bit of money. He also said that if I was ever back in Glasgow and wanted to use the club's facilities, I was more than welcome.

He must have seen the look on my face, because he added: 'By the way, there's going to be a lot of players going out of this place and I won't be asking them back. I like you, I think you're a good guy.'

And I thought: 'Fuck, you never showed it before!'

Here was a guy I never had a conversation with, apart from the phone call saying to go down to West Brom. I thought to myself: 'Thanks but I won't be back.'

I wished him all the best and I walked out on to Edmiston Drive and that was it. Rangers, for me, was over.

I knew Souness would succeed with Rangers. He brought in top players and did magnificently – instigating a revolution not only at Ibrox but throughout Scottish football. Things would never be the same again. I had a bit of an inferiority complex when I first went to Rangers. If I had stayed, with the quality Souness brought in, I would have been surplus to requirements. But it was a privilege and an honour to have played for the club.

I was determined to put my disappointment behind me. I was looking forward to going to West Brom and hopefully getting an opportunity there, playing well and scoring goals. I never gave Rangers much of a thought. It was not until after a couple of months down in the Midlands and seeing players at Rangers, players who were getting injured and players who were getting their opportunity, that I wondered whether, had I stayed, I would have got my chance. But I doubt it. I don't think I got – or would have got – an opportunity at all, to be honest. Souness explained to me he was going to bring in big-name players and, when you look back now, he certainly did that. So, maybe it was better I did move on.

I don't think I was treated badly … but all I wanted was a chance.

CHAPTER 7
THE BAGGIES AND BIG RON

WEST BROMWICH Albion had been relegated from the First Division when I joined them, so they were coming to terms with life out of the top flight. I certainly wasn't disappointed initially – the stadium was good and the training ground was more than up to standard. They had a lot of quality in the squad, good, experienced players, but they weren't featuring. Guys like Imre Varadi, Mickey Thomas and Tony Grealish. Garth Crooks didn't play at the start either. A lot of it was about wages. That is the impact of relegation – a club has to cut its cloth accordingly and big-name players on big contracts can be a serious problem. It was for that reason that I felt manager Ron Saunders was happier that he had got Jimmy Nicholl off the books than he was in signing me. I'm sure I was on half the wages Jimmy had been on – perhaps even less.

One of the first guys I clicked with was Derek Statham. He was a very talented left-back but was held back by a chronic problem with his Achilles. It stopped him from getting a big move to Liverpool and restricted how much he could play at The Hawthorns. We were training indoors one day and the young players had a drill where they were trying to kick the ball through a gap, slightly larger than a football, in the door. None of them could manage it – some of them couldn't even hit the door! Derek was stretching nearby, watching the farce play out in front of him, and decided he would show them how it was done. He placed the ball down and hit it clean through from 30 yards. I couldn't believe it and Derek could see the shocked expression on my face. Who was this guy, I was thinking, when he turned to me and admitted that was the first time he had ever done it! Derek was a great guy. But for his injury issues, he would have had far more than his three England caps.

I felt that when I left Rangers I left a football club and that when I joined the Baggies I had joined a social club. No disrespect to them, but after training on Monday, Tuesday and Wednesday, a few of the guys would go to the pub for some lunch, play some pool and sink a few beers. You couldn't do that at Ibrox. If we had lunch, it was soft drinks. The Rangers fans didn't want to see their players drinking in the afternoon. They would be right on the phone to the club to report you. And, by the way, I have no problem with that at all. The fans pay their hard-earned money to watch their team on a Saturday, so the least you can do is be professional on and off the park. But at West Brom, the fans would be glad to see you and would insist on buying you a beer and having a chat. I like a few beers and it didn't take much to persuade me to join in.

The first player who actually took the time to talk to me was a very young Carlton Palmer. It is only after you've moved around a bit that you realise the first players who talk to you are not really popular with the rest of the squad. Carlton went on to be a very good footballer, playing for the England national team. We were good at first but our relationship deteriorated after a few months – but more of that later.

There was an established group of players who weren't very welcoming and you had to prove yourself to be included in any conversation. As it happens, these guys would do lunch occasionally but not participate in the beer drinking. They were married guys with children and had to get home. It didn't stop me from staying out and shooting pool. With the family still up in Glasgow, I had little else to do, so I would hook up with our big striker, George Reilly, and our goalkeeper, Stuart Naylor. Stewart Evans, who joined us from Wimbledon, would also become part of our group.

Don't get me wrong, the social side never happened straight away. I went down there to do my best and help the club back into the First Division, where they belonged. And on the football side, it started off quite well. In fact, the manager pulled me into his office and told me that some of the directors were saying I was his best signing. It was early days but it was good to hear such positive feedback.

The family came down to join me after a few weeks and it was good to have Lorraine and little Emma with me. We were staying in an apartment but I had seen this house out on Lichfield that I really fancied. So, we bought it and moved out into the suburbs – a beautiful place. It's claim to fame is that it's one of the smallest city in England, as it has a cathedral. I regret that in the two years I lived there I never saw anything of that cathedral, other than its spire from a distance. I never went in, never had a look around. What a waste.

Life was good and I was feeling at home within the Baggies squad. We had a young striker called Steve Bull who was trying to break into the team. Steve was a strong lad with a ferocious shot and worked his socks off. Before training every morning, our groundsman at the training ground would put on the keeper's gloves and go in goal. Bully would be outside the box firing these balls at him. I feared for the groundman's health, such was the power of Steve's shot.

Sadly, we never played too many games together but, given time, we could have been a good partnership. We were similar in the fact we never gave defenders a moment's piece. We played Ipswich at The Hawthorns and although we lost 4-3 – Bully got two and I scored the other – we showed real signs of being a productive partnership. It was easy to see just what a talent Bully was going to be, along with a young midfielder we had called Andy Thompson. But for some inexplicable reason, West Brom let them both leave, for only £60,000, to local rivals Wolves. The pair of them would wrack up hundreds of appearances for the Molineux club – Bully would go on to play for England 13 times, even scoring a goal at Hampden against Scotland but I won't hold that against him.

Christ, how different things could have been for me if the gaffer had recognised what a player Bully was and what a partnership we could have made – even though we couldn't understand each other! He struggled with my Scottish accent and his Black Country twang was too fast for me.

Andy's departure was also a huge mistake. I always felt the gaffer could be quite cruel to him. We used to line up in the hall in the morning and the gaffer would walk down the line and say 'stay here' or 'go on the minibus', the latter meaning you were being sent off to train with the kids. When he got to young Thommo, who was a happy wee guy, always smiling, Saunders would regularly tell him to get on the minibus and I thought that was unfair. I'm so happy he had such a successful career with Wolves. Saunders once tried his mini-bus line with me and I just started walking. The gaffer said he was only joking – he had a very dry sense of humour and rarely laughed but he could be cutting.

I was disappointed to see Bully leave the club but Saunders came to me and said he had found a big 'un to partner with me up front. Stewart Evans came in from Wimbledon and we became good friends – although we weren't great together on the park. He actually moved in with us, as we lived in rented accommodation before moving into the house at Lichfield. It was a recipe for disaster. We would travel to training together and then, on the way back, stop off at a pub for a few and play pool. My drinking levels went up again and we would arrange to meet up with big George Reilly at some pub with a pool table and have a round-robin competition. George was a shark and only told us the rules when we made a mistake but he was a good pool player and also a good footballer, who had played at Watford and Newcastle. George was unfortunate – he had done his cruciate ligament while water skiing, so he never featured much and would console himself drinking with us. As I said, I didn't need any encouragement to go for a beer and never blamed anyone for leading me astray.

My relationship with Ron Saunders had been strong at the start of the season. The target for the team was to get straight back up after relegation but that was always going to be tough, especially with cash being tight and top talent being shown the door. But I had scored goals away at Sunderland – a 3-0 win – and then in a 2-2 draw at Barnsley. By the beginning of December, we were fifth in the league and looking good to contend for promotion after I netted in a 3-1 win at Bradford.

Then the rot set in. We couldn't buy a win and, with only a couple of victories between December and April, we plummeted down the table. My goals dried up, too, and instead of pushing for promotion, the prospect of falling into the third tier became a real and worrying possibility.

It was at Christmas that my relationship with Saunders – and Carlton Palmer – rapidly deteriorated. The lads had arranged a night out in Birmingham. It was all very well behaved. These were responsible guys and good pros and we were moving from pub to pub. I was walking along the street, chatting with our keeper Stuart Naylor. I had my hands in my pockets because of the cold when Carlton, who was getting carried away, came up behind me and got me in a bear hug. He started swinging me and then, all of a sudden, let me go. As my hands were in my pockets, I couldn't break my fall and smashed my face on the pavement. It was to be the end of my night. My nose was broken and my teeth smashed. I was a mess and big Stuart had to take me to A&E. Then I had to go home and explain to Lorraine why my face was so smashed up. I looked like I had been hit by a bus.

The next day, we all had to be in for training. I certainly wasn't going to miss it and turned up. The boss was going to make us run off the night before. That was a crazy idea – one I would never have considered as a manager. I would never run players after a night out, because that is when you risk serious muscle damage. My timing couldn't have been worse. As I walked in the door, the manager was on his way from the training hall and couldn't miss me. He ordered me into his office and demanded to know what had happened.

I wasn't going to drop anyone in it, so I said I fell.

'I don't believe you,' Saunders replied. 'I'm going to ask you one more time, what happened?'

I wasn't going to change my answer, so I told him again that I had fallen.

He was raging and marched me into the training hall, where the rest of the players were gathered.

'Right,' said Saunders, pointing at my wounded face. 'What happened?'

That's when Carlton piped up.

'It was me, Gaffer,' he said. 'I dropped him.'

Saunders turned and looked me up and down. 'I knew you were a liar,' he said, before walking away.

I was raging. If I had just been able to get to Carlton beforehand, I could have told him the story I had come up with. I was the victim but he was the good guy for telling the truth and I was the bad guy, the liar with the smashed face. I thought I was doing the right thing, keeping Carlton out of trouble the way I had done with McCoist a few years before. But it backfired badly. We played Shrewsbury in our next game on Boxing Day and I was on the bench. We lost 1-0.

Off the field, the relationship with the gaffer was strained, to say the least, and on the field, it was getting worse and worse. We were plummeting down the table and I was unable to make any kind of impact, struggling to score as winter turned into spring. We were in big trouble and an away trip to Millwall in April was the last place we wanted to go. A win was vital and we dug in, with yours truly getting the only goal of the game. There was relief in the dressing room afterwards – a buoyant feeling that the threat of the drop had been erased. Saunders was his usual emotionless self in the aftermath. Christ, I didn't want hugs and kisses but we had kept him in a job, so some recognition would have been nice.

With our place in the second tier secured, a few of us were given the green light to attend the season's PFA awards in London. The event was on a Sunday, so we asked Saunders if we could get the Monday off and he agreed. Everything was arranged. I was to stay in Stewart Evans's flat. Derek Statham was staying in a hotel and his driver would drive us down and back in his car. All good. But we lost to Barnsley and the gaffer cancelled the Monday off. As everything was paid for, we decided to go anyway and drive back up early on Monday morning for training. We had a Saturday night in London, then went to the function on the Sunday. It was great to catch up with some old friends I hadn't seen for a while and meet a few players I had played against and get to know them better.

The plan was to get to Derek's hotel early in the morning and drive back up for training. But Derek was a bit worse for wear and we couldn't wake him. When we eventually got into his room, he reckoned that the manager was way out of line and he was going to take the day off anyway. I couldn't talk him out of it. As it was, he was injured and would only be going in for treatment. The physio and Derek were good mates and I was pretty sure he'd cover for him. That left me on my own and I felt even more vulnerable when Derek phoned his physio pal, told him the cover story and neglected to mention me at all. Yep, I was on my own! Derek wanted to find a pub and play pool but all I wanted to do was get back to Birmingham for training. It was a good hour before I persuaded Derek to get his driver to take me back.

We got back to The Hawthorns about noon and when I went in the door, I caught the boss in mid-sentence cursing me and calling me a liar. I told him that was unfair, that I had been let down but had got back as quick as I could and that I wanted to go out and train.

'No, you're not,' said Saunders. 'You get home and face your wife. I've already spoken to her and told her I was fining you two weeks' wages. She said I was quite right!'

He told me he would take the fine in the close season. I was raging. I should have taken it to the players' union but I didn't. I thought, or hoped, that Saunders would forget about it but I had to pay up.

At the end of the season, the manager told me he was putting me on the transfer list. I was so disappointed. I liked life at West Brom and the family were very settled in Lichfield. We had a strong friendship group, including my pal Micky Reece and Jimmy and Mandy Kelman. I didn't want to uproot the family all over again. That summer was not a pleasant time. I didn't hear of any team making an offer for me. To be honest, I wasn't even sure if Saunders had put me on the transfer list. When we returned for pre-season, I was still a West Brom player, still in the bad books with Saunders, yet still determined to prove myself all over again.

But we had a terrible start to the season. After games with Oldham, Blackburn, Swindon and Leeds, we had only one point. We had scored just two goals and one of those was an own goal. Nobody was surprised when Saunders was sacked. I believe that, for many of the Baggies fans, it was a relief.

Within 24 hours of one Ron leaving the manager's office, another one breezed in, with Ron Atkinson taking charge. Big Ron was an FA Cup winner with Manchester United and had managed at The Hawthorns before. In many respects, his return had parallels to Jock Wallace's return to Ibrox – a legendary figure returning to save a club in the doldrums.

Colin Addison, who came in as Big Ron's assistant, was a very experienced manager in his own right. He had managed a team out in Qatar called Al Ahli and had also held the reins at Spanish side Celta Vigo. He certainly wasn't cut out to be a No.2 and never got into any banter with the lads. I maintain that a key part of a No.2's job is to pick up the pieces after a manager has had a go and to be open for a few laughs. Big Ron had a sense of humour and was up for a laugh at the right time. Addison certainly didn't do that.

Ron also brought in former Manchester United player Stuart Pearson as part of the coaching team. Pancho, as he was known, reminded me of Ray Wilkins – a lovely speaker and a real gentleman – and I took to him immediately.

At first, it was good, but the problem was Ron brought in another striker with him – Andy Gray. He was a top player, a Scottish international who had starred at Everton, Villa and Wolves. Andy was a great guy and a great addition to the squad – very sociable and a good laugh. As well as playing, Andy was a bit of a go-between for the manager and the players. The type of role a No.2 should fill.

Andy was a winner. That was just his mindset and he hated losing – even at five-a-sides in training. He was soon to forge a partnership with fellow frontman Don Goodman, who joined us from Bradford City. Don was a good lad, had a good football career and is now having a good career as a pundit. I wish him well. But their double act meant I was going to have to get used to spending a lot of time on the bench. I wasn't happy but Andy tried to keep me going and told me to keep my head up, that the manager rated me, liked me and that I would get my chance. But it never came and I became despondent. I admit now that my attitude was not great.

I remember sitting on the bench and giving Carlton Palmer stick when he made a bad pass or did anything wrong. In a way, he was becoming the target of my frustrations. Big Ron noticed and turned to me. He asked why it was only Carlton I was singling out and not any of my mates in the team?

I think that's when the manager switched off on me – and rightly so. I was wrong. Big Ron asked me if I was racist, as I didn't like Carlton. I couldn't believe it. Nothing could be further from the truth. The fact was, and this is what I told Ron, Carlton would be a far more popular kid if he weren't so mouthy in the dressing room.

My relationship with Carlton had deteriorated badly and never got better. I had a conversation with Robert Hopkins, a guy I got on well with after he joined us from Manchester City, regarding Carlton. Hoppy told me that Carlton was criticising me when he was on the bench, loud enough for the manager and assistant to hear. I took it on board and that was why, whenever I was on the bench and Carlton was playing, I would do likewise. In hindsight, Hoppy might just have misled me and I believed him, as he was not a big fan of Carlton's either. So, I took the bait.

If that was the case, I owe Carlton an apology but we never got on. It all came to a head on one Christmas outing.

We were travelling back in the car from a pub, heading to TGIs on Edgbaston Road. Carlton was in the passenger seat and me and two others were in the back. I was giving him some stick for being the manager's favourite – although I have to admit that if I had managed him, he would have been my favourite, too. If we were running at training, the manager would encourage Carlton to go faster, which would mean we would all have to go faster. Carlton was a fit lad and when he got in his stride, he could shift. He bit off more than he could chew when he took on a challenge to race Don Goodman. The race was over before it started, because Don was one of the fastest players I knew and was quick off the mark. He was ten yards ahead of Carlton before Carlton had done two and the race was over. We went into the pub and, as there was so many of us, we split up into little groups. I was drinking with Gary Robson, brother of the legendary Bryan, and their father, who was a great guy and good company. They had heard about me and Carlton in the car and proceeded to wind me up, saying I should get it off my chest, take him outside and sort it out – that's what they would do! The more I drank, the more it sounded like a good idea. I went over to Carlton, told him we needed to sort it out and we headed for the door. I had been getting advice from the Robsons to hit him as soon as we got out the door. I led the way down to the car park and through a side door that looked on to Liberty's nightclub. As we got down the stairs, Carlton slipped. I never gave him a chance to get back up. It was over before the fight started. Andy Gray and Stuart Naylor pulled me off him, taking an arm each to hold me back. I was draped over the bonnet of a car but nobody had thought to hold Carlton back. He threw a punch and one of his rings must have caught me and bust my lip.

Writing this now, I feel so ashamed. Carlton was four years younger than me and I should have known better. But it happened and I regret it. I wish Carlton no ill will. I hope he is well. I heard he went into management and is still involved in the game, so the best of luck to him.

But it was the beginning of the end for me at the Baggies. Ron Atkinson more or less banished me to the reserves and, despite banging in the goals – I scored 30 for them that season – I was hardly getting a look-in for the first team.

I did get a run-out at Wimbledon in the FA Cup. We lost 4-1 and Dennis Wise scored a goal for them from distance. I was tracking back and knew I wasn't going to get there in time but still launched myself into the tackle. Dennis managed to get his shot away but I was committed to the challenge and clattered into him. The ball flew into the net and Dennis nearly followed it! As he lay there rolling about, the famed Wimbledon Crazy Gang surrounded me. They were all in there – Vinnie Jones, Lawrie Sanchez, John Fashanu. The physio was on with the treatment bag, which got kicked up in the air. It was mad. Dennis got stretchered off and then came back on. I think he was overdoing it just to get me booked.

The respect I had for manager Ron Atkinson was diminishing day by day, especially when he would take part in the five-a-sides and have yours truly and others doing laps on the outside of the park. It was demoralising. In fact, he had us doing a 12-minute run round the main park and I even got lapped by one of the young players who was still trying to push for a first-team place. My morale had gone.

Big Ron had destroyed me. At first, he had been brilliant. He was jovial, funny, but not now.

So, I stopped putting in the effort and for that I need to apologise to the Baggies fans. My heart wasn't in it.

There were still some high points, mind you. We played away to Reading and I scored one of the best goals of my career. I picked up possession just near the touchline and headed goalwards, moving diagonally from right to left, beating players as they came. I found myself one-on-one with their keeper, took it round him and tapped it in. My team-mate, Tony Kelly, a Scouser, ran up and raised my arm to the Reading fans as if I had won a boxing match and, credit to their fans, they actually applauded! Andy Gray scored a good header and we won 2-1. We were on the bus heading back up the road and the manager produced a bottle of champagne and gave it to Andy. I asked him where mine was and he dismissed me out of hand, saying I'd get a bottle when I reached the 200-goal tally. I didn't realise Andy had reached that landmark. What a player.

Mid-season, Big Ron came into the dressing room and told the players that he had booked us on a trip to Portugal for some sun and to recharge the batteries. Great news, especially when he said there was no training planned; we were to relax and switch off. Sounds good, right? Wrong! It was a disaster. The worst football trip I had ever been on.

Big Ron wasn't coming with us. He put Colin Addison in charge, along with Pancho. The first night, we were told we had to go to some pub for an event that was organised by some fans to meet and greet and have a few drinks with them. We had been on the beach all day, having a few beers and the last thing we wanted was to get dressed and head out to this function. On the bus, some of the lads were already merry and a bit boisterous and loud. I don't know why it happened but Hoppy threw a little mixer bottle down the bus and it hit David 'Budgie' Burrows on the head. It was pretty dangerous, Budgie wasn't happy and the shouting started.

By the time we reached the pub, it had calmed down but it all kicked off soon after arriving when Don Goodman hit Hoppy in the face with a bit of ice from his glass. Don thought it was funny, Hoppy didn't and, before long, the two of them were fighting. Pancho tried to get to it to break it up, pulling Hoppy by the hair, which only made things worse. Punches were getting thrown, women were screaming and it all spilled out of the pub into the street like something from a Wild West movie. Order was only restored when Hoppy forced Don into an apology.

We should have ended the night there and then but we didn't, heading off to a nightclub. The place was dead and, in the dark, Tony Morley spotted Tony Kelly pissing in the corner. Morley was no fighter – he was a really placid guy – but he wasn't having it and went over to chastise Kelly, who responded by punching him in the face. Andy Gray saw this and, being a pal of Morley's from their Villa days, jumped in for his mate!

It was a nightmare. God knows how it all ended. But the next day, Addison had us all up bright and early. Big Ron had told us there would be no training but Addison was going to punish us for the night before. We did every run imaginable, using every line on the park as markers and doing laps and sides. Everything!

The thing is, if Addison hadn't arranged that night and allowed the players to do their own thing – as Big Ron had instructed – the fights would not have happened. Players would have gone out in smaller groups, with guys they were comfortable with. Instead, they were under orders and that raised the tension.

And, bugger me, were we not all ordered to attend another dinner the very next night. It was with this couple of really boring guys who nobody seemed to know. By the end, we were going mad and Stuart Naylor and I escaped to a nearby pub. On returning to the hotel, Addison was waiting for us. Fuming. He said he had given orders that nobody was to go out after the dinner and that we had breached his rules. It was nonsense. We'd not heard him say that and why should we be punished and not the guys who had been throwing punches the night before? I was in the bad books, though, and he was more annoyed with me than the guys who had been fighting.

Thankfully, we left the next morning. I couldn't wait to get home. When I was checking out, the receptionist told me that one person hadn't returned his room key. When I asked who it was, she said it was Mr Addison.

I climbed on board the bus and, in a loud voice, announced: 'Some idiot hasn't handed in their room key.'

Addison immediately realised it was him and he turned to Terry Neill and said: 'Terry, go and take my key back.'

This was Terry Neill, ex-Arsenal and Spurs boss, Northern Ireland international and legend. And here was Addison ordering him to take his key back. What a sign of disrespect to a guy who had done so much in the game.

Back at The Hawthorns the next day, Addison was going through us and I was getting the most of it. But it was such a ludicrous situation that I was beginning to find it funny and I was struggling not to laugh.

Colin noticed this and said: 'This isn't funny. This is serious.'

I told him the sun was in my eyes.

But I had given them another reason to resent me, another reason to keep me in the reserves, another reason not to have me in the first team, another reason to have me running around the pitches. It wasn't fun. I hated it. Even after the season had finished – and we escaped relegation by the skin of our teeth – he had us in for a cross-country run. When I queried it, he said it would benefit us for pre-season. It was nonsense. It was just more punishment. We ran on the Monday and then he had us in on the Wednesday to tell us our fate. New contract or freed?

There were a few of us waiting and, to be fair, it didn't take long – in and out. I went in and Ron told me I was being released. There was no small talk. I stood up to shake his hand and he flinched. He thought I was going to hit him!

All that nonsense about preparing us for pre-season by running us into the ground was just a last-day punishment. He knew he was freeing us.

I let myself down at West Brom. I could and should have done better and it was time to have a good look at myself and where my career was going. I'd gone from a player Rangers had paid £100,000 for to a swap with Jimmy Nic and now I had no club at all.

I have no problems with Ron Atkinson. I disagreed with how he treated the players he wasn't interested in and I made sure that, when I became a manager, I never treated players like that.

Big Ron was later accused of being a racist for a remark he made when he thought his mic was off while commentating on a game. He is most definitely not that and I felt he was hard done-by, because he was a very good and amusing analyst. He accused me of being a racist with that incident with Carlton Palmer and that is utter bollocks as well. I live in Kenya and am married to a Kenyan for crying out loud!

But my days at The Hawthorns were over – and I had no idea what was going to happen next.

CHAPTER 8

MEET THE MILLERS

BEFORE I left West Brom, I had to go back into The Hawthorns to pick up a few things. When there, Colin Addison pulled me into the manager's office and sat down in the manager's chair. Colin wasn't a No.2. He had to be the boss. He told me that Dave Mackay, the Doncaster Rovers manager, wanted me to give him a call. I said 'thanks' and left but I never called Dave. I always felt it was up to the manager to call me – like Graham Turner did at Wolves, like John Rudge did at Port Vale and Billy McEwan did at Rotherham. However, I do regret that now. Dave Mackay was a Scottish legend. He played 20-odd games for his country, hundreds of games for Spurs and won multiple trophies as a player in Scotland and England, as well as the First Division title as manager of Derby County. Yes, out of respect to him and what he was, I should have phoned him. But I didn't.

I had a few managers interested in me and made arrangements to meet up with them. The first manager I spoke to was Graham Turner at Wolves. I went down to Molineux and was very impressed with the stadium and the set-up. Also, with the club being in the Midlands, it meant I wouldn't have to relocate, as it wasn't far from my place in Lichfield.

We had a discussion and Graham was very honest with me. He said I would be playing second fiddle to Steve Bull who, to nobody's surprise, was doing great things at the club. His partner was a guy called Andy Mutch and they were banging in the goals together and taking Wolves up the divisions. I wasn't happy about playing a supporting role and left Graham's office telling him I'd think it over and get back to him. The money wasn't great but I knew I had to get back in the game. Still, I said 'no' to them, which, looking back, was probably a mistake. I shouldn't have taken Graham so literally. If I had joined Wolves, I'm sure I'd have got an opportunity through injuries and suspensions and I had enough faith in my ability that, if I got that chance, I would make the most of it. I should have had faith in myself. Plus, it would mean I would have been playing in front of their brilliant, passionate fans.

I then went to speak to John Rudge at Port Vale. That would have been a sensible move as well, with Vale Park just a short jaunt up the M6, so, again, no need to move. In those days, the stadium had seen better days but that wasn't the reason I didn't accept their offer. When I spoke to John, he said he had watched me a few times and complimented me on the number of goals I had scored. But he then added that I had missed a lot of chances. That last statement didn't impress me. I mean, at least I was there to miss them! I left his office saying I would get back to him but I'm pretty sure I already knew my answer.

My last port of call was at Rotherham, up in South Yorkshire – the best part of two hours from our home in Lichfield. Manager Billy McEwan had said to bring Lorraine, as he knew we would probably have to relocate and it would be only fair for her to see the area and have her own thoughts. I was impressed with Billy and his wife, Maria, who took the time to meet Lorraine and look after her while Billy and I spoke business. They then took us for a drive around the place, showing us some nice areas where we could live and then took us to a restaurant for a meal. Billy had taken the time to make us feel welcome, to feel wanted, and that made such a difference. The money they were offering was not the best but I needed to go somewhere. I needed a fresh start. But, more importantly, I needed to prove to people that I wasn't finished, that I wasn't nothing. I phoned Graham at Wolves and John at Port Vale and told them 'thanks, but no thanks'. Billy had impressed me, so I was joining the Millers.

Billy McEwan was probably the coach I learned the most from on the training field. He was 24/7 football. He was doing shadow play most days. It was pretty boring but absolutely necessary. He had us very well organised and very fit. He used to run us on a Monday, which was not great if you over indulged at the weekend, which I usually did. When I became a manager, our physical day was usually a Tuesday. Monday would be light work to let the players get over the weekend – win, lose or draw. There was one day we turned up for training on Monday expecting a blast after a defeat on the Saturday and ready for a hard day's running but the gaffer walked us out of the gate down into the village to the local café and we had rolls and coffee together. It was very relaxed and I learned that, as a manager, you have to change your routine now and again and not become too predictable. I would argue, though, that repetition is, generally, the key to success. It might be boring but if you're doing the right things, why change?

I was excited about joining my new team and had worked hard during the off-season to make sure I was in the best possible condition. Being freed by West Brom had been a wake-up call. It had forced me to have a good, long, hard look at myself and where my career was going. I needed to prove myself, to show to everyone that I wasn't done. But this might be the last-chance saloon. Rotherham were in the bottom tier. If I couldn't make it here, then I was back on the tools. That prospect made my blood run cold.

Pre-season was hard but I was ready for it. Besides, the surroundings were easy on the eye. Rotherham didn't have their own training ground and in my first year we trained at this stately home, just outside the town. It had huge grass areas and we had to set up the portable goals. The place was stunning and, during training, it wasn't unusual to see a stag or a deer wandering around.

When I arrived for my first-team meeting, I discovered there were two other Scots in the squad. John Buckley was a right-winger and Billy Russell a right-back. Both had come through the ranks at Celtic but, like so many, had never managed to make the breakthrough at Celtic Park and had to move on to further their careers. Tony Grealish, who had been with me for a short time at West Brom, was also there. Tony had been one of those players at The Hawthorns who didn't feature much after the club were relegated from the First Division. That was a real shame, because I soon discovered what a quality player Tony was. He was a terrific presence in midfield, always in a position to make a tackle and break up an attack, because he read the game so well. He had about 45 caps for the Republic of Ireland at that time and had played in the FA Cup Final with Brighton. You know, that one when Gordon Smith was clean through. 'Smith must score,' the commentator said. He didn't ... but I always felt it was a great save, rather than a bad miss.

Tony and I used to car share, so we got to know each other well. He had been based in the Midlands for a while, his family was settled and he had a beautiful house, which had a swimming pool. There was no way he was going to move but I felt if I was really going to get my career back on track, I was going to have to relocate from our beloved Lichfield.

We put our house up for sale and we were inundated with offers. I hadn't really been monitoring the property market and was pleasantly surprised to find our house had doubled in value in the two years we had lived there. People were prepared to commute to London from Lichfield – it was such a beautiful place and you got so much more for your money. Every weekend, we would travel up and house-hunt but we couldn't find anything in Rotherham, in any of the desired areas, so we had to look further afield into the Sheffield suburbs. We found a nice place about 45 minutes' drive from the ground. It was just outside Beighton, right on a man-made lake that I used to jog round and watch all types of water sports.

Off the field, we were settled, which makes things easier when it comes to your mind being in the right place on the field. We got off to a great start and never looked back. Our first game was against Dave Mackay's Doncaster Rovers – a home game against our local rivals. Their goalkeeper was red-carded when conceding a penalty and I grabbed the ball to take it. As the Doncaster team were regrouping, putting an outfield player in goal, as there was no keeper on the bench in those days, I jokingly rolled the ball into the back of the net. The Rotherham fans loved it. With the stand-in keeper in place, I knew any effort left or right of him and there was no way he was getting it. I fired the penalty to the right and opened my scoring account for the club. The fans were chanting my name and would do for all the time I was there. My days at Rotherham were to become some of the happiest of my career. I loved the club and the fans – and my son, Steven, was born there.

Billy McEwan had built a great team. We would go on to win the league and promotion. There was Kelham O'Hanlon in goal, who would go on to play at Dundee United. We had Martin Scott or Pat Heard at left-back and Billy Russell at right-back. Andy Barnsley and Phil Crosby could play anywhere along the back line. Nigel Johnson was at centre-back alongside John Green, our skipper. Nigel would attack everything, while John would read the situations and take the ball. Sadly, Greeny's knees were shot and he was in and out of the team.

Big Nigel was an ever-present. He was very steady and would chip in with a few goals and assists from set plays. I thought I got on well with Nigel, who was nicknamed 'The Chief'. But one Friday, we were doing some shadow play against the defence and Nigel was marking me. He was coming through me every time I received the ball. I told him to settle down; there was a game the next day. I don't know what was wrong with the big man. Maybe he was having domestic issues but you don't bring it to work! He went through me again and I gave him a final warning. The next time, I was ready for him. As the ball was coming to me, I threw an elbow back and caught him flush on the chin. He went down in a heap. As I turned around, he was struggling to get back to his feet, like a boxer trying to get up from a haymaker!

As he climbed up, he asked me: 'Do you want a go?'

His legs were shaking, his eyes were glazed over and the manager stepped in, ending the session there and then. I went in to see the gaffer.

I said: 'You saw what happened. He was kicking me all over the place. I warned him and warned him.'

The boss replied: 'I saw you, you're right, but you could have broken his nose and he would have been out for the game tomorrow.'

'If I hadn't done it, he would have injured me – and who would you have missed most?' I asked.

When I walked out of the gaffer's room, Nigel was going in. We shook hands. He apologised for the tackles and I apologised for the elbow. I found through experience that these altercations in training did more good than bad. The players involved usually found more respect for each other. Some incidents are really bad and a bridge can't be built, with one or both having to move on. This was not one of those occasions.

Des Hazel had pace to burn on the left wing and John Buckley would batter up and down the right. If they had been counting assists back then, Buckie would have been up there, as he supplied me with most of my chances. He loved a nutmeg and tormented full-backs.

The aforementioned Tony Grealish kept the midfield ticking over alongside a very young Shaun Goodwin and another talented young player called Nigel Pepper.

Mark Dempsey also joined us from Sheffield United and was a good addition for us in midfield. I was up front, either paired with a young Clive Mendonca or Paul Haycock. Haycock was my initial partner. He was a hard-working guy, not prolific when it came to goals but he got his fair share. Young Clive was a work in progress. We could all see the potential and he would go on to have a great career until injury cut it short when he was at Charlton.

Football is a small world and my old pal from West Brom, Stewart Evans, would later join us. Evo introduced me to a few working men's clubs – we'd go with his brother, Steve, and see these hairy-arsed Yorkshiremen playing bingo on a Sunday afternoon! That was until the break, when the stripper would come on at one in the afternoon!

Evo was a talented big player with a good left foot. He was tall but he wasn't a target man. He could play and there was much more to his game than simply dealing with high balls. We were mates from our time at West Brom and we stayed in the same hotel. One weekend, I had gone back to Scotland and Evo's room had been broken into. He suggested they check mine and when they opened the door, the cops confirmed my room had been done as well. My stuff was all over the place. Evo took one look and corrected the officers, telling them that I always lived like that!

After games, I would head into our players' lounge for a few beers. There was a guy who used to help out behind the bar by the name of John Newey. He was a policeman but a big Millers fan and became a good friend of mine. He passed away a few years ago and I was pleased that I was back in the country to be able to make his funeral. I miss the guy; he helped me enormously. John came on a few club trips with Rotherham and again with Killie and was a good guy to be around. He was tight as a drum when it came to money but, as a friend, he would be there for you. He would work behind the bar and if he felt I had drunk too much, he would insist on driving me home in my car and his wife would follow in his car. When I pointed out he had drunk as much as me, he would just flash his badge!

I remember coming in one Monday morning and a black guy was rapping away in the centre of the dressing room. I didn't take much notice but it was a lad called Shaun Goater, who had come to the club and was introducing himself to the squad in his own inimitable style. Shaun certainly wasn't shy but I didn't know at the time he had been brought in to replace me further down the line. Shaun was strong and fast; his finishing needed to improve but you could see the talent. One of the reasons Rotherham ultimately cashed in on me was to open the door for Shaun. And, boy, did he make the most of that opportunity. His finishing developed and he went on to bigger things, becoming a legend at Manchester City. He was honoured with an MBE – not bad for a young lad from Bermuda. Shaun may have ultimately replaced me but he was a great lad.

The manager, Billy McEwan, was the key to our success. I finished top goalscorer and won all of the player of the year awards but the gaffer was the man. He was ably assisted by Phil Henson and got us promoted in my first season. We would go on to hold our own in the Third Division the season after.

I got a hat-trick in a game towards the end of the promotion season, the fans celebrating in the sunshine. It was

Crewe away and it set us on our way to finish champions. We wrapped it up taking a point against Stockport.

At the end of the season, the gaffer took us away to Majorca for a week in Cala Millor. He joked that if it was good enough for Cloughie, it was good enough for Rotherham. Sure enough, Forest were there at the same time. I never met the great man but it was a decent trip and not without incident.

The players were good together and we all headed off to the bar to socialise and celebrate our promotion. Mark Dempsey and Clive Mendonca were the dancers and they were entertaining the holidaymakers. Clive was showing the young kids some of his dance moves and the mums and dads were loving it. But as the day went on, he had more and more to drink and, eventually, the mums and dads were keen for Clive to be removed. We got him out the pub and carried him back to the hotel before locking him in his room to sleep it off. We got back to the bar and were stunned to find Clive was there waiting for us. The idiot had only climbed down the balcony and beaten us back to the pub!

Clive's roommate was Nigel Pepper. They were a loveable but troublesome double act! One night, I got back to my floor, only to find this older gentleman walking up and down the corridor in his pyjamas. I was bemused and was wondering what his story was? It turns out Pep had kicked his door off its hinges by mistake and ran in screaming. He realised his error when he saw the old couple jumping out of their bed thinking they were about to be attacked. Pep legged it back into the corridor, crashed into another room, where two of our other players were sleeping, and ran out on to the balcony before climbing over to his own room. The old guy had seen him and called security, who contacted the police. Our two players were huckled to the police station, where they pleaded their innocence, and the gaffer had to go out and get them out. He told the police that he would find the culprit and, so, the inquest began. The boss got us all in a room and asked who kicked the door down. Nobody responded. He then said that if the guy didn't own up, we would stay in the hotel for the rest of the week with no alcohol. He told us we had five minutes to sort it and then he walked out of the room.

The only people who truly knew what had happened were Pep and the two players whose room he had run into and they weren't for dropping him in it. Eventually, Pep said he would own up – only to deny it all when the boss came back in. Finally, though, he held up his hand, saying he did it for a laugh after thinking it was one of our rooms. It was an expensive mistake – he had to pay for all the repairs!

I was actually glad when that trip ended. A week was too long. By the end of it, we were laying in our rooms with the curtains blowing over the beds. Nobody could be bothered even drinking any more. The weather was pretty poor and the red flags were up on the beaches, as it was too dangerous to go swimming. Unfortunately, a couple of Germans never heeded the warning and drowned.

As a team, we were more than capable of holding our own in the Third Division. I had managed to get my game back together and finished top scorer in my two full seasons. I even got in the Third Division team of the season. The game that stood out for me was Birmingham at Millmoor. I scored three goals that day and I loved the fans singing my name. For the third goal, I cut in from the left and was maybe just a yard off the by-line. I looked up and saw the keeper off his line but also saw Clive Mendonca lurking at the back post for a tap-in. I looked up at Clive, fooling the keeper into thinking I was about to pass, and blasted the ball in at the near post. It was great to hear the cheers but the best thing was the look on young Clive's face. He didn't join the celebrations and just turned and headed back for the restart with his head down. But when you're on a hat-trick, you're never going to pass.

I scored another hat-trick the following week. The local butcher in the town centre had promised three steaks for any player who could score three goals. I was in there a few times!

I was loving life at Rotherham. I had rediscovered my love for the game and things were going well, on and off the field. So, it was a shock when the manager phoned and told me there was a club in for me and that they were considering a sale. It was not what I wanted. I didn't want to uproot my family and I didn't want to leave Millmoor. Billy told me to stand by the phone. If any deal was to be done, it would be done in the next two hours. It is an odd situation; your future is being decided elsewhere and you don't seem to get a say in anything. But Billy didn't phone back, so, whatever the move was, it didn't happen. I later discovered it had been Neil Warnock at Notts County. It would have been good to work with Neil but some things just aren't to be.

However, it was becoming clear that, sadly, Rotherham were prepared to sell if the right offer was on the table. I wasn't happy, as I said I didn't want to go, and I was taken aback when I was told about Kilmarnock's interest. Neither Lorraine nor I wanted to move back to Scotland and we talked about it, both of us wanting to stay where we were.

I felt that I should at least show Killie the courtesy of talking to them and if their plans and ambitions matched my own, maybe we could agree terms. I drove up to Kilmarnock and met with Jim Fleeting, the manager. His brother, Bobby, was the chairman and he was there alongside goalkeeping coach Jim Stewart, who wasn't involved in the discussions but was in the boardroom at the time. The money wasn't life-changing and some of the players would be part-time. But Jim sold the club to me and if I could get Rotherham to pay me what they owed and a bit more – as they were getting £100,000 for a guy they picked up on a free – I would sign.

I called Billy McEwan and he agreed everything. He told me to sign and wished me all the best. On the road home, I phoned him again to see when I would get paid and was stunned when he told me the chairman wouldn't pay what we had agreed. I wasn't happy and felt Billy had let me down. If a manager promises you money, you expect him to do his best to get it. I suspected Billy, without speaking to the chairman, had said it to me just to get the deal done. I never held it against Billy, as he helped me get my career on track and I learned so much from him – but it hurt.

It meant I would have to go in and see the chairman myself. Ken Booth had made his money out of scrap metal and had owned the club for a couple of years. To be fair, he had got them out of the shit financially. I never liked this side of the business but I wasn't going to be treated like a fool and was more than prepared to fight my corner. The office was just like Mr Booth – very old – and I began to state my case. I told him they had got me for free, that I had scored a barrel of goals to help them get promotion. I also told him what I had agreed with Billy.

Mr Booth told me he wasn't paying, surprising me by insisting that, as I had asked for the move, he didn't see any need to fork out. I was astonished. I'd never engineered this. I wanted to stay but Rotherham clearly didn't want me. I told Mr Booth that I was not looking to move and he seemed surprised. Then he opened one of his desk drawers and pulled out a huge bundle of cash. He counted out an amount and handed it to me. I was stunned. He had all this cash and here he was haggling over a few grand. I suppose that's why he was a millionaire.

In my last game for the club, I had missed a penalty and Mr Booth asked me if I had missed it on purpose. Why would I do that? I loved the club, loved the fans and would have liked to have left on a high. I didn't want to leave. I was happy, the family was happy. But football can be a cruel game and I was out. My time at Rotherham was over.

CHAPTER 9

IN FOR THE KILLIE

I ALWAYS thought I would finish my career in England but in football you never know what is around the corner. Jim Fleeting had really sold Kilmarnock to me and I could see there was a grand plan there. The club had been close to the bottom of Scottish football and were on their way up. I felt it would be exciting to be a part of that.

We bought a house in Robroyston and we began to settle in – Lorraine, me, Emma and Steven. It was probably the right time for the move and meant we could get the wee one settled in at school, even though she found herself repeating a lot of the things she had already completed in England.

I was shocked to find that some of the players at Killie were part-time. I hadn't even considered that and hadn't been part-time since my days at Clydebank. There was a small core of full-time guys there, including myself, Ian Porteous, who was known as Sid, Willie McStay, Tommy Callaghan, who was the son of my former coach at Clydebank, and the great Tommy Burns.

Tommy was a legend at Celtic and had joined up at Rugby Park in a player-coach capacity for a transfer fee of £50,000. He was a great lad, so down-to-earth and respectful. He never swore. I never heard him curse once in all the time I knew him. That doesn't mean he didn't get angry – believe me, he did. But you would watch your language around Tommy, who was a deeply religious man and would attend chapel every day. As well as being a class act off the pitch, Tommy was a Rolls-Royce on it. He played with his heart on his sleeve and gave his all. His biggest strength was his man-management. He knew how to get the best out of everyone and led by example. He liked to play a pressing game and, when he had caught his wind, he would implement it pushing forward from midfield. It wasn't sustainable for 90 minutes, as Tommy wasn't getting any younger, but in the early parts of the game, when it is most important, we could do it successfully. For someone whose eyesight was so bad off the pitch, he had tremendous vision on it. You would make a run and think he hadn't seen you and then, the next second, the ball would be at your feet. Like most top players, he was very vocal on the park, always shouting for a pass. I would be running with the ball towards the opposition's goal and I would hear him shouting for a pass. When I turned around, he would be 30 yards behind me! But what a player. Class.

Training was Monday during the day, Tuesday evening with the part-timers, Wednesday daytime, Thursday evening, Friday daytime. It was difficult when the part-timers came in, because we did a lot of running, both with and without the ball, to get their fitness levels up. I found it hard to adjust and it really did take me a lot of time to get used to it. It wasn't helped by the fact that in my last weeks at Rotherham before I moved north, I had been getting treatment for a knee injury and was taking injections to play on a Saturday. In all my career, I can't remember once waking up on a Saturday and feeling 100 per cent.

I had, and still have, the utmost respect for the manager, Jim Fleeting, and his brother, Bobby, the chairman. They helped to get Killie back where the club belonged.

Jim had a very difficult job with the team trying to go full-time, because we had so many talented part-time players but they had well-paid jobs outside of football and, understandably, didn't want to take the chance in the precarious world of the full-time game. Jim would always try and keep the training different for the full-timers but it was tough and there was very little variety in coaching so small a group. It was always ball work or fitness and very little team shape or game awareness. I've experienced working with not even half a squad and it's difficult to make the training game-related. You are mostly working on ball skills.

But, all the same, Jim was a very good coach. When I started learning the trade down at SFA courses in Largs, Jim was one of the educators and he gave me a great piece of advice. He told me that, as a coach, I should try to look ahead of the ball to see who is making themselves available and that when you are attacking, look at your defence to make sure they're in the right positions. It's not easy when you've got to try and do both but I always thought that if we score, great, I'll see it later, but it was better to ensure the defence was organised in case we lost possession and the opposition broke away. If we conceded, I would always know whose mistake it was, if there was one. I found Jim to be a good manager and coach and very well organised. He was also a gentleman.

The boss had Jim McSherry and Frank Coulston assisting him. At times, it felt like we had three managers, as they were both more than capable in their own right. They worked well together but I always felt Jim and Frank could have shown more of their personalities in the dressing room. I later worked with both down at Largs on the coaching courses and found that, as well as being extremely knowledgeable about the game, these guys had a great sense of humour. If the players could only have seen that side of them, it could have been better. Wee Jim liked to dish it out but he behaved like a manager when receiving it and you knew you couldn't step over the line.

I wasn't long at the club and we had a game at Rugby Park. Frank was having a go at the strikers for not following in a rebound.

I piped up: 'Frank, I was at the other side of the goal, I could never have got there!'

Frank turned around and stormed into the treatment room. The next day, at training, he never said a word to me. The next time was the same. We were training on an Astro somewhere in Ayrshire and as we were packing up to go back to Rugby Park, I asked the manager if I could have a word with Frank. I had to clear the air. I hate things festering away.

'I'm sorry, Frank,' I said. 'I wasn't doing it to undermine you but if I've got something to say in a dressing room, then I need to say it. I've been like that all my career. There was certainly no way I wanted to cause you any offence.'

Frank looked at me, smiled and jovially replied: 'Ach, Bobby, that's okay.'

We shook hands and as I walked back to the group, he shouted: 'Just don't do it again!'

See, I told you it was like having three managers. Frank was letting everybody know he was the boss.

Wee McSherry, as he is affectionately known, later became our commercial manager and he was brilliant and well liked. He was very popular in that role, more popular than he was as an assistant. If you're ever in Ayr town centre, pop into his pub, the Wee Windaes. He's a bit like Basil Fawlty behind the bar and you will get a good laugh.

My first game for the club was at home against Brechin City, who were struggling in the table, and we were expected to win easily. It didn't turn out that way and we had to work hard for the victory. I was delighted to score the equaliser, after we had gone behind, from a corner that had been knocked on by Billy Stark. Tommy Sloan, who had joined the club around the same time as me, got the winner quite late on.

Our next game was against Dundee, who were top of the league and had ambitions of earning promotion that season. But I discovered on that day that this Killie team had a bit about them. We had experienced pros like Bobby Geddes in goal and Dave McKinnon, who was brilliant that day, organising the back line alongside Ray Montgomerie – a really under-rated but not under-appreciated player. Paul Flexney was a no-nonsense defender. Then there was Willie McStay and, of course, Tommy Burns, plus a great lad called Robert Reilly. Robert was a decent player but had a good job and wouldn't go full-time. He was also a great character about the place and still is. When he and Jim McSherry are together, the banter flows. All you've got to do is listen; nobody else gets a word in. It's hilarious. There was also Billy Stark, who unfortunately suffered from injuries and missed out a lot of the time, Tom Callaghan, Tommy Tait and Tommy Sloan. John Sludden was always good for a goal or two. The team was packed with experience – and maybe that was the problem. We looked like Dad's Army!

But that day we were outstanding. I got the first when I raced through, leaving at least three Dundee defenders for dead before I blasted a shot past Tom Carson in the Dundee goal. Minutes later, Tommy Burns floated in a brilliant free kick and Tommy Tait lashed a header into the back of the net. Dundee didn't know what had hit them but we gifted them a way back in when Tommy Callaghan tried a pass back to Bobby Geddes from all of 40 yards! I couldn't believe it and neither could the Dundee striker Keith Wright, who slotted home. But we held on. In fact, despite the loss of that crazy goal, we never looked like dropping points.

But it was soon to turn into a season of one step forward, two steps back. We couldn't get any consistency going or put a run together and our ambition of being in the promotion mix slowly ebbed away. There were still highlights. We beat Ayr in Ne'er Day derby, which was a great experience, even though I didn't score. And I went on a run of scoring in five consecutive games – the highlight of which was a hat-trick against my old club, Clydebank. Gus MacPherson had joined us by then, having failed to make the breakthrough at Rangers and after a spell on loan down at Exeter, and he played in that game, nearly getting a goal as well. For me, the reward for my three goals was a family trip to Malta as part of a sponsor's prize!

The goals kept coming for me – there was a double in an 8-1 win over Meadowbank – and Calum Campbell was adding his fair share as well. But the season fizzled out and we would end up fifth. I finished highest scorer in the league with 14 goals. John Sludden's overall tally was one better than mine, because he had scored in the cup. But with the nine I had got before I had left Rotherham, it was another season with more than 20 goals in the bag, so I was pleased.

The last game of the season was at Somerset Park against our bitter rivals, Ayr. Despite being pretty meaningless for both sides, it was a towsy affair. We went behind to an early goal from Ally Fraser and, no matter how hard we tried, we couldn't get a leveller. It would have been a great way to end the season, getting a third win over our bitterest rivals, but it was not to be. Eventually, the frustrations boiled over. Ray Montgomerie was the first of three quick bookings, including Calum Campbell, who went in late on the Ayr keeper, Cammy Duncan. The two of them squared up and it riled the Killie fans, who started throwing things on to the pitch – one of them hitting the Ayr keeper. Jim Fleeting and the rest of the coaches in the dugout had to appeal for calm and, for a short time, the atmosphere was unhealthy.

We never did get the equaliser.

At the end of the season, I organised a trip to Magaluf, where we met up with my former Rotherham team-mate Kelham O'Hanlon and my mate John Newey. My Killie pal Paul Flexney was there and he brought along a good pal of his who worked on the railways, so was called Choo-choo. This guy was Celtic-daft; everything he wore was green. And he loved a beer. We would go on a pub crawl and each time as we moved from one pub to another, Choo-choo would be opening up another can just for the walk. One morning, we were sitting at the pool and Choo came down late. He explained he had met up with another bunch that night and went back to one of their rooms to carry on drinking. When he woke up in the morning, there were bodies everywhere and he hadn't a clue where he was. He crept out of the room and made his way down to reception, noting that all these hotels looked the same. He stepped outside, blinking into the sunlight, to try to get his bearings and work out how he was getting back ... when he looked around and realised it was his hotel all along.

The man had us in fits laughing.

It was a decent break – these trips are always good for letting off steam after a long, tough season. I don't remember how we acquired these massive water pistols but I woke one morning to find one in my room, so I loaded it up and went looking for a victim, knowing that Flexney was next door. I went out of the patio door and looked in. He was asleep on the couch and I went in blasting! He jumped up, grabbed a pistol and went into the toilet! I was on empty and I had a good idea he was going to load his, so I ran for the patio doors but Stuart Burgess was holding it shut from the outside. I looked around and noticed a glass of clear liquid on the table, left over from the night before. I filled my gun as best I could, just as Flexney was coming out of the bathroom whistling the tune from a Clint Eastwood Western. He grabbed the end of my gun, confidently predicting that I was empty and held it right up to his eye. I pulled the trigger and, as much to my surprise as his, this liquid shot out. God knows what was in that glass! It could have been neat vodka! But Flex tumbled on to the couch, dropping my gun as I made a hasty exit.

Christ! His eye was red for the whole day!

When we first arrived, it was a case of dropping the bags and heading to the pub. After a couple of beers, Robert Reilly piped up: 'I never came here to sit in a pub. I came for the sun. Who's with me?' He headed to the door on his own and came back a couple of hours later, burnt to a crisp. Robert's a really funny guy. We were in a pub that had one of those boxing machines and Robert decided to have a go. Honestly, he had that machine bouncing all over the pub. It nearly went out of the door! He stripped to the waist, as the sweat was pouring off him. It was so funny, people outside were looking in the window. In the end, he had to go back to the hotel for a shower.

A new season began with fresh optimism that we could push for promotion but our start to season 1991/92 was nothing short of a disaster. Eight games in and we had won only once – and that was against a poor Meadowbank side when I netted the winner with an 85th-minute penalty. Our opening game of the season had been against newly promoted Stirling Albion and, even with them down to ten men, we struggled. Truth be told, our keeper, Bobby Geddes, had to bail us out a few times. It was a nightmare for boss Jim Fleeting and his backroom double act. No matter what they tried, we just couldn't hit our stride. Ross Jack had come in from Dunfermline to bolster the attacking options, Ally Mitchell came down from East Fife for about £100,000 and Shaun McSkimming was brought in from Dundee to add some steel to our midfield. My old mate from Rangers, Hugh Burns, also joined us and, midway through the season, we brought in Craig Paterson.

But the mood in the camp was not good as our season threatened to implode before it had even got started. We eventually steadied the ship but the win over Raith at the tail end of September was our first league victory at Rugby Park for six months.

There were highlights, don't get me wrong. We travelled to Somerset Park in the November and won 3-0 with all the goals scored before half-time. It is always great to put one over our nearest rivals but we were immense that day. Tommy Burns and Ally Mitchell had put us two up inside 20 minutes and I got a third right on the stroke of half-time. We actually did the double at Somerset Park that season, with a 2-0 win over Ayr later in the campaign.

We travelled to Clydebank in the week before Christmas to win 3-0 on the day Ally Mitchell really announced to everyone just what a talented player he was. He was outstanding that day – I set him up for his goal – and Hugh Burns and big Calum Campbell also netted. But Ally, 'Super Ally', was everywhere. I don't know if I realised then that he would go on to be a legend for the club but I knew we had one hell of a talented player in our ranks. So, despite the poor start to the season, we were keeping ourselves in the promotion race and were within touching distance of the pacesetters, Dundee, Hamilton and Partick Thistle.

But it was against the Jags in April when our title ambitions were brought to a crashing halt – and it was all a piece of madness from one of the country's most experienced referees. We'd already suffered at the hands of a ref just a few weeks before up at Dens Park when Doug Yeats had sent off Tom Black for a foul on Ian McCall. Even the Dundee players couldn't believe that decision and we did well to battle to a 1-1 draw. This time, it was Brian McGinlay who killed us.

There were nearly 6,000 inside Rugby Park that day, with both sides pushing for promotion. We got off to a good start and Hugh Burns should have put us ahead when he lobbed over the Thistle keeper, Craig Nelson, but his effort hit the bar. Thistle went ahead when Bobby Geddes could only parry Geordie Shaw's effort, leaving Davie Irons with a tap-in. It got worse when we switched off at a corner and big Gordon Rae nodded Thistle's second. But we were still in it. Nelson was forced into a couple of decent saves and then, a minute into the second half, Jim Duffy sent Tommy Burns to the ground for a penalty. Tom Black was one of the most reliable penalty takers I had ever seen and he got us back in it. We were pressing and pressing. Gus MacPherson had an effort blocked, Nelson pulled off a great save to deny Tommy Burns. We were on top and an equaliser looked inevitable. Then Shaw, who was a pacy wee frontman, nipped beyond our defence. He was clearly offside, the linesman's flag shot up and our back four stopped. Even Geordie Shaw stopped for a second – before realising that the ref was ignoring the linesman and waving play on. He couldn't miss. Big Bobby in goal could do nothing and Shaw, unchallenged, fired in their third.

All hell broke loose! We went mental and you could feel the venom of the Killie fans towards McGinlay. We confronted him but he was not for listening to any of us. The experienced players in our ranks were leading the assault. Tommy Burns, such a quiet and composed man off the park, was seething and got booked. Ross Jack also saw yellow but the ref could have picked any one of six or seven to be booked. I couldn't believe what I had just witnessed. It might well be one of the worst decisions I had ever seen. McGinlay wasn't even going to consult his linesman until we 'persuaded' him. God knows what the pair of them said but McGinlay trotted back on to the pitch and signalled that the goal stood. It was awful. Our season, our hopes of promotion effectively died there. Okay, we still had to find an equaliser but I had no doubt we would have and may even have gone on to win the game. But not now. The frustration was boiling inside me and I was booked for a lunge at some Thistle player. I didn't care. It was over.

How do you lift a team after that? This is their livelihoods, their profession, and failure to gain promotion could have a massive impact on careers, both on and off the park. To have it taken from us, because that is what effectively happened that day, is criminal. That one decision by a referee cost us – and it cost Jim Fleeting his job.

Nobody saw it coming. There was an odd dynamic at Rugby Park, with Jim Fleeting as manager and his brother Bobby as chairman. It meant that if Jim was being put under pressure by the board, ultimately that news would be relayed to him by his brother. We didn't think he was at any risk of losing his job, so, when the announcement was made, we were as shocked as anybody. Jim was such a great guy and, as players, we felt we had let him down. Refereeing decisions had killed us but we were to blame for starting the season so badly, which had really killed us. That season would end with us missing the second promotion spot by three points. Three points! I could think of a dozen we threw away.

Whether Jim resigned or was sacked, I don't know. I suspect it was the former, because that was the kind of guy he was. He would have taken that difficult decision so that his brother didn't have to. All I do know is that we lost a good man and we had lost Jim McSherry and Frank Coulston, too. They were all good guys and I was very disappointed.

Then Tommy Burns was made player-manager, with Billy Stark as his assistant. I have to admit that my mood changed almost immediately. I was gutted that Jim had lost his job but I can't lie – I was thrilled Tommy was put in charge. The pair of them were still young and had such enthusiasm. They were ambitious, hugely respected by the players and loved by the fans. It was a great appointment. Tommy played with his heart on his sleeve and he gave everything. I knew he would be the same as a boss. He was just a guy you wanted to play for, wanted to do well for. Every player wanted to do their best for him and he made you feel like a million dollars. Initially, he was put in temporary charge but we finished the season with four wins and a draw, conceding only one goal. We also thumped Ayr 4-0 to win the Ayrshire Cup, so at least we had some silverware in the cabinet. Giving Tommy the job full-time was a no-brainer. Guys called Burns always do well in Ayrshire after all!

After a season that had started so badly and ended in heartache, there was no way we were going to miss out again. Tommy drilled into us in pre-season that promotion was all that mattered and that he strongly believed we had a squad more than capable of achieving it.

'We have got to look to win the league,' Tommy said. 'Just to say we'll settle for promotion would be wrong. We'll be aiming for good results all through the season and, if we can get that bit of luck you need, we can go all the way.

'I want people to sit up and take notice of how well Killie can play. I want teams to come to Rugby Park and be apprehensive about facing us – knowing that they're not going to get anything apart from a cup of tea and a biscuit.'

Tommy brought in George McCluskey – not just because he was a pal but because he had great ability. He was maybe coming to the end of his career but he still had great skills and loved a nutmeg. He was not one for closing down defenders but he contributed greatly to the Killie cause. I remember one game at Cowdenbeath when he was unfortunate to get injured and had to go off. There was no stretcher and they came on with a wheelchair! He's the first player I've ever seen being 'prammed' off the park. The rest of the players had a field day. George is a legend – great talent, zero work rate!

Under Tommy's charge, chances were few and far between and when they did come along, you had to take them. I was not a one-in-two striker, more like one-in-four, but it wasn't just about scoring – I had to defend from the front and put pressure on defenders so they couldn't put quality balls forward. But I had a problem – the pubic symphysis injury I had experienced when I joined Rangers was flaring up again. It would go on to impact my entire season and I would see a few specialists before the situation was remedied. It kept me out of the first two games of the season – wins over Morton and Dumbarton – but I came back in the third game against Raith, who would be our rivals for promotion.

I had to wait until September for my first goal – a headed effort against Clydebank at Kilbowie – but the league was already shaping up as a race between Raith, Dunfermline, St Mirren, Hamilton and ourselves for the top two places. We had a nightmare in a game against Accies in which we missed two penalties. I was the first sinner when my effort came back off the post, then George McCluskey had his saved late on by Accies keeper Allan Ferguson. We escaped with a point thanks to Mark Skilling's goal but it was a real warning to us that, in a title race that was always going to be tight, every point was crucial.

We got a tough draw in the Scottish Cup when we had to face Raith at Rugby Park but everything went for us that day. First of all, they had their keeper, Tom Carson, taken off after he pulled a calf muscle. This was in the days before you would have a sub keeper on the bench and defender Davie Sinclair had to go in goal. Then their centre-back, George McGeachie, got himself sent off after two yellow cards. It was open season for us after that – wave after wave of attacks. I got a hat-trick, George McCluskey got a goal and Gus MacPherson also netted in a 5-0 win.

Off the pitch, I was starting to think about my future. It was clear to me that football was all that I knew but my career could not go on forever, so I would have to start thinking about what else I could do when the boots were hung up. I considered all options, because the last thing I wanted was to go back on the tools. I thought about being a prison officer, joining the police or the fire service. But I knew that I wanted to stay in the game and decided to start taking my coaching badges.

For someone who had hardly been the best academically, I loved learning more about the game. The Largs coaching programme does have its critics but I thought it was brilliant. You were surrounded by football people – guys like Walter Smith and Archie Knox. You would work hard on the training ground and then in the pub at night, where you would talk even more football.

On the park, we stumbled around October and dropped careless points with draws against Raith, Clydebank and

Meadowbank, and then lost up at Dunfermline. The East End Park game was a real bad-tempered affair and I was to see red for a high challenge on their winger, Chris Sinclair. It was late on in the match and was an act of frustration. But I always felt there was a 'wee black book' attitude in Scottish football that I never experienced when I played in England. It's because teams in Scotland played each other so many times – a minimum of four in the league and more if you met in cup competitions. Any vendettas carry over, whereas in England you play each other only twice and by the time that second meeting comes around, all the bad blood is forgotten about. In Scotland, your team-mates certainly don't let you forget either. Before a game, there is always someone reminding you that this player or that player had 'done you' in the previous meeting. I used to have run-ins with Neale Cooper, who, by coincidence, was playing that day for Dunfermline, but the guy I always used to look forward to meeting was Jock McStay – a tough full-back at Raith Rovers. I would go out of my way to kick him and, with him being at full-back, it was always easy to get to him. We had many altercations but it wasn't until many years later, down at a coaching course at Largs, that I met Jock and discovered he was a really good lad! After a few beers, he asked me why I was always wanting to fight with him. I told him that when he was at Motherwell, playing in a reserve game against Rangers, he had badly injured a mate of mine called Billy Mckay in a tackle. Billy would eventually have to pack in football. I wasn't even at that game that day but I was told it was Jock who had done him and each time I tried to kick him it was retribution for my mate. Jock looked at me and informed me that he remembered the incident well but my information was wrong – it was the Motherwell keeper that day who was the guilty party! I felt terrible. All those times I had tried to kick him and Jock was totally innocent. I apologised profusely and we had some more beers.

After our tough run of dropped points, it was clear Tommy was getting frustrated. He would tell us that we were the team playing all the football and that we were controlling things in the middle of the park but we were getting punished for our carelessness and our missed chances. We were dominating games but not killing off teams. Up next were our greatest rivals, Ayr. My red card against the Pars meant I would be sitting this game out because of suspension. I was gutted. I always enjoyed playing against Ayr and scoring against them. In fact, over my career, I had a decent record against them as a player.

Tommy was looking to shake things up anyway. Ian Porteous and Mark Reilly were left out and Shaun McSkimming dropped down to the bench. Tommy's plan worked. At last, not only were we dominating a game, we were also getting the reward for our domination. George McCluskey got us off and running early doors, Mark Skilling added a second and then Ayr's John Traynor hammered into his own net.

It began a run of six wins on the bounce – and it was where our foundations for promotion were cemented. The problem was that I had dropped out of the team and when you are out and the team is winning, it's difficult to get back in. In addition to that, my pelvic problem was beginning to bother me again. I got back in the squad for the visit of Dunfermline but had to settle for a place on the bench. We got beat 3-2. Then I got my first start in eight games when we travelled to Cappielow to face Morton. We got beat 2-0. As we approached Christmas, there was not a lot of festive spirit about the place. Still, we were in second place in the league and still on track for promotion. And it was Ayr, once again, up next.

I'm delighted to say I had a hand in the winner that day in front of nearly 8,500 fans at Somerset Park. After the two previous disappointing results, a win was a must and when I raced past the Ayr defence, I looked up to pick out 'Sid' Porteous, who coolly back-heeled it into the net for the only goal of the game.

The promotion race was getting tighter and tighter. Raith at the top had put clear distance between themselves and the rest of the pack but Dunfermline, St Mirren, Hamilton and ourselves were split by only a couple of points. It was an exciting time to be a player, pushing for promotion, desperately wanting to find out how your rivals had done before you had even reached the dressing room. It is a cliché but there was a buzz about the place, a buzz about the town. Kilmarnock is a town that deserves a team in the top flight. The fans are terrific and we all so wanted to get back into the Premier League.

But my pelvic problem, which I had already been playing through, was not getting any better. Eventually, the issue would be solved but it was to curtail my involvement through to the end of the season. I still weighed in with goals here and there but just being fit to play was getting tougher and tougher. My last goal of the season came in a 2-2 draw at Cappielow in March.

With the end of the campaign fast approaching, the matches came thick and fast. We kept our heads above water in the promotion race. Raith were way out in front but we grimly held on to second spot. But it was tough not to be involved as the final few games approached. Obviously, you want the team to do well and to keep winning but you feel removed from the action, standing on the sidelines at the party. I did my best not to let my mood affect the boys and was always working to get fit to play a part in the final few games. But it didn't happen for me. Our second last game of the season saw us cruise to a 3-0 win up at struggling Cowdenbeath – meaning that a point in our final game against Hamilton would be enough.

Nearly 13,000 crammed into Rugby Park that day. The town was electric. You could feel it in the build-up all week. Sadly, I was to be watching from the stand. As a player, it is the worst place to be. There were obvious nerves from the start but soon it filtered through that our nearest rivals, Dunfermline, were trailing against Morton and that seemed to ease the pressure. Suddenly, the boys began to relax into it. Tommy Burns didn't play that day either but he was roaring them on from the touchline, trying to keep the younger heads calm and imploring the older players to take control. When the final whistle went, it was our only 0-0 draw of the entire campaign and never has a goalless encounter been celebrated so loudly. Thousands of the Killie faithful spilled on to the park. Ten years of hurt and pain had been erased. The club had been as close to the bottom as you can get and here we were, climbing back to the summit of the Scottish game. I'm sure there were tears as well as cheers. But as I write, I struggle to recall the celebrations that followed or any parties that took place. It was great that we were going up but I hadn't felt part of it as the season came to an end. I was determined to make up for that as I returned to the top flight. For both Killie and myself, it was a return to the Premier League for the first time in ten years.

CHAPTER 10

TOP-FLIGHT RETURN

THE SEASON finished with everybody at Kilmarnock in a celebratory mood but I had my contract to sort out. It was coming to an end and chairman Bobby Fleeting had given assurances that the old guard would be kept on. I went in to see Tommy Burns, who told me that, while there would be an offer of a new deal, they couldn't increase my wages and nor would there be any kind of signing-on fee. I wasn't happy with what was on the table, so I told the club I wouldn't be signing. This was long before the Bosman rule came in to change things for out-of-contract players and I didn't have an agent to sort things for me. I was in limbo, waiting to see if any club would come in for me.

I used the summer to complete the intro for my A Licence down at Largs. Every time I was there, I would take the opportunity to talk to the educators on the course. These were great football people who knew the game inside out – off and on the field. Each and every one of them would listen to you and give advice. Largs gets a bad press but these guys are just there to help and guide you. Some players don't welcome the advice but you take out of it what you think is best for you. One night, I found myself chatting to Alex Miller in the pub. Miller had been a legendary full-back for Rangers and, at that time, was the manager at Hibs. I was having a beer and Alex was supping his favourite soft drink, an Appletiser. I told him about the situation I was in at Killie, out of contract and not happy about the new offer. I explained that I had been thinking about trying a move abroad. Alex listened to what I was saying and then warned me that any move to the continent would mean I would be forgotten about back home and when I wanted to get back in, it would prove difficult. I took on board what he told me but when I returned to Killie to start the new campaign, I still hadn't signed anything.

We started the season well. Our opening game was against Dundee at Rugby Park and Tom Brown got us the only goal of the game. With the contract issue still not sorted, I missed out again but was back in for the trip north to face Aberdeen at Pittodrie. We played really well that day but Paul Kane scored for the Dons and that was it. Again, we fell victim to a refereeing mistake when Gary Smith, the Aberdeen defender, clearly handled in the box but play was waved on. We lost again the following week to a single goal against Motherwell. It was hardly the best preparation for the visit to Ibrox, which was next on our agenda, but despite the back-to-back losses, we had been playing well.

We would be facing a Rangers team packed with talent. Gary Stevens and Richard Gough were at the back, Trevor Steven and Ian Ferguson were in midfield and up top they had Mark Hateley and Duncan Ferguson. In the summer, we had brought in Andy Millen from Hamilton to anchor our defence and we led the line with myself and George McCluskey, the pair of us having a combined age touching the 70s. But

Tommy was going to give youth a chance that season and we had a young Mark Roberts in for his first start at just 17. The sun was shining that day and Ibrox was full, with more than 40,000 there. As expected, we were on the back foot in the early stages and Bobby Geddes in goal had to bail us out a couple of times. But, as is often the case, as we settled in, we were more than holding our own. At the interval, it was goalless and Tommy, who had preached a positive, attacking policy from the start, wanted more of the same. In the 62nd minute, Shaun McSkimming went on a marauding run down the left but he seemed well marshalled by Gary Stevens, an experienced England international. But Shaun did brilliantly, managing to get in a cross and there was young Roberts to put a diving header past Ally Maxwell. To score his first Premier League goal for the club at Ibrox, in front of the massed Killie travelling support, was the stuff dreams are made of.

We held on until the 78th minute when Ian Durrant floated in a cross and Steven Pressley beat Bobby Geddes to the ball to head in an equaliser. Big Bobby bailed us out once again with a brilliant save from a Davie Robertson header and it looked like we would share the spoils. That was until four minutes into injury time when Tom Brown robbed Pressley as he was shepherding the ball out at the by-line. He cut it back to Ian Porteous, whose shot was parried by Ally Maxwell straight into my path, no more than three yards out. Gerry McNee in the commentary of the game would say I'd never get an easier goal in my life and he was right. It was a tap-in, and as I raced to the Killie fans behind the goal, they dragged me in for a celebratory embrace. The boys were going mental. I could feel them jumping on my back and the place erupted around me. What a moment it was.

The dressing room was ecstatic and Tommy was beside himself. We were all buzzing and I thought to myself that I would never be in a stronger position to negotiate an increase on my deal. I left it a couple of days and then went in to see Tommy again. I'd just scored the winner in the 94th minute at Ibrox – surely I held all aces? But Tommy was not for shifting – it was the same deal on offer. Bugger it, I thought, I love the club, I love the fans and I loved scoring that goal. So, I signed. It was one of the best decisions I ever made in my career.

The result at Ibrox seemed to inspire us and we went on a nine-game unbeaten run which included a win at Tynecastle, a win over Partick Thistle and a goalless draw away to Celtic. The biggest cheer that day was for the returning Tommy Burns, although I had a great header late on that I put just past the post. In October, we travelled up to Stark's Park to face my old mate Jimmy Nicholl's Raith Rovers, who had won the First Division the previous season. As often happens with a team, for some inexplicable reason we weren't firing in the first half. In fact, we were 2-0 down when we returned to the dressing room. Tommy went ballistic. He slaughtered us in the dressing room and he saved the worst of it for me. I still remember his team talk. He pointed at me while looking round the dressing room, shouting: 'Don't pass to his feet, he can't play!' I was stunned and I could feel the anger coursing through me. I got up and threw my strip on the floor.

'If I can't play, then get someone who can,' I shouted and stormed into the shower room.

Billy Stark, the good cop in the partnership, came in after me.

He had my strip in his hand and said: 'Come on, get your gear back on. He's lost it for a bit and doesn't mean what he said.'

'Stuff him!' I responded and I was not for backing down. But Starky is a born diplomat and he talked me round. I pulled my strip back on and went back out.

Jimmy Nic had his team well organised and they played with a sweeper that day. I was up front on my own and I just couldn't get on the ball. Anything over the top was swept up by Ronnie Coyle, who had a few yards on me, and Shaun Dennis and David Sinclair. I just couldn't get on the ball. My first touch was never the best and Tommy was right, I lost a lot of possession. I couldn't get anything over the top, which I preferred, but I was never one to hide and I knew Tommy appreciated that, so I went looking for the ball and looking to get involved. My efforts paid off. Tom Black put in a great cross and I headed past Scott Thomson for our first and then Ally Mitchell got the equaliser. After being two down at half-time, a share of the points was a good reward for our fightback. But I couldn't get Tommy's outburst out of my head. It gnawed away at me all weekend and first thing on Monday I went in to see him.

I asked Tommy why he had said what he said but he told me that I just took it the wrong way. That was nonsense. What other way was I supposed to take it? We both had our say over what had happened and I learned a lesson that day. Firstly, I couldn't hold a grudge with Tommy. I respected him too much for that. And secondly, a clear-the-air meeting is always a good way of letting off steam. It was something I would take with me into my own managerial career. In the end, we shook hands and put it behind us, which was the perfect outcome and the best way to handle it.

The result in Kirkcaldy also kept our unbeaten run going – and we kept it up with our next game when Aberdeen came down to Ayrshire and we battled to a 1-1 draw. Twelve games into the season and we were level with Rangers, above Celtic and only two behind league leaders Hibs.

Celtic were really struggling at the time – in fact, they were a shadow of the club everyone knows now. On the pitch, under their new manager, Lou Macari, they were a shambles, and off the park, they were a financial basket case hurtling towards bankruptcy until Fergus McCann rode to their rescue. It may have pained Tommy Burns to see his beloved club in such a state but when they came down to Rugby Park in the November, there was only one thing on his mind. He and Billy Stark had us so well drilled in the build-up to that game. It was a lesson in how to coach a team for a specific game and every tiny detail was taken care of. In the days leading up to the game, Starky took me to one side and told me that he had heard Mike Galloway – normally a midfielder or sometimes a centre-back who hadn't played at all in the last six games – was to be playing at right-back. He told me that if the ball was played over Galloway and he was facing his own goal while he was running, he would have a glance over his shoulder. Starky said that was when I should stop my run and when he turned to face the ball again, I should start my run once more.

'Mike has got a habit ... when he reaches the ball, he flicks it back blindly with the outside of his foot,' Starky said. 'If you time it right, you could snatch it.'

Midway through the first half, Packie Bonner in the Celtic goal booted a kick upfield and it was won in the air by Tom Brown, who headed it back into Celtic's right-back position, where Galloway was under no pressure at all. But Starky's wise words were in my head. I checked my run and, just as I had been told, Galloway looked up, glanced at Bonner and prepared to make his pass back. It was as if the move had been scripted. Galloway was short with his pass and I pounced. One-on-one with the Celtic keeper, I clipped it past Bonner as he went to ground and I was in. Even a despairing dive from Dariusz Wdowczyk couldn't stop me as I rolled it into the empty net. Starky had taught me a lesson that week about how important it was to analyse opposition players, get to know their weaknesses and their bad habits. Any little thing you can capitalise on can prove crucial when it comes to game day. The match finished 2-2 but in the dying moments, I pounced on Galloway again after he made a shocking heavy touch. Racing in on goal, I saw Ian Porteous on the edge of the box and cut it back to him but Sid fired well wide.

We went another six games without defeat after that Celtic game but, because there were only two points for a win at that time, the league table was very tight. Aberdeen were flying high and we travelled north to face them just before Christmas.

To be honest, we were well beaten that day. Joe Miller, Duncan Shearer and Lee Richardson had the Dons three up and my pass for Mark Skilling to tap in late on was no more than a consolation. But I'm afraid that was not the talking point of the game. Just the week before, in Dundee United's 3-0 win over Rangers at Ibrox, the Arabs defender Gordan Petric was twice highlighted for use of the elbow – first against

Mark Hateley and then, more clearly, in a challenge with Ian Ferguson. The Rangers midfielder was red-carded for reacting by spitting at Petric and while that made big headlines, it was the use of the elbow that became a matter of debate. Against Aberdeen, I was playing up front with Tom Brown and one of their centre-backs, big Brian Irvine, caught Tam and later Shaun McSkimming with a flying elbow. Both needed treatment and, soon after, I ran across Irvine, saw his elbow coming out and ducked under it. Now, when players jump up and challenge one another in the air, elbows will fly; it's common nature but this was different and I decided that if I got an opportunity on Irvine, I was going to take it. That opportunity wasn't coming, so I manufactured one. Late on, an aimless high ball was played out of our defence and, although my position or my timing weren't good, I reckoned it was the last chance I would have. So, I ran at the big Dons defender and, as he headed clear, I caught him with my elbow. Big Irvine went down in a heap and lay there motionless. I immediately regretted what I had done. I could have really hurt him and I had a terrible weekend, unable to get it out of my thoughts. Thankfully, Big Brian was okay but what if he hadn't been? What if I had done serious damage? Referee Andrew Waddell took little time to reach for his red card and I could have no argument.

In those days, *Scotsport* on a Sunday would have a viewers' phone-in and the next day I cringed as it was dominated by my challenge. Well-known journalist Gerry McNee and Scotland legend Gordon McQueen were studio guests.

McNee said: 'This was a shocking situation yesterday and it was a lot worse than the Petric incident at Ibrox last week. He [me] just flies in here and that is unacceptable.'

McQueen then added: 'When you have a centre-half and a centre-forward going for the ball, it's inevitable that arms and elbows are going to be lifted and you're going to get accidental clashes. But when you do something that Bobby Williamson did there, a deliberate blow to the face, it is a very, very dangerous thing to do and can leave a player with a serious injury.'

I thought twice about using my elbows in the future but when the adrenaline is running through your veins, all logic goes out of the window. I didn't have a reputation as a dirty player and I wasn't about to start now. I was physical, I admit, and defenders always knew that they had been in a game but I always felt I was fair and the incident with Irvine really shook me.

The season continued with the usual run of results – but two more games really stand out for me. For once, we were putting together a run in the Scottish Cup and had beaten old rivals Ayr, Morton and Dundee to set up a semi-final clash with Rangers at Hampden. As always, we were very much the underdogs and Rangers were building a side that cost millions. There was Mark Hateley, Alexei Mikhailitchenko, Richard Gough, Stuart McCall – Christ, they brought Duncan Ferguson and Ally McCoist off the bench in the second half! Still, we more than held our own in the sunshine that day and fully deserved our 0-0 draw and a shot at a replay, which was to be played just a few days later. I still remember the match report from Alex Cameron in the paper the next day: 'Every ounce of what could pass for glory at Hampden yesterday went to gallant Kilmarnock.'

Apart from our brave showing, the main talking point of the first leg was the performance of match referee Les

Mottram, who looked like he was going to run out of yellow cards. It should have been a warning ahead of the second match, with the same whistler in charge.

Tommy rewarded the team that had done so well in the original game by keeping the same starting line-up but Rangers changed things and brought in McCoist and Ian Durrant to start. We began the game really well and looked up for the challenge. We deservedly took the lead when a short corner was knocked on to the back post and Tom Black sneaked in behind a sleeping Gordon Durie to slot past Ally Maxwell. What a moment it was. Here we were, on the threshold of making a Scottish Cup Final if we could just hang on, which we did comfortably until half-time. Tommy was incredibly calm in the dressing room, telling us only to keep doing what we had been doing but to be ready for a Rangers onslaught. We came back out in determined mood and, in the opening seconds, Ally Mitchell came close to lobbing Ally Maxwell in the Rangers goal. Then up stepped Mr Mottram to have a say in proceedings. The second half was barely two minutes old when Durrant put in a cross to the back post, the ball arced over Andy Millen's head and Hateley pounced with a diving header. The ball bounced up and Ray Montgomerie knocked it on to the bar, before it landed on the stomach of the prostrate Bobby Geddes, who was able to gather up McCoist's weak follow-up. I defy anyone to tell me the ball crossed the line but Mottram was in no doubt and gave the goal. I don't think any of us could believe it and big Andy Millen was irate, talking himself into a booking.

Shortly after that, Ian Ferguson, the Rangers midfielder, went down with an injury. I didn't think there was much in it, so agreed with Mottram when he waved play on, refusing to let the Rangers physio on to the pitch and telling Ferguson to get up. The ball had gone out for a Rangers throw and big Goughie had it in his hands but was refusing to take it, as he wanted the physio to be allowed on. Goughie could intimidate refs and was accused a few times of calling the shots. When Mottram told him to get on with it, Goughie threw the ball into the Rangers fans behind him. I couldn't believe it when Mottram turned round and waved the physio on! I was furious.

'Who's refereeing this game?' I shouted, pointing to Goughie and asking: 'Him or you?'

Mottram told me to shut up or I was going in the book.

Rangers and Celtic believe that most decisions go against them. I've been on both sides and when refereeing any half of the Old Firm, it is difficult, because the ref is under immense pressure to make sure anything he gives against them is spot on, as the scrutiny from the press can finish a referee if he makes a mistake. Against the so-called lesser teams, the press barely mention it!

But Mottram had history, I'm afraid. This was the guy who failed to see Dundee United's 'goal' at Firhill against Thistle when they clearly scored but he waved play on – even missing the handball when Jags defender Martin Clark picked it up! It wasn't long after that that Mottram relocated to finish his career in Japan.

Our cup dream ended when Hateley got his second to kill the game. Defeat is never easy but that was a sore one.

Still, we lifted ourselves just three days later when we hosted Celtic and beat them 2-0. Our target for the season of avoiding relegation was looking more than achievable and we took a big step to safety with a 3-1 win away at Dundee United. I was the lone striker that night and worked my proverbials off and was rewarded with two goals. The win was vital. With just a few games of the season to go, Dundee and Raith were cut adrift but there was a third relegation spot and we were very much in danger of falling into it alongside Thistle and St Johnstone. We lost 1-0 at Motherwell but when Rangers came to Rugby Park on the penultimate day of the season, Tommy Burns had us ready to run through walls. Knowing how important his experience would be in such an important game, he unusually named himself in the starting line-up alongside his No.2, Billy Stark. It was a tight affair. Rangers looked certain for the title but they seemed as nervous as we were. Then disaster for me. I could feel my old pelvic injury flaring up again and, no matter how hard I tried to ignore it, I knew I was done. Tom Brown replaced me at half-time and I knew my season was over.

I was gutted that I wouldn't be able to help the team but my sorrow lifted when Tom Black rattled in a piledriver of a strike past Colin Scott for the only goal of the game. The win, and the two points in those days, was vital. It meant survival was in our own hands, yet it couldn't have been closer. I was injured but still travelled with the team for the last-day encounter at Easter Road to give them some moral support. The 0-0 draw meant we survived on goal difference above Thistle, with St Johnstone taking the final relegation spot. My seven goals that season helped us stay up.

The euphoria surrounding our success at retaining our top-flight status was short-lived, however. Nothing in football stays the same for very long.

We were all well aware that Celtic were a struggling team under Lou Macari and when they parted ways, no one was surprised that Fergus McCann came knocking on Tommy Burns's door. The problem was they didn't inform Killie of their approach and would ultimately be fined £100,000 for 'tapping up'. The SFA decision also ruled that Killie would retain Tommy's playing contract, which effectively ended his playing career. But there was no way Tommy – nor Billy Stark, who would go as his No.2 – would possibly say 'no'.

During the course of the close season, we were all wondering who the club were bringing in to replace Tommy. I got a phone call from the chairman, Bobby Fleeting, asking me if I could take the team for pre-season until they found a manager. I told him it would be an honour and a privilege. I found out later that Bobby had spoken to his brother, Jim, our former manager, to ask his advice. He had told him that there was no need to bring anyone in, as I was a qualified coach and more than capable of taking the team.

Bobby then shocked me by saying I shouldn't apply for the job, as he didn't feel I was ready. Billy Stark called all the players to thank them for their services. During his call to me, he insisted I was perfect for the job and should throw my name into the hat. But Bobby was right, I knew that I wasn't ready. I had my badges and was doing some coaching with the kids up in Castlemilk, along with George McCluskey, but that was miles away from being ready to be a manager in my own right.

The club had fixed up a pre-season tour in the Republic of Ireland to get our match fitness up to speed. We weren't there long when our new manager joined us – none other than Alex Totten, who I knew well from my Rangers days. I met Alex in his room at the hotel. I'm not sure if Alex had interrupted his holiday to join us, as he was well tanned. Alex loved the sun and the sun seemed to love him! He asked me to organise a room for him to introduce himself to the players, which I duly did.

I didn't realise at the time that Andy Millen, our centre-back, did not like Alex one little bit. They had a massive falling-out when they were both at St Johnstone. Alex was the manager at the time, so there was only going to be one winner and that would be the case again. There had been too much water under the bridge for a reconciliation. Andy had suffered a lot at St Johnstone and wasn't prepared to let it go. I think Alex tried, as Andy was a great player for us and a top professional. Losing him would be hard for us. But there was no way back and he found himself training with the reserves and the kids, which is not a great place to be. Andy became an angry man and he was taking his frustrations out on the young lads and was kicking lumps out of them. It got so bad I had to have a word with him. I told him that, if he wasn't careful, he was going to really hurt someone and it wasn't their fault he was in this position. Andy is a great pro and he took on board what I said. Instead of kicking them, he began passing on his advice and knowledge from years in the game, which was brilliant for all the young guys. I knew then that Andy would go on to be a great coach and so it proved. He would soon leave us in a swap deal with Hibs for Billy Findlay.

When we got back to Scotland, Alex brought in Kenny Thompson as his assistant and let me take the reserves while I still competed for a first-team place. Kenny was very quiet and a really likeable chap – I don't recall any player falling out with him. Alex never really delegated much and took most of the training. I would train with the first team each day but juggle with my coaching commitments, including taking the youngsters in Castlemilk on a Wednesday night. I never looked forward to it, as it clashed with Champions League games on the telly, but once I was there, I enjoyed it. I got so much out of coaching the kids and I think I loved it because they did.

But you had to be on your toes on the Astro at Castlemilk. The local kids were always around trying to steal balls and if a ball went over the fence, you had to move fast to get it before someone legged it. I had put the balls in the back of the goal so we could start the session and, as I was briefing the players, I kept one eye on the kids loitering behind the goal. I assumed the balls would be safe but I could see them dwindling in number before I realised that the net had a hole in it! I took off and chased them through the fence, the kids throwing balls over their shoulders as they ran down the hill into the housing scheme. I didn't fancy chasing them in there, so headed back up the hill, finding balls as I went. At the end of the session, I counted the balls and discovered we had one more than we started with. When I checked, one had Q.P. written on it – Queen's Park also trained there.

I was even responsible for taking some of the kids to training and dropping them off afterwards. One night on the way back from training, there was a strong smell coming from the back of the car. When I asked them if they were okay, one of the kids said his tummy was hurting. I told him to hang on and I would get him to the toilet. As it happened, he couldn't hang on! My sister-in-law lived close by, so I decided to take him there. We ran in and I showed him to the toilet and explained the predicament to her, and then fetched a pair of shorts for him to wear the rest of the way to his home. Back in the car, I asked him what he had eaten before training and he told me mince and tatties! I explained that, in future, he should eat something light like egg on toast. I still remember his name but I'll keep it to myself to avoid causing him any embarrassment!

But I learned so much working with the kids – much of which I took on when I became a manager in my own right. One of the hardest parts of the management job is releasing players, especially the young ones who have just missed out on getting a contract. Most of the players coming out of YTS were young players I worked with in Castlemilk, so to tell them they weren't getting contracts was emotional, not just for the player I had such hope for and their families but for me as well. Sometimes, it's better for a player to move on to get first-team action. I made sure it was always done with great consideration by me and the staff. I used to look at the position they played in, how many players were ahead of them and make a decision from there. I used to speak to them individually around Christmas and tell them what they had to do and that if they could improve, there could be a contract. But I wanted them to be prepared for the worst so that it wasn't sprung on them – but it was difficult. I would tell them they had to give their all, day in, day out. If they did that and they were still released, I would always be able to recommend them to another club. If they didn't put in the effort, then it would be difficult for me to give my recommendation.

Juggling with my coaching responsibilities meant I was always struggling to make an impact in the first team. I did start the season in the team but Alex was looking for new blood. Colin McKee and Neil Whitworth were brought up from Manchester United and we had kids like Jim Lauchlan breaking through. I do remember coming on in a game against Falkirk when we were 3-0 up at half-time and eventually drew 3-3. I came on in the 85th minute, was yellow-carded almost immediately for a challenge on Bairns keeper Willie Lamont and then red-carded two minutes later for another challenge on the same player!

I scored against Celtic at Hampden – their temporary home while Parkhead was being transformed. The ball was played over the top and defender Mark McNally and keeper Gordon Marshall left it for each other. As they dithered, I nipped in to toe-poke it home.

But goals were few and far between, even though I was still in the squad. In the end, we finished in mid-table in an unremarkable season. At the end of the campaign, we went to a tournament in Seoul, South Korea. It was an eight-team tournament and quite a prestigious thing to be invited to. We were in a group that included the host nation and Costa Rica. South Korea hammered us 5-1 and it was then that I realised it wouldn't be long before they would become a force in world football.

In our first game against Costa Rica we didn't have any recognised full-backs, with both of them back in Scotland recovering from injuries. Big Neil Whitworth, who had just finished his first season at Killie and won many player of the year awards, picked up a bad injury. He had his nose broken in a challenge. I would go as far as to say that injury, psychologically, set the big man back. He had been a big aggressive centre-back and I don't think he was the same player again.

To make matters worse, not long after I took over as manager, big Neil was diagnosed with a bad case of tuberculosis. It took a long time for the doctors to figure out what it was, as it was the last thing they would expect to see in a fit young footballer. Everyone who had been in contact with him had to go to Crosshouse Hospital on a regular basis for checks. Had those two knock-backs not occurred, I'm sure Neil would have gone on to bigger and better things.

The gaffer had given us the night off after the last game and the guys hit the town. Technically, I was still a player, so I joined them. I felt that some of the newer guys didn't trust me, seeing me as part of Alex's backroom staff. But they had nothing to worry about. I went into the bar with four or five other players and we were immediately surrounded by gorgeous women. I was happily married and not interested but, looking around, I noticed one of the players engaged in conversation with one of these women. When I looked at her closely after a couple of hours, her face looked slightly darker – and when I looked even closer, I noticed she had an Adam's Apple! When I told my team-mate, he was extremely disappointed he had invested a lot of time and money buying booze, although he did admit he was finding it odd that he was being outdrunk by a young woman!

Before the start of the next season, Alex had invited me and Kenny Thompson over to his house to talk about pre-season. I felt pleased that he was treating me as part of his inner circle but when Alex handed me the squad sheet and I looked at the striking department, I noticed my name wasn't there. I scanned it again just to make sure but this was Alex's way of letting me know my playing days were over. He said he wanted me to concentrate on developing the players within the squad and told me I could still play in the reserves. When I asked him if I would be considered for the first team, Alex replied that I wouldn't. I thought about it. How could I deny a young player the chance of progressing his career when my playing days were over? I told Alex that if that was the case, I wouldn't play.

When I assessed it, I hadn't achieved much as a player. I had won the Tennent's Sixes with Rangers, helped Rotherham and Kilmarnock to promotion but that was it, end of story. I had always wanted to go into coaching and was being given a chance to do just that with a great club. It was far too good an opportunity to knock back. Nothing lasts forever and my playing career had to come to an end at some stage.

I told Alex I'd accept the challenge he had given me of developing players. The boots were being hung up.

That's it, then, I thought.

CHAPTER 11
TEARS

I DIDN'T realise Alex Totten was under pressure and it was a complete shock to me when he was sacked. I really enjoyed working with him. He was instrumental in my move to Rangers and he helped me tremendously starting out in my coaching career, even though I felt I had a season left in me.

His greatest talent was identifying a player and fitting him into the team. This didn't come cheap, though, and he brought in Paul Wright, John Henry, Colin McKee and Neil Whitworth for a good bit of money. He had also brought in a talented goalkeeper in Drago Leković. I brought Dylan Kerr up from England and Alex signed him. Gary Holt came in pre-season but was too late to go to the training camp, so Alex left him behind with me and asked me to assess him. When Alex came back, I told him he had to sign Gary and he followed up on my recommendation.

I was coaching around seven or eight kids and maybe a couple of pros who were on their way back from injury. It wasn't easy. You could hardly do any game awareness or organise a back four with so few players and I had to think of new training sessions every week to keep them interested and focused. But I enjoyed the new role and the added responsibility, although it wasn't all straightforward.

I remember one episode down at Troon, when we had a reserve game. Gus Hollis was our head groundsman and doubled up as the kitman. As he was packing up, he said to one of the young players that he would have to come back to Rugby Park with him to help unload the gear – but Gus wasn't asking, he was telling! I learned a lesson that day. Players are still full of adrenaline after a game and wee Rab Vincent told Gus there was no way he was going back to the stadium. It made sense. Rab lived near Troon and it was crazy to demand that he go all the way back to Kilmarnock. Gus wasn't happy but when he looked to me to back him up, I took Rab's side. Anyway, if Gus had asked him properly, he may have had a different answer.

'He already told you he's not going, Gus,' I said. 'I'm not getting into an argument with you. Ask one of the lads from Kilmarnock.'

Gus wasn't happy and went in to see the boss the next morning. When Alex asked me for the story, I told him as it was, end of. I had a good relationship with Gus when I first arrived at the club but it deteriorated over time. He was a big mate with Tommy Burns and I think Gus thought he would take him to Celtic with him. When that never materialised, his attitude changed, even though he had been a great guy until Tommy left. He was a really dominant character and everybody who entered Rugby Park was aware of him. When I became head coach, it became more difficult with Gus. We had a separate dressing room and some mornings when I came in, there would be a boot missing. When I asked Gus, he had never seen it. There were a couple of occasions when players' boots would be missing. We played St Johnstone in Perth and Paul Wright had to borrow a pair. We played Rangers at Ibrox and Christophe Cocard wore his trainers. Ironically, he had a great game and scored the opener for us in a 3-0 win.

After the game against St Johnstone, I went into the dressing room and found Gus whistling away. He asked me the final score and when I told him we had equalised in the last minute, his whistling stopped.

Eventually, Gus had to leave. It's hard to explain. I really liked Gus but the relationship soured. Still, I hope he's in good health.

Despite these minor headaches, I was enjoying what I was doing and didn't see Alex's sacking coming at all. It was December and the first team had just been beaten by Raith Rovers, which left them separated at the bottom of the table from the Kirkcaldy club only by goal difference. It was their eighth league defeat of the season, so I suppose the warning signs were there. Second bottom was not what the club powerbrokers would be looking for and Alex and Kenny were called upstairs by the new chairman, Ronnie Hamilton. I didn't know Ronnie well but was aware of his association with the club. He had played for Killie in their greatest era in the 60s, finishing top scorer in the year they won the league championship in 1965. Ronnie had only taken over from outgoing chairman Jamie Moffat that morning. By the afternoon, he had called Alex and Kenny to a meeting.

When they came back down, they told me that they had been sacked. The club put out a statement which read: 'The directors felt that a younger man should be put at the helm and, coupled with the three younger directors taken on board this year, now was a time to make this change, given the club's present position.

'We felt we should have made progress from last year. I take on board the fact that last season was our highest-ever position in the premier division but we were looking to improve on that. Apart from Rangers and Celtic, we feel we have the best set-up and our position does not mirror that. That was the deciding factor to make the change.'

Alex told me that Ronnie now wanted to speak to me. I went up fearing the worst. I sat down and Ronnie explained what had happened, why the decision had been made and that he wanted me to take the team until they found a replacement. I was surprised, as usually when a club sack a manager, they have a replacement lined up.

I had no option but to accept, although I made it clear that I would need help. We had just gone from three coaches to one – me – and I was going to need some support.

When I went back down the stairs, I could see Alex packing up his stuff. It was awful. I don't mind admitting I had a tear in my eye. Then I had to tell him that I was being kept on to hold the fort. Watching those guys walk out that front door of Rugby Park was emotional.

I gave an interview to the press that day and said: 'The players are very upset and so am I. We've all worked hard for Alex for the last two and a half years and none of us saw this coming. We are all stunned.'

And we were, although I didn't find the move from reserve-team coach to manager a problem at all. I had been down to do all the coaching courses and I sailed through them and I felt very comfortable talking to groups of players. Anyway, I had always piped up in the dressing room when I was a player.

A week later, Alex walked into another job, this time at Falkirk. He phoned me and offered me the job as his assistant. I knew that there was already a safe pair of hands at the Bairns in the shape of Walter Kidd, who I had got to know well on the SFA coaching courses. So, I declined Alex's offer. Besides, I had already started building my own backroom team, with Jim Clark and my old mate, Gerry McCabe.

I called Cabey first. We had kept in touch over the years and we had agreed that if one of us got a job, we would team up. So I was true to my word, though I'm sure Cabey had that agreement with quite a few players going back to our Clydebank days. When I called him, I was shocked when he initially turned down my offer. When I asked why, he said he had just signed for Shettleston Juniors! He was 40 and still wanted to play. That's why he's had two hips replaced! He also told me Shettleston had given him a signing-on fee.

'Well, give it back to them,' I said. 'And come and help me out.'

'I cannae,' Cabey replied. 'I've already spent it putting in new radiators at the house.'

But I got my way and Cabey did come and join me, with the club coming to an agreement with Shettleston.

The other No.2 I had in mind was big Jim Stewart – known to his pals as Shadow. He was training the keepers at the time and when we sat down, he told me he wasn't an assistant, he was happy as a goalkeeper coach, but he could recommend someone who was very trustworthy and more than capable. When I asked who, he said it was Jim Clark. I didn't know Clarky well but I had seen him around the stadium, as he was a community officer, and his wife, Anne, had been at the club before me. When I spoke to Clarky, he also declined the offer but with good reason. A community officer's job is steady and he could retire doing that, while an assistant's job is precarious. If results don't go your way, you're out of the door. Plus, I was only there as a caretaker and he couldn't take the chance. I totally understood, so it was me and Cabey on our own.

Days later, the pair of us were sitting in my office when the door burst open and there stood Clarky, soaking wet with a bag of footballs over his shoulder. He threw them down to the floor, looked at the pair of us and asked if the offer was still on the table. It was. Two had become three.

My first game in charge was against Dundee United at home. It was a typical west of Scotland December day, dull and dreich, which matched the feeling of the fans in the stadium. We lost 2-0 to a Kjell Olofsson double but, in truth, it could have been more and the result left us marooned at the bottom of the table.

Afterwards, the mood in the dressing room was sombre, to say the least. I told the players to go home, think about the predicament we were all in and that we would talk about it more on Monday. Right after a game, when you have lost, is an important moment and you've got to get it right as a manager or you could lose the dressing room. Over the weekend, paranoia started creeping in. You can't sleep and you overthink things. But when Monday came, those nerves had gone. I felt brand new and was confident I could handle the situation.

The players filed in and I sat them down and asked them a few questions. I told them Saturday's performance against United wasn't good enough.

'We need to work harder and show more desire,' I said as they listened to me intently. 'This is your career we are talking about. Do you want to drop down to the First Division, maybe get released at the end of the season? And even if you're not released, your money is going to drop significantly. It's not about me, it's about you guys. I'm sure I'm out of the door anyway when the new guy comes in.'

I also told them that I was going to shake up training, with the defenders in the morning and strikers in the afternoon, reverse it the next day and then bring them all together later in the week. Even I could see our squad was too big and, with such bloated numbers, there was never time to work on game awareness or shape. We worked hard on the defensive side of the game; all our defenders alternated, so they all knew how to defend anywhere in the back four. I even had Gary Holt, a midfielder, play at the back in case of injuries or red cards. When we were going up against one of the Old Firm, I would have us training with ten men just in case someone got sent off.

After the United game, I sensed a bit of hope in the squad – that all was not lost. I knew we had young players desperate to get an opportunity. Alex had watched a lot of reserve games and I had told him there was a few of the young players who were ready to step up. Alex never got the opportunity to use them but I did and I wasn't going to pass it up. I felt that if I was replaced by a new boss, at least I would have given young, hungry players their chance. The two I was most excited about were Alex Burke and David Bagan. I've never been afraid of throwing young guys in and I certainly wasn't going to falter this time. I also felt that when the new manager came in, I would have at least left him with more options. I had no doubt they would make an impact. I had worked with them for a few years and knew they were ready. Burke was predominately left-sided and had good pace and could beat a man. Bagan had two good feet, was perhaps not as fast as his pal but was clever and could pass and create. These two were the catalyst for an entire change of attitude in the team. They lifted the whole place with their enthusiasm and ability, which rubbed off on the senior players, who got a fresh lease of life. We had a good shape about us. Ray Montgomerie and Kevin McGowne were good, honest defenders and, with the work we had put in, became hard to beat. At full-back, we had Gus MacPherson and Dylan Kerr. Gus joined Killie just after me and was an ever-present. He was so steady, read the game well and was a good organiser, who also went into coaching and management. Dylan has still got a great enthusiasm for the game. He had a decent left foot and he could talk and organise. He was, importantly, a player's player and very popular in the dressing room.

In midfield, Gary Holt and Mark Reilly covered each and every blade of grass. They never shirked a tackle. Their work rate was phenomenal. Burke came in on the left, Bagan on the right and we had Jim McIntyre as our main striker, with Paul Wright playing off him. Wright caused teams all sorts of problems when he dropped off and he had a terrific shot. He could score from distance but also got his fair share of tap-ins. McIntyre was a terrific striker with a great touch. He was decent in the air and scored tremendous goals for us.

There were also guys like Ally Mitchell who, as I write this, I realise didn't have as much game time as he perhaps deserved. Looking back, I felt Ally, a Killie legend, was carrying so much weight on his shoulders as he tried to turn around a failing team and I suppose I was trying to take that burden off him. What a player he was, though, and we developed him into more of a midfielder than a wide man. Once he found his feet there, he never looked back. There was John Henry, who offered so much to the team as well and was always able to get into the box and supply goals. Aside from that, we had Colin McKee, Tom Brown and I even brought in my old Rangers mate, Robert Prytz. Originally, the wee man had come in to train with us but I could see he was still fit, so I signed him until the end of the season. The entire team was marshalled at the back by Drago Leković in goal. As I list all those names, I'm at a loss to explain why the team was struggling!

The hope I detected in the squad, despite that United defeat, manifested itself in the next game when we hosted Hearts. Colin McKee got our first goal in the second half and Ally Mitchell made the points safe. While we remained in bottom spot, we were clawing back the gap on those in front of us. Some had tipped us for the drop but we were still fighting and getting the fans back onside, which was hugely important. We had a good win over Aberdeen and then against Hibs but lost away at Ibrox and then got a real doing when we went down 6-0 at Parkhead. But other than that, we were fighting, and if we were beaten, it was only by the odd goal. I could sense something was building, even though the pressure was always on our shoulders.

The Scottish Cup in January offered us a pleasant distraction from our problems in the league but our first game was against a very resilient East Stirling team who stuck to their task admirably. Goals either side of half-time saw us through but it was anything but straightforward.

Next up were Clyde. I had drilled it into the players that, in many respects, this was Clyde's cup final. They were two leagues below us and would be well up for the challenge of humiliating a struggling Premier League team. Clyde had beaten Ayr United and St Mirren, so they were no mugs and, with Eddie Annand up front, were always likely to be a goal threat.

The game at Broadwood was a messy affair, not helped by a typical Scottish winter pitch – muddy with barely a blade of grass. In fact, the pitch proved our friend on one occasion when Clyde's Paul Brownlie was clean through but the ball took a terrific bobble just as he was about to strike it and he missed it all together. Our luck was to get even better later on as Clyde defender Jamie Prunty and Paul Wright tussled in the box. Referee Mike McCurry must have seen a pull on a jersey, because he was well placed and pointed to the spot. But I'll admit now, if I was Gardner Speirs, the Bully Wee boss, I'd have been fuming with the decision. Paul kept his nerve to net from the spot and that was that – we were through a very difficult tie.

We were away again in the next round when we were drawn to face Morton at Cappielow – a great wee ground that was almost full when we travelled down on a sunny afternoon in March. We were cruising that day and were 3-0 up at half-time after a John Henry double and a strike from

Paul Wright. Our case was helped all the more when Morton defender Steve McCahill saw red for a shocking tackle on Wright. The great fear as a manager in those circumstances is that the players switch off and assume the match is already won, so I quickly shut down any of that talk in the dressing room at half-time. But, typically, Morton got a foothold back in the game when Alan Mahood, a player I would later sign, got their first and he added a second soon after. Surely we weren't going to throw it all away? I have to credit the players for the character they showed that day. It could have all gone so wrong but Jim McIntyre got our fourth and then John Henry wrapped up his hat-trick for a 5-2 win and a place in the semi-finals.

The cup results kept the mood in the camp high but, boy, did we need it. In the league, we lost to Motherwell, Aberdeen, Hearts, Dundee United and Raith. I was still operating on a caretaker basis and the club had shown no signs of appointing a permanent boss. Of course, I was in pole position but we were going to have to turn things around and next up was the visit of Celtic. It was probably the last thing we would have wanted and they were on a high themselves after beating Rangers in their own cup quarter-final just days before. Tommy Burns had his side pushing for the title and were they to win the midweek encounter at Rugby Park, they would cut Rangers' lead at the top to just two points. We had met just weeks before at Celtic Park and lost heavily. Despite our run of results, we had climbed off bottom spot and were five points above Hibs. But we had lost our first-choice No.1, Drago Leković, who was away with Yugoslavia on international duty, so young Colin Meldrum stepped in.

I don't know if Celtic had their eye off the ball that night. They were pushing for the title and had a huge game against Rangers the following weekend, which was rightly being looked at as a title decider. Tommy had spoken in the build-up of taking each game at a time and while he believed it, I'm not sure his players did. Everyone outside the town of Kilmarnock was waiting for Celtic to roll us over and march on to the big Old Firm derby. But we knew differently and the game at Cappielow showed what we were made of.

Quite simply, the boys were immense that night. We won 2-0 but, in truth, it could have been more. Wee Alex Burke absolutely terrorised Enrico Annoni, pulling him out of his back-three position so that the Italian didn't know whether he was coming or going. The wee man deserved to get the second goal, a sweet strike from the edge of the box. When he scored, I thought he was going to run up to the back row of the stand with his celebration.

Tommy kept his players locked in the dressing room for some time, such was the impact of that defeat on their title hopes. As for my team, I couldn't have been more delighted or more proud of them. And it set off a run of results that effectively turned around our season. From March to May, we lost only once – to Dunfermline. We beat Motherwell at home, went to Ibrox and won 2-1 and then beat Hearts when they came down to Rugby Park. I was thrilled with the way the team were playing and was always delighted that after each game the press would ask the players about the managerial situation. Each and every one of them was behind me for the job, even though I had been acting in a caretaker capacity since Alex's sacking in December. It was beginning to prey on my mind but, to be fair to the board, they kept me informed week by week. Then, in the build-up to the cup semi-final against Dundee United, I was called in and given the job full-time. I was only 35, one of the youngest managers in the top flight, and I understood why the directors had taken their time. I was untested as a manager, I was inexperienced and they had to be sure they were getting the right man. My audition for the job had lasted nearly five months but we were off the bottom of the table, even though relegation was still a possibility, and I had taken the club to a Scottish Cup semi-final. I felt I had earned it by getting the players performing to their capabilities on the park and I was bringing through young players, something that is so important to a club like Killie. Until they had made the decision, though, there was always the chance they would go in a different direction. When they confirmed it was to be me, I couldn't keep the smile off my face.

The day the news was made official, the four managers of the semi-final teams were meeting for a media event – Tommy McLean of Dundee United, Tommy Burns of Celtic and Alex Totten of Falkirk. I wouldn't say I was apprehensive of meeting Alex but it meant so much to me that he was delighted with my full-time appointment. He congratulated me and then spoke at length to the media about how it was the right decision and how I had earned it.

We had been drawn to face Dundee United in our semi-final, a game that was to be played at Easter Road on a Monday night. It was a crazy decision, made no doubt for TV purposes, with the match live on Sky. Apart from anything else, the Easter Road pitch was not in good nick. United had been beaten there to end a decent run – 17 games without defeat – and Tommy McLean was not pleased at having to go back there. His argument was that United and Killie were both teams who liked to get the ball down and play. He was right, of course, but perhaps it played into our hands that United were so unhappy.

The first game was, let's be honest, dreadful. For any neutral watching, it was a dull encounter, but for those of us with a dog in the fight, it was an extremely nervous affair. Losing a semi-final is always a heartbreaker – so close to the final and it is taken away from you. And players are so afraid of making that one mistake that could cost their team that they forget to perform in the way that has got them to this stage in the first place. It finished 0-0, meaning a replay at the same venue the following week. And guess what ... it was the same nerve-jangling, dull affair! Nearly 180 minutes had passed of the tie, with extra time beckoning, when we flung a corner into the box, Gary Holt gathered the loose ball and hammered over a low cross which Jim McIntyre anticipated brilliantly to knock past Sieb Dijkstra.

Cue bedlam among the travelling Killie fans behind the goal – and it was the same in the dugout! The players were all over each other and the ref, Jim McCluskey, was trying to get the players back to their own half. Jim was a great guy. I had enjoyed his company at many functions. He was an Ayrshire lad but he could never do us any favours. In fact, many a time it almost seemed that he gave decisions against us just because he feared being accused of favouritism! But when Jim was ushering the players back for the restart, he had his whistle in his mouth and I'm sure he was smiling. Stuart Murphy, a well-known Killie fan, was in the main stand behind the dugout. I could hear him shouting: 'Bobby, you're a legend now!'

Those last few minutes felt like an hour. United had one last chance, which they put past the post, and that was it. For the first time in 26 years, Killie were in the Scottish Cup Final.

Getting to the final lifted all the players and they were all fighting every day to get in the team. The competition for places was fierce but I didn't feel any pressure then regarding team selection – that came later in my career. Our last game of the season was against Aberdeen at home and we needed a point. It was an incredibly tense afternoon. The league at that time only had ten teams in it and Raith had been doomed in bottom spot for some time. But the play-off position – second-bottom place – was still very much a possibility for us, as it was for our rivals, Hibernian and Motherwell. As the afternoon's matches ebbed and flowed, each one of those clubs occupied the second-bottom spot at some point. I always had the cup final at the back of my mind, even though I had drilled it into the players that the only game that mattered was the league game with the Dons. I was anxious that we took a positive attitude into the cup final and the nerves of being involved in a tense play-off with Hamilton would have obliterated that. I knew that the whole town of Kilmarnock was buzzing for the cup final but that we had to concentrate on our league situation, knowing that the spectre of relegation was still hanging over us. It was hard to keep the players focused on the job at hand. I wanted them to be 100 per cent zoned in on the league but players may only ever play in one cup final in their careers, so it wasn't easy to get it out of their heads.

There were nearly 10,000 inside Rugby Park that afternoon and it was a tight game until about half an hour in, when Joe Miller swung in a cross and Billy Dodds rose to head Aberdeen into the lead. That was the score at half-time and, while I wanted to read the riot act, I reckoned a calm head was the better approach. It paid off. Midway through the second half, Jim McIntyre went on a mazy run inside the Aberdeen box and there was the unlikely hero, Gary Holt, to head home his first-ever goal for the club to earn us a crucial point. When the dust had settled, we finished a point above Motherwell and Hibs, with the Easter Road side facing the dreaded play-off. I was delighted. I knew how important the game was, not only in the context of the league and avoiding relegation but also in regard to the cup final, with a positive mood flowing through the players.

The cup final was two weeks away but before that, I had to make some difficult decisions. The SFA had put a deadline in place by which you had to release the players you weren't holding on to for the next season. I didn't feel good doing it, I never did. But it was especially difficult with the final approaching, when I thought I could use as many options as possible. I sought leniency from the SFA blazers, hoping that they would relax the rules, but they stood their ground. It meant I had to show some of the players the door. I had 18 left and the rest were released. That included my mate, Robert Prytz, who I had signed until the end of the campaign. He was such a great influence about the place. He was still fit enough and was a great help to the younger players. Prytzy was, in fact, on the bench for the semi-final and I would have dearly loved him to be involved, in some capacity, for the final. But the rules were the rules and, with one eye on younger players coming in, I had to release him.

Unusually, we did all our training in the build-up to the final on the Rugby Park pitch instead of travelling around Ayrshire looking for facilities, as we were forced to do throughout the season. With no league games, we didn't have to worry about the condition of the pitch, and being able to use it as our base, walking from the dressing rooms out on to the pitch, was a huge help.

On the Saturday a week before the final, I took the players to Seamill Hydro, a nearby hotel down the coast, which was an old favourite of Tommy Burns's from his Celtic days. I took the leash off the players and let them go and socialise together to relieve the pressure. But there was one condition – they weren't to bring women back to the hotel. Myself, Clarky, Cabey and big Jimmy Stewart had drinks in the hotel. We talked about old pals, old games, laughed and joked. It was a release valve, easing the pressure on everybody and I felt it was important. With a week to go, it was going to be full-on.

CHAPTER 12
FINAL ACTS

I HAD decided against taking the team away the night before the final. Some people criticised me for it and insisted I was making a mistake but I had my reasons. I felt that if we took the players away to a hotel, there would be too many distractions for them. Despite having them strictly under control, there was always the chance they could over-eat. I remember Tommy Burns telling me he went there when he was with Celtic and he had a go at some of the players for having a dessert! He was right. If you get something put down in front of you, chances are you're going to eat it. I also thought the players would stay up all night, playing cards or talking. All these little things could add up and make a huge difference when it came to performance. I wanted it to be as normal as possible, so I decided the players would be better off staying at home on the Friday night, following their typical routine, eating the usual things and going to bed at the time they normally did. We would meet at the hotel on the morning of the game for the pre-match preparations but I said we would stay at the hotel after the game, no matter what happened. I think that was important and my decision was a significant one. I believe, to this day, that it helped a lot.

With Hampden being rebuilt and unavailable for the final, the game was played at Ibrox. We boarded the front coach, with the wives and families in the coach behind. A camera crew tried to board the bus to film the guys and I turned them away. I wanted the players to relax on the way to the stadium and that would not have happened with a camera crew on board. They wouldn't have been themselves and the adrenaline would be flowing. Nowadays, cameras are everywhere – fly-on-the-wall documentary teams would be following their every move. I would have hated that. This wasn't a normal day but I was battling to make it seem as normal as possible to the players.

The team had already been picked. The only question mark was over who would fill the three places on the bench. John Henry had been struggling in the build-up and would only be able to fill one of the sub spots. I was also determined that Ally Mitchell would get a place on the bench. That left just one spot, which went to Tom Brown. I felt it was a good mix – an impact bench, if you like. But the starting XI picked itself … Leković; MacPherson, Montgomerie, McGowne, Kerr; Bagan, Reilly, Holt, Burke; Wright, McIntyre.

On the bus to Ibrox, I was pretty relaxed. The usual chatter could be heard behind me but, as we got nearer to the stadium, the nerves began to jangle. The closer and closer we got, the more and more Killie fans I could see. There were thousands of them, cheering the bus on its way. I don't think there could have been many folk left back in the town. It dawned on me then just how important this was, not just to the players and the club but to the people of Kilmarnock. We were carrying their hopes and dreams that day and I did feel a sense of responsibility. The team hadn't been in a Scottish Cup Final for about 30 years and hadn't won it for 60. Playing a team from the league below us meant we were firm favourites but that tag didn't sit well with me. I was up against my mentor, Alex Totten, who was a wily old fox and had performed miracles with a Falkirk side that had seen off Celtic in their own semi-final. Alex had done a fantastic job with Falkirk and they were there on merit.

It had dawned on me that, in many respects, both the sides were Alex Totten teams. I had brought Burke and Bagan up from the reserves but hadn't brought in a single new signing, although I did manage to get a reaction out of them. So, this was still very much a Totten team. He had been instrumental in starting my coaching career and encouraging me from the very start. Alex helped me throughout my career. When I was going to Rangers, he was one of the coaches who gave Jock Wallace a steer about signing me. When he came to Kilmarnock, he let me coach the reserves and the youth team. When you think about it, he gave me my start in coaching and signed Paul Wright and, when you consider what was about to happen in the final, it's certainly ironic.

With the team confirmed in the dressing room, the players were stripped and went out for their warm-up. I don't know about other managers but I always found this the hardest part of the build-up. The dressing room is pretty empty and you are alone with your thoughts. Question after question races through your head. Have I got the line-up right? Will they cope with the expectation, the pressure? You're thinking about the game ahead and hoping the players can play to their best and the referee doesn't make any mistakes. It is hard just sitting there with your own thoughts – the hard work has been done. Once the players come back in, they start to get their match gear on. I was walking around, reminding the players of their positions, their roles at set pieces, for and against. I know you may think that strange, having to remind them, but they are so caught up in it all, caught up in the moment, that they forget the most basic things. I actually took one player on to the park and showed him where he should be when we were defending a corner. Would you believe it ... during the game we conceded a corner and that player was nowhere near where he should have been! There are some players you just can't depend on in these situations and you need to delegate accordingly.

With that, it was the call to go. We left the dressing room and, for the first time, I laid eyes on Alex. He looked fantastic, dressed in the full kilt set-up in the Falkirk tartan. He looked like he was going to a wedding. All of a sudden, I felt really under-dressed in my club suit and buttonhole. Had I under-done it or had Alex over-done it? Then I thought, what we were wearing mattered fuck all – it was about the fucking game.

Our mascot that day was the son of one of our directors, Robert Wyper. I'm sure he pulled rank to get his boy out there, which was none of my concern, but the bugger was nearly as tall as I was. When I led the team out of the tunnel, into the May sunshine, we walked into a cauldron of noise. There was blue and white everywhere; it was just a different shade of blue for each team. The place was rammed. It was fantastic – such a great occasion to be a part of.

I was delighted with the way the team started. Any fears I had about youngsters David Bagan and Alex Burke being overawed by the occasion were dismissed by the runs they were making down either wing. Paul Wright also was at it from the off, dropping deep to pick up the ball in midfield, with the Bairns' defence unsure whether to go with him or not. It meant he could ping balls out left or right. But, despite settling the better of the two teams, neither side was able to create anything in front of goal.

That all changed when wee Burkey floated in a corner, which Kevin McGowne did brilliantly to get his head to and knock it back to where Paul Wright had been left unmarked at the back post. I don't think, even now, Paul could claim it was his cleanest of strikes but it went past Craig Nelson in the Falkirk goal and we were ahead. If there had been a roof on Ibrox that day, the noise would have blown it off. In the dugout, we were ecstatic. Taking the lead was exactly what we deserved. The rest of the half played out in exactly the same way and at half-time I asked the players for more of the same. We were terrorising them with our balls into the box and even with Kevin James, their giant central defender, they were struggling to cope.

But with only one goal in it, no matter how dominant you think you have been, the opposition always has a chance. I'm sure Alex would have given them both barrels in the dressing room and, to be fair, Falkirk started the second half brightly. Alex had made some tactical changes and they had a powerful force in Andy Gray, who had played a barrel load of games for both Crystal Palace and Spurs before Falkirk picked him up. He was driving his side on and using all his experience to plug the holes in midfield that we had exploited in the first half.

Paul Wright was struggling and had run himself ragged in the deeper role he had been given. He deserved his goal but it was time for a change and I knew John Henry could do as good a job. I also switched Jim McIntyre with Tom Brown, again because McIntyre had emptied his tank. Alex also shuffled his pack and he put the giant Kevin James into a forward position. We braced for a late Bairns onslaught. All game, Gray's long throws had caused us trouble and, with just minutes to go, he launched one in from the right. We defended it as if it was a corner, with Tom Brown on the back post. Kevin James met Gray's throw-in and nodded it down for Neil Oliver to net. The Falkirk fans went crazy but my players had been well schooled on the fact that those on the posts had to clear the six-yard line. Tom had done just that, meaning Oliver would be offside. I was glad John Henry hadn't been on a post, because he would still be standing there! The linesman's flag went up to break Bairns' hearts but it just showed that all the hard work on the training ground beforehand had been worth it. The fine detail of defending a corner or, in this case, a throw-in had proved crucial.

Minute after minute, second after second ticked down before referee Hugh Dallas blew the final whistle. My emotion was one of overwhelming relief. Paul Wright and Jim McIntyre doused me in water and orange juice, soaking me. I was fuming and, for a nano-second, seriously considered throwing a couple of punches. Getting wet wasn't the problem; what annoyed me was that I hadn't been able to acknowledge my counterpart, Alex Totten. All I could do was shake his hand, I couldn't embrace him as I wanted to and give him the recognition he deserved. He had actually managed two clubs that season to the cup final. I shook Walter Kidd's hand and made my way on to the park to shake hands with the

Falkirk players. There was plenty of time to congratulate my own guys. As you can imagine, the Falkirk players were gutted and rightly so. They had fancied their chances but I made sure there was no way we would underestimate them and I drilled into my team that Falkirk were full of Premier League players – Andy Gray had been capped by England! They were a good side and we had given them the respect they most surely deserved.

With the game being played at Ibrox, there was no climb up the steps to get the trophy. The presentation was made on the field, and watching the MP Sam Galbraith present it to my captain Ray Montgomerie was a magical moment. It was beyond my expectations – such a magical experience just to be part of it. I'm sure we had a bit of luck getting to the final and we had a bit of luck in the final as well. But it was a fantastic achievement, which doesn't really sink in immediately. It was 60 years since Killie had won the Scottish Cup – and they've not won it again since. You think: 'Wow! What a brilliant experience! Let's do it all again next season.' Obviously, it's never happened again.

We headed back to Kilmarnock and stopped at Fenwick to climb aboard an open-topped bus. When we reached the town, there were fans at the side of the road and we acknowledged them but I'm sure I was not alone in thinking it was a bit underwhelming. But then we turned into John Finnie Street. There was blue and white everywhere. The whole town had come out. There must have been 100,000 people there. Anybody who was there will never forget it. I remembered after the Morton game that I had dedicated the cup run to the memory of Jean Molloy, a lovely lady and loyal servant to Kilmarnock Football Club. Her husband, Freddy, had also worked at the club and played for the club as well. They were two great people and I was so happy we had delivered the cup success for people like them. At the time, you don't appreciate the magnitude of the achievement; it's only now, all these years later, that you realise just what you have done.

A journey around Kilmarnock that would usually take ten minutes took us two hours. We headed back to the hotel for a quick change and then to Rugby Park for a celebratory function. As you can imagine, the place was heaving. We entered the function suite to discover there was no seating for the players or their families – and there was no food left, despite the fact the players hadn't had anything since their pre-match meal. We only had about eight directors but they all had a table for ten. Folk weren't happy – and I can't say I blame them. One of our directors, Robert Wyper, the father of our lucky mascot, thought it would be a good idea to take the trophy into the Killie Club, where some fans were gathered. I went along with it but I had only taken one step through the door when I was mobbed. Robert took a couple of steps backwards and reversed back out of the door. I wasn't happy but I was pleased the fans got to touch the Scottish Cup. When I had extracted myself from the crowd, I headed back into the function suite to be confronted by a disgruntled player's wife. I was in no mood to get upset and was just going with the flow but I realised it wasn't fair on wives, children or the players, so I instructed everyone to get back on the bus. We went back to the hotel and I told the players to order anything they wanted and to charge it all to the club. I expect the club would not have been happy but I didn't care. It eased the tension and we went on to have a great evening.

But the headaches from the cup success didn't end when the hangovers cleared. A couple of days after our win, there was a board meeting which I attended and I faced the wrath of one very unhappy director. I understood where former chairman Jamie Moffat was coming from. His largesse and financial support to the club was unmatched – he was a great old gentleman whose company, A.T. Mays, was a huge success and whose name and logo was emblazoned on the front of our strips. He was disappointed, to say the least, that in the immediate aftermath of the win at Ibrox, the players had pulled on Sports Division T-shirts. It meant that in many of the pictures in the press and TV that followed, his A.T. Mays logo was hidden. I was as disappointed as Mr Moffat and I had no idea the players planned to do it. I understand that they had to make the most of every opportunity but I hadn't a clue they had cut a deal with Sir Tom Hunter. I had to make profuse apologies to Mr Moffat. The whole thing was embarrassing. He also wasn't happy that some of the players stripped to the waist and then saw fit to lob their club blazers and ties into the crowd. I told Mr Moffat these were mementos for the fans and that I had actually heard one fan talking about how great it was he had got Jim McIntyre's jacket. That seemed to appease him but I'm pretty sure I made it up!

Things changed after the cup win. We were now an established top-flight team, with the Scottish Cup in our trophy cabinet and a European adventure to look forward to. The expectation levels went through the roof but you just had to deal with it and handle it, which I thought I did quite well. I just took it in my stride and treated it as a learning curve. I'd only recently started managing and had taken charge of only 20-odd games. Now, all of a sudden, we were playing in the Cup Winners' Cup!

The team got stronger, as I brought in a lot of good players to add to what we had.

I had heard that Pat Nevin could be available from Tranmere, so I contacted their boss, John Aldridge, and Pat was keen to travel north. We were sitting in my office chatting, before he met our chief executive, Ian Welsh, who would negotiate and conclude the deal. I was just about to walk out of the door to get something when I remembered reading Pat's own book, in which he admitted that when he was about to sign for Chelsea he was in chairman Ken Bates's office and when Bates left the room, Pat seized the opportunity to rifle through his paperwork! I immediately recalled this and told Pat not to touch anything!

It took Pat a bit of time to get back into Scottish football but, once he found his feet, he was great. He was living around the border area and travelling was a problem. So, in the early part of the week, I would tell Pat to stay at home – he had a young lad who needed attention. But his influence on the team was immense. Ally Mitchell would watch Pat working on his ball control, dribbling round cones, and he proceeded to do it as well. That knowledge, from experienced pros rubbing off on younger players, is like gold dust. I knew it would be good for both Alex Burke and David Bagan to work alongside Pat, plus his arrival meant I could rest the two younger lads and not fall into the trap of overplaying them.

That pre-season, we headed over to France for a week. I always felt that staying and training in the same place for maybe four to five weeks can be soul-destroying for the players and the coaching staff. Pre-season is the hardest time of the year for a footballer and if your club can afford to go on a trip, it is huge. With new players coming into the club, it gives you an idea if they are going to fit in. I got fed up bringing trialists over to Scotland, putting them up in a hotel for a week, only seeing them for a couple of hours a day and leaving them up to their own devices in the evening. Plus, playing a trialist in the reserves is to the detriment of a young player who has committed himself to the club. Pre-season on a trip was best for me, where it was 24/7 watching how they behaved, how they fitted in with the squad. We were in France when I got a call from Willie McKay telling me he had a French striker who was top-drawer – his words not mine. I had only met Willie once years previously when I was walking up Queen Street in Glasgow with Ally McCoist and I bumped into an old team-mate of mine from Clydebank, Shug O'Rourke, who was with Willie and introduced me to him. We exchanged pleasantries and that was it. So, when I got his call, I remembered who he was and he then proceeded to tell me he was a football agent and had top players from France looking for clubs. I kind of humoured him, all the time thinking, 'He knows nothing about football.' How wrong was I? Look at Willie now – top agent, racehorses, mega rich. Who's the mug? Anyway, he told me he had this French striker in at Ayr and asked if I would like to have a look at him? I said the only problem was that we were in France. Not an issue, said Willie, he would get him to join up with us in

France. The player's name was Jerome Vareille. He fitted in really well and would go on to play nearly 100 games for us.

The funniest story about Jerome was told by the club's chef, Ernie Bolton, who came to me just after Christmas with this belter. Turns out Jerome had approached Ernie and asked for a table for four on Christmas Day. No problem, says Ernie, and, on Christmas morning, in comes Jerome, who is shown to his table in the Park Suite. The table is looking splendid and is bedecked with all the Christmas decorations. Jerome walks up, removes all the decorations, lifts the table and walks out to put it in the boot of his car. Turns out he had friends coming on Christmas Day and needed a table for his flat. I'd have paid good money to see Ernie's face!

We started the new season with a goalless draw away to Aberdeen and then a 4-0 defeat at Easter Road against Hibs. In between, we got our first taste of European football in the Cup Winners' Cup preliminary round against Irish side Shelbourne.

The Scottish press had us down as firm favourites, naïvely dismissing the quality or strengths of Irish sides they knew nothing about. The fans, of course, bought into it and had already assumed we would win to set up a tie with French cracks Nice. Gerry McCabe and I went over to watch them in Dublin. I wasn't very impressed but knew it would be difficult when they faced us. We went back to the hotel and settled ourselves in the bar. Cabey loves his Guinness and I settled for a lager. There were a couple of women sitting at the next table and, hearing our accents, started talking to us. One of them was staring at me and she said I looked like an actor but she couldn't remember his name.

'It'll come to me,' she says.

I'm waiting for the usual – Danny DeVito or some like. Then she shouts up: 'I've got it, Mel Gibson!'

Cabey nearly fell off his seat laughing. I told the lassie she'd had too much to drink if she thought I looked like *Braveheart*! Christ, Gabey got some mileage out of that one.

The tie itself was tighter than even I had expected. In the first leg, they took the lead early on before a double from Paul Wright, one a penalty, at least had us taking a lead over to the second leg. But I was a relieved man when we held on for a 1-1 draw in Dublin, losing a ridiculous goal after a mistake by Drago Leković. I was just glad to get out of there and still be in the competition.

In the first round proper, we were drawn against Nice, who were in the French second division but had won the French Cup, which was a magnificent achievement. Again, our press made us favourites! Ignorance is bliss.

When we arrived, the Nice PR team had set up a tent on the beach to do the press conference. The place was stunning and they had laid on this magnificent spread, full of French delicacies and local fresh seafood. The French media were out in numbers but when I arrived with our club secretary, Kevin Collins, the only one thing missing was the Scottish press! I had a good idea where they were. The conference started, with me, the Nice manager, Silvester Takac, and an interpreter for me and one for him, which wasn't needed, as the Scottish press never gave us the pleasure of their company. One Scottish journo did pop in, head down, lifted a pile of press releases and headed back out. I tell you, they missed a great spread and the champagne was flowing.

The atmosphere in the stadium was electric and the French fans were extremely passionate and noisy. They were throwing these paper darts at our players. I know it sounds daft but they were pretty sharp! We conceded early on to a header from Stefan Kohn – the German striker who had won the UEFA Cup with Werder Bremen. He scored again in the second half and, although we got one back through a Paul Wright penalty, our cause wasn't helped when Martin Baker was sent off for two completely unnecessary yellow cards. The first was for a deliberate handball when he jumped with a player for a throw-in. The second, a minute later, was for a carbon-copy offence. Shortly after, Mickaël Rol headed in a third.

We were up against it in the return leg at Rugby Park. A rare Mark Reilly goal gave us a lifeline until a smashing Zoran Milinković header put the tie beyond us. Our first taste of Europe had ended almost before it had begun but I was hungry for more and knew that we would have to strengthen the squad to achieve it.

Powering up the dreaded sand dunes at Gullane in pre-season under Jock Wallace. I wanted to do so much more at Rangers but my broken leg put a stop to that. (Credit: Eric McCowat)

Above: Early success in the Auchengill Star team. That's me, bottom left.

Left: Posing for the pre-season pictures after joining West Bromwich Albion. I didn't even know they had been relegated.

I found a new lease of life at Kilmarnock and helped take them back to the top flight with a great squad and the perfect manager in Tommy Burns.

I was fuming when the players drenched me at the end of the cup final because I had wanted to shake hands with Alex Totten properly. (Credit: Eric McCowat)

Lifting the Scottish Cup in 1997. I'll never forget it – nor will I forget the fans lining the streets when we got back to the town. (Credit: Eric McCowat)

Gerry McCabe and Jim Clark were key lieutenants and are great pals. The three of us were a brilliant team. (Credit: Eric McCowat)

I swapped Killie for Hibs. They are a great club but my relationship with Rod Petrie quickly turned sour. (Credit: Eric McCowat)

We had to sell big-name players almost immediately at Easter Road but we discovered gems in the reserves like Scott Brown. (Credit: Eric McCowat)

I brought Jimmy Bone to help me at Chester.
He was a great friend and I miss him dearly.

With assistant Kevin Summerfield, as a new challenge began at Plymouth. I loved my time on the south coast.

With the players and backroom staff at Gor Mahia in Kenya. I loved my time there and turned the team into winners.

Holding the balls as manager of Uganda! Moving to Africa was a real challenge but I managed to get some success with the national team.

My battle with cancer put everything in perspective. It changed my appearance and my outlook on life.

Happy days with the newest addition to the family – my beautiful grand-daughter Hannah.

CHAPTER 13

NO-BRAINERS

IT IS always a gamble bringing a new player into a club. No matter how talented they may be, there is no guarantee they will fit into your set-up, into the dressing room or, if they are a foreign player, into Scottish culture. Sometimes, however, it is a no-brainer.

We had finished the 97/98 season in fourth place, not bad for a side that had come close to being relegated the season before, meaning we had qualified for the UEFA Cup. But there was building work needing to be done along the way. Jim McIntyre and Mark Reilly had gone to Reading – although we soon got Reilly back – and our goalkeeper, Drago Leković, had hot-footed it to Spain when Sporting Gijon matched the £150,000 release clause in his contract.

Drago was a good keeper and had fitted into the team well. I can't remember him having many howlers. I did have a go at him at half-time during a game against Hearts at Tynecastle. It was 0-0 and we were well on top but I was furious we hadn't capitalised on our pressure and I was having a go at the players in the dressing room when one of them piped up and said something like: 'We're battering them.'

'Battering them?' I fumed. 'It's 0-0 and they won't play as badly as that in the second half and then what happens?'

Out of the corner of my eye, I could see big Drago rubbing his bottom lip with a piece of ice. I lost the plot and smacked the piece of ice out of his hand.

'You're six feet two and you're acting like a child,' I shouted. 'Grow up. Your lip's fine. Get out there and smash anybody who comes near you.'

As it happens, we did win the game. Drago was a good lad and I was disappointed not to keep him but he had to go and make money in Spain. But I was delighted to bring in Gordon Marshall from Celtic. He was a very imposing and confident lad, who organised the defence well and was a top pro. When you sign Old Firm players, you know you're getting a player who has that desire to win. It's indoctrinated in them. Gordon did tremendously well and I only remember having words with him once, when we played Rangers at Rugby Park and lost 5-0, with Rod Wallace scoring a hat-trick. Every time we got a corner, I worried because Rangers would defend it so well, put two players on the edge of their box, win the ball and race up the pitch to carve out a chance. We were well aware of this and organised the players the best we could to combat that, until one of our defenders – who shall remain nameless – was delegated to stay back but decided he was going up for a corner. We lost possession and Rangers scored through Neil McCann. Our experienced full-back, Gus MacPherson, was injured and missing for the game, so I played young Steven Hamilton in his place. When I shouted an instruction to Steven, he told me to 'Fuck off!' I wasn't going to take that from a senior pro, let alone a young kid, so I subbed him for

Ally Mitchell, who was capable of playing anywhere on the right. But Ally was caught in possession almost immediately by Neil McCann, who raced on to cut back for Wallace to slam past Gordon Marshall for their second. That was in the 75th minute and they would go on and score three more. I didn't blame Ally Mitchell at all – I knew who was at fault. But big Gordon and I had words afterwards. He wasn't happy I had subbed our young full-back at 1-0.

I told him: 'I don't care who you are or who we are playing, you talk to me like that you're off!'

No manager would accept a player being disrespectful. It was the only time the two of us had a confrontation. Apart from that, I felt we had a good relationship.

The comings and goings at Ibrox were always worth keeping an eye on and I had been aware for some time that both Ian Durrant and Ally McCoist would be becoming available. While they were falling down the pecking order at Rangers, they would be top of the pile at Rugby Park if we could persuade them to sign.

We got Durrant first. It was a bit harder to get the deal done for McCoist. Don't get me wrong, signing Durrant was not easy. He was a wanted man and could have played down in England or moved abroad. He had lots of options but I pestered the living daylights out of him, as you do. Phoning him all the time ... 'Come and sign for Kilmarnock ... it's only ten to 15 minutes down the road ... you'll enjoy the football ... no bigotry, none of that pressure ... we're a family club ... your kids will enjoy it.' But it wasn't really him I convinced. It was his wife. I phoned her and said: 'Look, if he moves down south, you'll never see him. He'll be out playing golf all the time and you don't want to be uprooting the family at this stage of his career. We're only down the road. You'll love it. You'll love the atmosphere, you'll love the players' lounge, there's not so much pressure, the kids will enjoy it as well.'

Durrant wasn't too difficult to deal with. I don't know how it went when he sat down with Ian Welsh, because it was our chief executive who did all the final negotiations to finalise the deal, but we managed to get him.

Coisty dragged on a bit. Hibs were trying to get him. They were interested and he was big mates with big Alex McLeish, who was boss at Easter Road at the time. They were definitely wanting him, as were Raith Rovers, but I just had to try and sell the club to him. McCoist had missed out on selection for Craig Brown's Scotland squad that was going to the World Cup in France and I'm sure that decision must have really hurt him. He was to be in France as a pundit but that was no substitute for being there as a player. He was determined to take his time to decide on the next chapter of his footballing career, so I couldn't put pressure on him. I could only try to explain all the benefits of joining the club, including that he didn't live too far away, just 15 minutes. I think he had just had a newborn and I told him he didn't want to be travelling all over the place with a baby to look after. We managed to get the deal done – a deal that didn't bankrupt the club.

They were both superb signings. I'm sure people would be thinking they were past their best and that we were signing a 'couple of jokers', mates who were more interested in having a laugh than focusing on football. But I knew what we were getting; two serious individuals who, when it came down to business, were on it 100 per cent. Sure, in the dressing room they were great fun, but when it came to the serious stuff, training and playing, they were top-drawer. They were respectful, too. I had been a team-mate of theirs but when they came in, it was 'Gaffer this' and 'Gaffer that' and I admired them for that. They took us to a new level. With their professionalism in training and in games, our other players reacted to that. Especially wee Durrant in midfield, taking touches on the ball and not panicking, showing composure. The other midfield players started to do likewise, learning to take time on the ball and be far more composed than they had previously been. The two of them were fantastic and big Ian Welsh and the chairman deserve a lot of credit for doing the deals to get them. I don't know why but Durrant was staying in a hotel and after every training session, he'd be looking for ice to put on his knee – the fallout from THAT tackle from Neil Simpson up at Pittodrie all those years before. I don't know if the chairman thought it was ice for his alcohol but he was certainly a bit concerned that his knee would last a season. To be honest, I was concerned about it as well. But Durrant played every game for us that year and he was outstanding.

On the day the two of them signed, we brought in a third signing – and one who, in many ways, was to prove just as influential. I had always been a fan of Alan Mahood at Morton – ever since that cup quarter-final on the way to our Scottish Cup win. In my mind, he was one of the best players in the First Division and I was determined to get him. As ambitions continued to grow, to get such a high-quality trio was huge for the club.

McCoist was superb for us but there were some challenging moments. With his career coming to an end, he was beginning to carve out a life away from football. We had a crucial game away at Ibrox at a time when we were still very much chasing a place in the UEFA Cup. The game against Rangers was on 12 May, the same day as the FA Cup Final in Cardiff between Arsenal and Liverpool, and it suddenly emerged that Ally was booked to be one of the ITV pundits alongside Terry Venables and Des Lynam. There was no chance I was going to let that happen.

I fumed: 'I pick the Kilmarnock team, not the guys at a television studio. I've not made any decisions about my squad for the Rangers game but Ally could be part of it. He's aware of the ground rules about his TV appearances, of course he is. The team requirements come first and he knows that.'

I won that argument but if I thought the controversy would end there, I was wrong. I put McCoist on the bench at Ibrox but we were well off the pace and were trailing 3-0, with the whole of Ibrox desperate for McCoist to go on for a grand farewell in what would be his last game there. But there were 500 Killie fans in the away corner of the stadium and they were my main concern. I remember Dick Advocaat, the Rangers manager, saying after the game that I should have put him on. I thought, 'That's good coming from him, he released him!' But he was my player and I had to do what was best for my club, my team and our fans. I turned to McCoist and told him that I couldn't put him on, to think of our fans, not the Rangers ones who wanted to give him his big Ibrox farewell. I had to be professional but I know that, to this day, a lot of Rangers fans have not forgiven me for not putting him on and will probably never forgive me. It was a difficult decision – it hurt me as much as it hurt McCoist. But, as a manager, you have to be stubborn – to think of your fans, not the opposition's.

As it happens, McCoist's final game was against Celtic the next week at Rugby Park, when he came off after 50 minutes in a game we won 1-0 through an Alan Mahood goal to secure a place in Europe. Making his debut that day off the bench was a certain Kris Boyd. Perhaps a baton was being passed.

McCoist was also central to another big decision I made as Killie boss and one that I do regret – or certainly the way I handled it.

We had managed to get to the League Cup Final in 2001 against Celtic after defeating St Mirren in the semi-finals. That semi was due to be played at Fir Park but I wasn't happy, because I felt Motherwell's ground would be too much of a leveller, being pretty tight and not as spacious as Hampden. I knew the national stadium's pitch would suit us better, with wide-open spaces we could exploit through the pace in our team. I phoned the St Mirren boss, Tom Hendrie, and told him we would both be at a disadvantage by not having the experience of playing at Hampden while the other semi-finalists would have that advantage. I was somewhat surprised when Tom agreed, so we got the game switched. On a very cold, wet night, Craig Dargo, a great wee player we brought in from Raith, scored a tremendous goal for us and we won relatively comfortably.

We had Celtic in the final, so I was up against Martin O'Neill. With all the talent in the Killie squad now, I found team selection so much harder. The team for the Scottish Cup Final had more or less picked itself. This was far more challenging. There were two key decisions I had to make – Paul Wright or Ally McCoist on the bench, Garry Hay or Martin Baker to start.

I selected McCoist, because I couldn't see us scoring many goals and was thinking that, if we could get to the hour mark level, I would put Ally on in the hope that he and Durranty could link up, as they always did, and conjure up a goal. But I felt terrible leaving out Paul – he was and is a Killie legend. I also decided to leave out Baker in favour of Garry Hay, which was not as tough a call. I had no doubt Hay would be a player and be a future Killie captain and I didn't have the same confidence about Baker. I always felt Martin lacked enthusiasm for the game and got the impression it was a hardship for him. Martin had all the attributes to become a top player but I felt he lacked the desire. Garry Hay would go on to feature in the Killie team that won the League Cup under the tutelage of Kenny Shiels in 2012, another magnificent achievement.

But I will always regret the way I handled those decisions. Normally, for such a big game, I would tell the players who were missing out the night before the game. But I knew these were two headstrong individuals and I feared there was a real chance the pair of them would just walk out of the camp. So, I chose to tell them on the morning of the game. But, for one reason or another, time ran away from me and I didn't manage to speak to them. I certainly wasn't going to do it on the bus to the game, so, when we got to Hampden and into the dressing room, I read out the starting line-up and walked out of the door. As a manager, I found dropping players from the team for a cup final very difficult. It's not just the player you're disappointing, it's his whole family. I knew Paul's wife and his wider family and knew they would all be at the game, expecting to see him play.

Durrant was magnificent in the game and I thought my plan, to keep it tight into the second half, was paying off, because it was 0-0 and the wee man was running the show. The likes of Neil Lennon and Paul Lambert couldn't get near him. Then his knee gave up on him and he had to come off. I don't think he kicked another ball. It was gutting. In the second half, Henrik Larsson raised it up a level and scored a hat-trick.

After a cup final, win or lose, you have to organise food and drinks for the players and their families and the guys had booked an Italian restaurant in Newton Mearns. McCoist has a good mate, wee Cliffy, who was a singer in a band, and he was the entertainment – a very funny guy. But would Cliffy let it go? In between songs, he would crack jokes regarding Paul and Martin Baker being left out the team, much to the amusement of the rest of the players.

I felt terrible.

One of the best players we brought in was French striker Christophe Cocard – after a tip-off from super-agent Willie McKay. He phoned me to say he had this player in at West Ham and manager Harry Redknapp wasn't going to take him, so did I fancy a look? We were due to play a European game against Kaiserslautern but I reckoned I could go via London, watch the player and make my way to Germany to meet up with the team. Willie also had a player he was looking after at Wolves and he suggested we first stop off in the Midlands and have an overnight at The Belfry. That sounded fine to me but I never realised big Willie's timekeeping was awful and he turned up at my house between 5pm and 6pm and the game was in the Midlands at 8pm. We were racing down the motorway, with Willie steering with his knees, his phone in one hand and his Filofax in the other. He must have set off every speed camera between Glasgow and Birmingham but he didn't give a toss, because he was based in Monaco! 'They won't bother sending me fines out there,' he said.

We missed the first half of the game but he saw his player and then, after the game, we went to The Belfry, had a few beers and bumped into former Rangers player Mark Walters. I left the two of them talking, because I was wanting up and away early. The next morning, I couldn't raise Willie. He didn't answer his bedroom door and he didn't pick up his phone. I thought the big bastard had been up all night drinking and we had to get to London and then I had to make it to Germany. Eventually, he came down. We headed to the car to put our stuff in the boot and Willie threw a box into my bag.

'Give that to the wife,' he said. I never thought anything of it.

We raced to London and missed the first half of the West Ham reserve game in which Cocard was playing. I watched him for ten minutes and knew immediately that he had the ability, he had the balance and that he could play. He would do for me.

We went into Harry Redknapp's office after the game. He's a great guy, very warm and welcoming, and we spoke about Cocard.

'Bob, the boy's a player,' Harry said. 'But he won't get in my team. He'd be lucky to make the bench. I've got a lot of really good players.'

He then proceeded to tell me a story of how he had been sitting at home and put on a video of Eric Cantona. 'Bob, my knowledge of European football is rubbish,' he said. 'I'm watching the video and the French team is lining up for the anthem – and there's Cantona, Desailly, Deschamps – and, all of a sudden, wow! There's that little geezer who's training with us.'

It was Cocard – Harry had no idea he had played for France!

What a signing he was for us – but you had to encourage him to be up for every game. He was always up for Celtic, Rangers, Hearts and Hibs but Motherwell away, not so much. Right at the beginning, in just his second training session with us, he went up in a challenge with Mark Reilly and his nose was broken. It was a mess and he walked off the park. Little did I know he also walked into the dressing rooms, got changed, walked to his car and fucked off back to France! I didn't see him for two weeks. I was on to his agent every day asking if he was coming back! He did, thankfully. He was a fantastic talent.

Oh, and that box Willie McKay threw into my bag? I arrived back home and put my travelling bag in the washroom for the wife to empty when I heard her shouting: 'Oh, thanks for the present.' I had forgotten it and reckoned it was probably perfume – before she came out wearing a designer watch!

Not every transfer worked out. Some you win and some you lose. We brought in a French striker called David Merdy. I really thought he would do well for us but he just wasn't suited to Scottish football. He didn't even learn the language and didn't play a single game for us. And I was frustrated losing out to the likes of Hibs and Hearts, clubs with bigger budgets. I tried to bring David Zitelli and John O'Neil to Ayrshire but they went for the bigger money they could get at Easter Road.

There was a French agent by the name of Jean-Luc Witzel who I got to know well. The big guy seemed okay and we had arranged that he would bring a left-sided player for a trial when we were at a training camp in Germany. They turned up and I noticed the lad had a lot of luggage for a training camp. I had told the agent we were on pre-season and it would be hard work, so he should make sure the player was ready – which he wasn't. I wanted to involve him in the double sessions we were doing to assess his fitness and then the next day in a match we had arranged. When we got to the training field, we had a head count and we were a player down. We discovered it was this French lad and I sent someone back up to fetch him. They came back without him and told me the lad was in bits and couldn't get out of bed. I phoned Jean-Luc, told him the story and told him to come to the camp. I told him that if I couldn't see the boy play, I couldn't even consider signing him. The lad then produced this contract, supposedly with three years, on which my signature had been forged. I told the lad it was fake and there was no way I was signing him. Jean-Luc was in a panic. It transpired that he was committed to another agent, who was quite heavy, and was offering me all sorts to sign the lad. He even told me Everton wanted to sign him but he had to get him to another club first and I would get a slice of the fee. I never signed him and felt sorry for the lad. He had brought so much luggage because he thought he was coming back to Scotland with us.

Jean-Luc would later recommend a striker he thought I would be interested in, so I travelled to France to have a look. I didn't fancy the striker – he was poor – but there was a big centre-back who did catch my attention. I couldn't take my eyes off him – he was massive and dominated the defence. I watched him intently and on one occasion when they had cleared the ball and the defence were jogging out, as he jogged past the striker, he nutted him! The striker went down like a ton of bricks but none of the officials saw anything and play carried on. Big Sam Allardyce was also there and I was hoping he hadn't been monitoring this player. I was certainly interested and made enquires and discovered he was available. We got his agent over. His name was Pape Diouf, a top agent in France. We met at Glasgow Airport and our chief executive, Ian Welsh, had the discussions with him. I wish I had joined him but I never got involved with the money side of deals. After a while, Ian came out and said they were not close to making the deal. I said we had to sign him, that we wouldn't have him for long and would sell him on for big money. But it didn't happen. The next time I heard the player's name, Bobo Balde, he was signing for Celtic.

The other player we missed out on was Shefki Kuqi, a big Finnish striker. He came over on trial for a couple of weeks and I knew he was a player. But we couldn't afford him either. He went down south, got himself a deal at Blackburn and was sold on for more than a million.

There was another trialist we brought over from France. It was a cold winter night at Rugby Park and I was taking the warm-up and noticed we were one short. I went back inside and the poor French lad was standing beside the radiator. He said it was too cold to play and I told him that's why we do a warm-up. He hadn't kicked a ball and I knew he wasn't for us.

CHAPTER 14
INTO EUROPE

MUCH AS I would have liked to have been involved in the negotiations of contracts, I knew people were better qualified and I didn't want to be the manager who put the club into debt.

My attention was fully on bringing in the talent that would enhance the team and making sure they gelled on the park. Over the years, as I have explained, we had some great players: McCoist, Durrant, Nevin; there was Craig Dargo, Alan Mahood and Andy McLaren; Cristophe Cocard and another Frenchman, Freddie Dindeleux.

But in order for these players to come in, others had to leave and sometimes they were legends of the club. It is a tough call for any coach but you must make these decisions to keep the team improving. I always hoped I was honest with the players but I think some of them hated me and I don't suppose I blame them. In order to get big Freddie in, I had to let Ray Montgomerie go. I wanted him to stay and start a coaching career but he felt he still had some years left in him and moved on to Partick Thistle. It's great, though, that Ray is still involved in an ambassadorial capacity at Rugby Park. Gus MacPherson is also someone I let go too early. He went on to have a very good spell at Dunfermline.

We had a lot of quality players about the place, so it wasn't difficult to manage them. Discipline-wise they were fine and they worked their socks off day in, day out. It was a pleasure to work with them. I never had any major problems when it came to discipline stuff. The expectation did grow and the fanbase grew as well. When I went to Killie, we were getting maybe 3,000 fans in but when I left, the average gate was up to about 8,000. I loved everything about it, the fans were passionate and I really enjoyed the place.

Things were changing on and off the park and expectations were always on the up, which brought its own pressures. But there was still time for levity. One day, the first minister at the time, Henry McLeish, was at Rugby Park to publicise some government-backed initiative – I can't remember now what it was. But I was to pose in pictures with him – just the two of us and some life-size cardboard cutout of a player. The cameras were flashing away until one of the photographers said: 'Can we just have one of the two of you now – without the dummy.'

I looked at the First Minister and said: 'Do you mind?'

The place fell about. McLeish gave me this look as if he was going along with the joke but I'm not sure if he found it that funny.

Bill Costley, our chairman and a successful hotelier, had brought together a few successful businessmen to make up our board. We had Ian Welsh as our CEO, who was very intelligent and knowledgeable. I remember our first conversation in the boardroom. Ian said he was looking forward to working with me but one day he was going to have to fire me and he hoped I wouldn't take it personally! Thankfully, he never did fire me.

After a game in Iceland, I remember Bill Costley getting the directors together and making it clear he wasn't happy. He said: 'We don't go on these trips for a jolly, we are here for work.' After he finished, I said: 'Mr Chairman, it's my staff and players that are here to work. Europe is a huge bonus for everyone but directors should enjoy it, get out and about, sightsee, socialise, network. Leave the work to me and my guys.'

I had some great trips with Bill, going to scout players in England and on the continent. We made a trip down south to see a player and, after only two minutes, Bill said: 'I don't like him. Too heavy in the hips.' And that was that. There was no way I could sign a player if my chairman didn't rate him.

We got back to our hotel and Bill asked if I fancied a nightcap? But we were told by the receptionist that the hotel, one of these Travelodge-type places, didn't have a bar, so it was off to bed. We surfaced in the morning and Bill wasn't happy. He had slept in his clothes on top of the bed and told me he was going to have a word with the secretary, who made the reservation. Standards, you see. Bill was a perfectionist – every little thing had to be pristine and spotless. His standards were so high that he once complained that the brass door plate on the main door at Rugby Park was too smudged and he cleaned it. I was thinking, 'That's how people open the door, obviously it's going to get smudged.' I would avoid using it after that, because I didn't want Kim, our cleaner, to get into trouble. Bill was brilliant to work for, though. I would like to think we are friends, even though we are on different continents.

Our club secretary, Kevin Collins, was another great addition. He made sure we never fell foul of any laws, always knowing when players were suspended or when a player was ineligible to play. In fact, it was Kevin who made me aware we had to release Robert Prytz before the cup final, much to my dismay. We travelled a lot together, going abroad to check out the venues, training facilities and accommodation of European clubs we had been drawn against to make sure there were no problems for the team. Kevin liked a beer as much as I did and the trips were enjoyable but, when flying, you had to be aware with Kevin. He was pretty clumsy and, whether it was drink or food, he was liable to spill it – much like Leonard Rossiter and Joan Collins in the old Cinzano adverts.

These trips with Kevin were not always a barrel of laughs. We were due to play in Sarajevo against Zeljeznicar in the qualifying round of the UEFA Cup. This was not long after the Balkans war, when so many atrocities had been committed. Kevin and I had travelled to check out the facilities but the first attempt to land was aborted, because the pilot wasn't happy landing in the dark after the airport had had its radar blown away during the war. We landed in Vienna, stayed overnight and tried again the next day.

Once there, it was really harrowing and disturbing. We were met by their club secretary and he showed us around. I started asking him questions, because you could clearly see that all the buildings were damaged – every one of them. Even the hotel we were staying in had a hole in the side of the wall. It was smashed in where something had struck it. In saying that, our hotel was the only building that had escaped relatively unscathed. Because of the dignitaries who had been staying in it, they made a pact that they wouldn't target it. The whole place would have been beautiful if it hadn't been blown to bits. They had cable cars to go skiing and it must have been a stunning place at one time. I hope it is back to what it was. It was heartbreaking just listening to the secretary talk about things and, after a short while, he just broke down in tears and couldn't answer any more of our questions, because he was so upset. Behind the stadium was a hill and wherever the eye could see, it was covered in white crosses where the casualties of the war had been buried.

When we got back to Scotland, the players were very inquisitive and wanted to know about the place. I think they were anxious to ease their fears. I looked at Ian Durrant and was about to say it was not any worse than Kinning Park but then changed my mind and said Castlemilk.

I couldn't believe it when, a few days later, there was a story on the front page of the *Evening Times* quoting what I had said. One of the players had said to the press: 'The gaffer said it's no worse than Castlemilk.' I meant absolutely no offence but I got dog's abuse. Even Glasgow's Lord Provost, Pat Lally, who represented the people of Castlemilk, waded in! I had to go to Castlemilk with a TV crew and publicly apologise to residents. It was all taken out of context.

There was a bit of concern about the game taking place in Sarajevo but I was glad it did. Their fans were very noisy and created a great atmosphere. Their lives had been so harrowing. God knows how many people they had lost but for the 90 minutes of football, they would support their team. Before we left Kilmarnock for the game, I was accosted by one of our fans looking for money to contribute towards a big flag some fans were getting made and I duly gave him some cash. At kick-off, the Killie fans unfurled their flag, which looked huge until I looked to the Bosnian end and, when they unfurled their flag, it made the Killie flag look like a postage stamp. The game finished 1-1 and we scraped through 1-0 at our place, with a rare but important goal from Alan Mahood.

In the first round proper, we were drawn against Sigma Olomouc from the Czech Republic – another team we knew nothing about. Kevin and I were on our travels again and we flew into Prague. In sharp contrast to the previous round, the city was absolutely stunning and we were taken aback by the architecture and grandeur of the place.

Olomouc was an hour's drive away and when we arrived, we discovered they had rooms at their stadium, so that's where we stayed. It's only when you travel that you realise how far behind we are in Scotland when it comes to facilities. Theirs were fantastic and they had a brilliant youth system. We were looked after by one of their coaches, Thomas Trucha, who I still keep in touch with. He was here in Kenya briefly but left, as he wasn't getting paid, and is now plying his trade in Asia somewhere. A top guy.

We were well beaten by Olomouc, 2-0 away, and by the same scoreline at Rugby Park. They were big, strong and fast and most of their players had come through their youth system. I was thinking at the time how it was that they developed players to become that big and strong? Was it just natural to their culture? Was it what they ate or was it just genetic? I remember years later, when Gordon Strachan was Scotland manager, he was on the same subject about the Scottish players being a lot smaller and it's true – we don't have many 6ft-plus footballers. It's a hell of a disadvantage in general play and at set pieces!

These trips away were always a real highlight – be they for competitive action or for a training camp. The camps were excellent for team bonding and getting to know new players.

I had discovered a great venue in Germany. It was Bayer Leverkusen's training camp and was a great facility, moulded for athletes. When I took teams away, it was designed to get players fit but it was a training camp, not a prisoner of war camp. So, after training, the players were left to their own devices. I told them to go out, have a drink if they wanted but not to bring back women! Paul Wright asked if there was a curfew and I told him that I trusted them, would treat them like adults and expected them to behave and not over-indulge, so there was no curfew.

But I warned them all that training would be intense the next day, so, if they overdid it, they would suffer. I never had a problem with players when away in training camps – they knew it was necessary.

One night, we were out having a few and were heading back to the camp through an American army base and noticed they had a club. We chanced our arm and they let us in for cheap beer. The place wasn't busy but they had semi-clad women dancing on the bar. Gerry McCabe was first in and headed straight to the bar. I told Jim Stewart I fancied sitting at a table away from the noise, so we got some beers in and sent one down to Cabey, as he was skint. There was a guy sitting beside Cabey and they were chatting away. We were watching them and we noticed Cabey putting money into the dancer's knickers. Jim and I were chuckling away. I mean, where did he get the money? The dancers took a break and Cabey came to join us, laughing away. I asked him where he got the money and he told us the guy next to him had given him some. I asked how he was going to pay him back and he explained the woman dancer whose knickers he was putting the money into was the guy's wife and he would get his money back when she finished! If I had never seen it with my own eyes, I would never have believed it – it was hysterical.

Please don't get me wrong. I know this makes these trips sound like one big jolly but it couldn't be further from the truth. And I was so proud that our success in the league led to continental challenges. I loved the test it gave me as a manager and for my team. But I would get frustrated that, each time, our media would have us down as favourites, in every tie, when they knew next to nothing about the strengths of the opposition. Our fans would buy into it and then would be angry when we didn't get past the first round.

The press really don't help when they put you down as favourites and the fans read that crap and they believe it. Then, when it doesn't happen, they are disappointed and they blame the players, the coach and everybody else instead of blaming the press for bigging us up. That is through their own ignorance.

We faced Kaiserslautern, who were a force in Germany but were struggling in the Bundesliga at the time. We should have beaten them over there. We had two one-on-ones, through Ian Durrant and David Bagan, but we missed both. The German fans were not happy but Kaiserslautern got their tails up and got a goal and then another before half-time. It was difficult for us after that. They had French star Youri Djorkaeff in their line-up and a few other top internationals and we had what we had. What right did we have to get past them?

Things came to a head when we were drawn to face Norwegian side Viking Stavanger in the UEFA Cup. As usual, our press had it down as a formality.

Craig Dargo scored our goal in a 1-1 draw in the first leg at Rugby Park – meaning we were up against it in the away leg. I always took the players for a walk a couple of hours before the game and we were walking about Stavanger town centre and the fans were all in a good mood, all drinking, all in good voice and enjoying the occasion.

But the way the game went, it didn't start well for us. I'd worked a kick-off where we'd shape up to play the ball to the left and Alan Mahood would let it go through him and play it out to his right. Paul Di Giacomo would get the ball and he had great pace and would get up the park as far as possible, maybe get a shot away, make another pass or whatever. That was the plan but when Mahood was setting up to take the kick off, Di Giacomo wasn't on the right side, he was on the fucking left side. Sometimes with players, you have to spell things out to them, write everything down, do it on the board and make sure they have retained the information but Di Giacomo wasn't the brightest and didn't retain the information. There was no way we could change it round, because they would know that was what we were planning. So, we took kick-off, lost possession, they got a free kick just outside the box and scored from it, all in the space of a couple of minutes. That is so costly at that level and, sure enough, it cost us on the day. We were always in the game, we were never out of it, but they got a second and that was it.

The fans weren't happy after the game. The technical area was the opposite side from the dressing rooms and the main stand and, as I was walking over, I was applauding our fans for their support and making the effort to travel. All I got was V-signs and abuse and all I heard was 'fuck off, Williamson!' and 'Williamson, get tae fuck!' We got to the airport and the police didn't want to let us up to the departure lounge. They said our fans were not in a good mood, that they were angry and there had been trouble. I told them not to be stupid. I wasn't hiding from our own fans and I was going to go up. When I got there, sure enough, blood had been spilt and noses broken – punches had been thrown. I addressed the fans and told them what had happened and explained to them what we tried to do. It seemed to calm them down a bit but I didn't like that experience at all. I didn't like the abuse I had faced after the game. I felt I had done a good job for the club, won the Scottish Cup, reached a League Cup Final, brought in talented players and taken the team into Europe. The team had been up there challenging at the right end of the league. For the first time, I started thinking that perhaps my time at Kilmarnock was coming to an end. Maybe I had served my time at Rugby Park and had run my course. Perhaps I had taken the team as far as I could.

The fans used to write to the club, complaining about this and that; tactical decisions and my way of management, that type of thing. If they had left contact details on their correspondence, I used to love phoning them up and coming back at them. I got a real kick out of it. One time, I phoned a disgruntled fan and this young lassie picked it up; I assumed it was the guy's daughter.

'Hello,' I said politely. 'I wonder if I could speak to your father, please?'

There was a short silence before the young voice replied: 'He's up in the attic.'

'Could you get him for me, please,' I said.

'Who's calling?'

'It's Bobby Williamson.'

There was a kerfuffle at the end of the phone before I heard the young voice shouting: 'Dad, it's the phone for you.'

Then, slightly less clear, a frustrated voice shouted back: 'Who is it?'

'It's Bobby Williamson!'

Crash! Bang! Wallop! Thud! I thought the guy had fallen through the ceiling, until I heard him exclaim: 'What the fuck does he want?'

That still makes me laugh.

There was another guy who was constantly writing in to complain – and I mean constantly – but the bugger would never leave any details, so I couldn't pin him down. It was as if he didn't want to be found! Then, at some point in the season, we were raising money for a charity or a testimonial, I can't remember which, and fans were kindly sending in cheques. Of course, this fellow did likewise, only he had to include his contact details with his donation. Got him! I enjoyed that call as well.

But I knew my time at Rugby Park was coming to an end. I needed a new challenge and to stretch myself. I thought then that if another offer came in, I was off.

I went to La Manga in Spain with our new CEO, David Heath, who had joined us from Celtic. He was a really nice guy, who I worked well with. Ian Welsh had moved on to pastures new, back into politics, and he never did get the chance to sack me! I don't think he ever wanted to and we remained friends in the years ahead. We had travelled to watch a tournament involving Scandinavian and German teams preparing for the restart of their respective leagues. On the flight, David was reading a book called *The Alchemist*. I can't recall what I was reading but I finished my book and David had finished his, so we swapped. *The Alchemist* was about people going in different directions. David looked at me and said: 'Don't get any ideas about leaving!'

As it happened, there was an agent who travelled with us and he told me it looked like Franck Sauzée could be on his way out at Hibs and asked whether I would fancy it? I said I wouldn't contemplate it until the role was vacant. A week later, Sauzée was sacked and the agent asked me again. I remembered the abuse I had taken in Stavanger and thought maybe it was the time to leave and test myself with a new club to see if I could replicate what I had achieved with Killie. I told the agent that, if he could get permission from Kilmarnock, out of courtesy to them, I would speak to Hibs. I had a few people to speak to when I got back. I spoke to my assistants – Clarky and Cabey – and asked them if they would join me. They agreed. I think they needed a new challenge as much as I did. We had been at Killie for a long time and the players knew how we operated and they probably needed to hear a different voice. It was agreed we would go to Easter Road and meet the Hibs board and see what their expectations and plans were. The night before the meeting, I had to speak to my wife, Lorraine, and the children. When it came to my career, I was very selfish and made my own decisions but I wanted to let them know my plans and see how they felt about it. My kids didn't want me to leave Rugby Park. They were Killie fans and that was the only club they knew. They had even been on the open-top bus when we won the cup. My son, Steven, couldn't understand why I was leaving a club who were pushing for Europe to go to a club who were fighting relegation. I told him Hibernian were a big club with a huge fanbase and it was probably the time to leave. I felt the Killie fans were fed up with me and they needed a manager with different ideas. I loved Killie and still do. When I'm back in Scotland, I always make the effort to get down to Rugby Park. I believe I've still got a good relationship with them and always get a warm reception and the staff give me great hospitality.

That Friday night, I sat with Lorraine and we shared a couple of bottles of red wine into the early hours to discuss the move. I was quite woozy when the agent picked me up to go through to Easter Road. We went up to the boardroom and we were introduced to the chairman, Malcolm McPherson, and the CEO, Rod Petrie. Ken Lewandowski was also there and a few other directors, whose names escape me. We talked football and Rod Petrie and the agent went into Rod's office. After a while, the agent called me in and went through the contract with me.

In my ignorance, I was too trustworthy and was only interested that the wage we agreed was there and the length of the contract was right. I insisted on five years, the same I was on at Killie. The agent never went through every page with me – something I have insisted on ever since. I thought it was just a meeting to get to know each other but Rod Petrie insisted I signed the contract there and then! I told him I couldn't do that, as I was still the Kilmarnock manager. He told me to resign and he even had a resignation letter written out, which he put before me. He told me to sign that first. He wanted me to start that Monday to prepare the players for the St Johnstone game the following Saturday. I called the Killie chairman, Bill Costley, and told him I was joining Hibernian. He was pretty disappointed and it hurt me – I felt that I was letting him down, as we had a good working relationship and he was a great guy. But I had come too far down the road and I had made up my mind, so I signed.

I had to have a discussion with Cabey and Clarky and told them I had resigned and they would have to do the same. Neither of them wanted to do it that way. I told them I understood but there was no option. Clarky is a very loyal and trustworthy guy and categorically said he wasn't resigning. But I needed one of them to join me and Cabey was loyal to me. He resigned and our time at Kilmarnock was over.

CHAPTER 15
HIBERNIAN

FRANCK SAUZÉE was a former captain of the French national team, had been capped 39 times by Les Bleus and had won the Champions League with Marseille. He had come to Hibs when they were in the Championship and captained them back into the top flight. He had a marvellous habit of scoring wonder goals – often against Hibs' bitter rivals, Hearts. He never lost a derby game. His passion for the Easter Road club was encapsulated one derby day in March 2000 when he climbed high to head home the second goal in a 3-1 win. As he did so, his face implanted into the back of a Hearts defender's head, knocking out the Frenchman and ruining his smile, as his four front teeth were smashed to smithereens. As he lay there, with his face in the turf, it was unclear whether he even knew he had scored. It slowly dawned on his team-mates the predicament their skipper was in. For a good few minutes, he received treatment, then got to his feet, stuffed some white gauze in his mouth to stem the blood and ran back to restart the game with a defiant fist pump to the fans to acknowledge his goal. The Hibs fans went crazy. He was – and is – a legend in the eyes of the Hibs support. They refer to him as 'Le God'.

How the fuck do you follow that?

I was the 'Weegie Hun' replacing him in the dugout. The fact that the team had not won in 19 games was but a minor detail to the Easter Road faithful. Sauzée had replaced Alex McLeish when 'Big Eck' swapped the Easter Road dugout for the one along the M8 at Ibrox. His appointment was, I suppose, the obvious choice but it was a risk, as he had never managed before. It also meant that he hung up his boots to concentrate solely on managing the team – taking arguably Hibs' best player off the pitch. His only win as boss came in a Scottish Cup game against Stranraer – and even that was after a replay. They reached the semi-final of the League Cup but lost to Ayr United. In the league, they picked up only five points – all draws.

But they loved him. Still do. Following Sauzée as manager of Hibs was like walking on stage after Sinatra.

When I first stepped into the dressing room at Easter Road, it was like entering the football equivalent of the United Nations. I think the squad had about ten different nationalities. There were French, Danes and Austrians in one corner, Swedes and Germans in another. Over there was an Ecuadorian or a Canadian. Over there, an Irishman. And that's without including all the Scots. I knew immediately that the squad was far too big.

It really was a split dressing room. Don't get me wrong, they were all good players, but confidence was at rock bottom.

First up was a game against bottom club St Johnstone, who were fighting for their top-flight lives. If we were to lose, we would be dragged into the relegation scrap. I was grateful that Donald Park remained on the coaching staff. He had assisted

Frank Sauzée but he was kept on until the end of the season. I really wanted him to stay on after that, because he was such a good guy to work with, but was disappointed that the club would not keep him. Donald was a very good coach and he helped me tremendously. I depended on him to assist me and, initially, to select a team for the game against St Johnstone. Jim Clark had agreed to stay at Kilmarnock until they got a new manager and would join us when they did. So, it was me and Gerry McCabe to start with and it was not easy.

I had added Mathias Jack into the team to add a bit of steel and brought back Craig Brewster up front for some experience but I was nervous before the game. Ian Murray took the heat off with a goal in just the second minute and he added another not long before half-time. Just a minute later, Saints had Keigan Parker sent off. We wrapped up the three points midway through the second half with a Garry O'Connor goal. I couldn't have asked for a better start, but all around at the end of the game, the fans were still chanting the name of Franck Sauzée. I know it was probably directed more at the board than me but it was a clear indication I was going to have to work hard to win over the fans.

We would go on to pick up wins against Livingston, Dundee United, Motherwell and, again, St Johnstone to end the campaign with a bit of our respectability restored.

If I thought our end to the season would give us a positive bounce into the new campaign, I was wrong. There was a financial crisis building in Scottish football and there was no way a club like Hibs was going to be immune from it. The SPL chief executive at the time, Roger Mitchell, had come up with a plan for an in-house SPL TV deal, which was backed by all clubs except the Old Firm. When they pulled out, the deal was doomed and, with Sky having no intention of coming to the table, it left clubs like Hibs, who were so dependent on TV cash revenue, in a financial black hole.

The first indication of this came in relation to my two assistants, Clarky and Gerry McCabe. I had a meeting with the chief executive, Rod Petrie, who was very honest with me about the challenges the club were facing now the TV deal had hit the skids. But Clarky and Cabey only had deals until the end of the season and when their new offers were put to them, they were on much reduced terms. It is fair to say they were not happy. Neither was I and I went to speak to Rod about it. He explained again how tough the financial situation was but I had come up with a solution. I told Rod to take the difference out of my contract and split it equally with Cabey and Clarky.

'How does that help the club?' Petrie asked, quickly realising that it wasn't saving any money, just distributing it to a different place.

'It doesn't,' I said. 'But it helps my two assistants, who are only here because of me and it makes me feel better.'

Cuts were having to be made across the board. Players were being asked to take reduced wages, and win bonuses were to be decimated – going from £900 a win to around £100. It also meant our high earners were to be sold. It was maddening. When I was at Kilmarnock, I had lost out on signing the likes of John O'Neil and David Zitelli because they had gone to Hibs for better wages, and here I was, at last managing them, and having to show them out the door. Ulrik Laursen went to Celtic and Ulises de la Cruz went to

Aston Villa – for £1.5m each. It was good money but it still wasn't enough. There was even talk of leaving Easter Road and moving to a new stadium, which we would share with city rivals Hearts, with the club debt erased.

De la Cruz and Laursen were sold when we were in Finland for a training camp or some friendlies. On the way to the training ground one day, Clarky suffered an epileptic fit on the bus. It was shocking to see. As far as we all knew, it was the first time this had happened to him. There was one time when we were still at Kilmarnock when we had an evening game against Rangers at Rugby Park. Before the game, I had gone to speak to Jim McSherry, the commercial manager, in his office and found Clarky sitting there. He looked terrible and we immediately got the club doctor in to see him. He took one look and sent him to hospital, where he was diagnosed with a bleed on the brain. Thankfully, he made a full recovery that time, so, when this happened on the bus, everybody was in a state of shock.

The night before, we had been out for a few drinks and had got chatting to a group of women on a hen night. They were dressed up in the typical hen-do gear – wigs, short skirts, stockings. It was a bit of fun and we wished the bride well and that was it. But the next morning, Cabey came into my bedroom with a pair of stockings. Apparently, one of the women had thrown them on our table. I thought it would be a good laugh if Cabey put them on under his tracksuit and, when he was taking the warm-up, he could remove his trousers and run around in the stockings. I thought it would be a great way to lighten the mood. But, given what had happened on the bus, I thought how lucky it was that it wasn't Clarky with them on, because he was now heading to the hospital to be checked over by the doctors and nurses and stockings under his trousers would have taken a bit of explaining!

Despite the players heading out of the door, we still had to build a team for the new season. Mixu Paatelainen had asked me if he could train with us to keep fit, as he was looking for another club, and I was only too happy to say 'yes'. Mixu had been at Hibs a few seasons before and had spent a season in France with Strasbourg. He had endeared himself to the Easter Road faithful by scoring a hat-trick in a 6-2 derby win. I loved having him on the training ground, because he is such a great guy and such a great player. Mixu always looked to be carrying a bit of timber, as they say, but he was one of the fittest guys I had ever known. I was so impressed, I asked Rod if we could offer him a playing contract for a year and, to my surprise, he agreed we could.

One of the pre-season exercises was a 45-minute run at Arthur's Seat in Edinburgh. It was a distant run, designed to improve player aerobics. The players set off and, once they were away, it gave me time to return calls and things. About 35 minutes in, I see this young lad in the Hibs kit heading towards the end of the run and going at a hell of a good pace. There was no one else in sight until I spotted Mixu some distance behind.

When Mixu came in, spluttering after the run, I pulled him aside and asked him if he had kept an eye on the boy the whole time, because I feared there might be some cheating going on.

'Honestly, Boss, I had eyes on him – I had him in my sights all the way,' Mixu said. 'The boy's a machine!'

I congratulated the lad on his efforts – funnily enough, one of my youngest players and my oldest had come in first and second – and then pulled one of the coaches to get the lad's name. I was told it was Scott Brown.

I thought to myself that if this kid could play as well as he could run, he'd be in my team before the season was out.

It was a blessing in such troubled financial times that Hibs had such a fantastic youth set-up. I wasn't slow in introducing youth players into the team. I had done it at Killie and I would do it again at Hibs. As a manager, it's 24/7 and I mean that. Even on a Sunday, I would find myself at the science park pitches in Glasgow watching our under-16s. It was there one Sunday that I met Alex Cropley, who played well over 100 games for Hibs and plenty more for Villa and Arsenal. He and his wife were watching his son, Jordan. He was a tidy little player, had great potential and went on to play for Berwick. It's important to know what you've got coming through so that you can release older players on big money to bring through a younger player on less without weakening the team in any way. Hibs was a huge challenge but John Park, Alistair Stevenson and the rest of the coaches and scouts were discovering great young talent and it was up to me to convince the parents that Hibs were the team who could develop their boys. Steven Fletcher was one who was on the books but was not on professional forms. Young Steven was painfully shy and it was difficult to get a word out of him. I don't suppose he's like that now, given the career he's had in the English top flight and with the Scotland national team!

His mate was a lad called Jamie McCluskey, another I gave a debut to. I didn't realise at the time that he had become the youngest player to play for Hibs. If I had, I'd have held him back a bit, because he took the crown from a true Hibs legend in Lawrie Reilly.

There was a long conveyor belt of talent coming through at Easter Road. Even further down the age groups, there were kids like Lewis Stevenson breaking through. I didn't get a chance to play Lewis but he can now proudly claim to have set a club record for league appearances before eventually exiting Easter Road for Raith Rovers.

With Rod Petrie in the process of showing the big earners off the premises, it was my job to bring in the young talent to the first team.

Garry O'Connor was already in the team when I got there. He was never a problem at training or on the park – in fact, he loved training and was always, and I mean always, working on some way or another to improve his game. It's a cliché but he was always one of the last off the training ground. Garry's problem was off the park. I remember him passing his driving test and I took him aside to offer him the benefit of my experience. I told him not to get some flash car but, instead, a wee runaround that he could use until he got used to the roads. Garry nodded his head as if he was listening and taking in what I was saying but then, a few days later, he arrived in this flash supercar. He had written it off within the month.

During the season, we were getting ready for a game up at Dens Park against Dundee and Garry was named in the squad. I was making my way into my office when I realised my desk phone was ringing off the hook. It was Hibs fans calling in to tell me Garry had been seen drinking in a pub. By then, he was already late for the bus, so I phoned Rod Petrie to tell him what I was hearing. Rod had imposed this fitness coach on me as part of my backroom staff. I didn't want him but, as he worked with Tom Farmer, who owned the club, I didn't see how I could refuse. He was good in the gym with the players but I wasn't impressed with him on the field. He kept telling us he wasn't a 'Trojan horse' but I reckoned he was reporting back to Rod. That wasn't a concern for me, as I was keeping Rod in the loop with everything anyway – and I certainly knew I had to fill him in on this situation, even though I suspected he knew already. Rod said he would send the fitness coach to fetch Garry and bring him to Dens.

I told Rod not to bother. How could I possibly select him if he had been in the pub and had been seen by the fans?

Rod was insistent I put him in the squad and, although I can't be certain, I think I named him on the bench. That was another alarm bell that Garry had problems but he had such a great support network around him. His wife, Lisa, was a gem, his mum and dad were great and Rod was also there for him. He was a great lad. When he made his big-money move to Lokomotiv Moscow, he donated his signing-on fee to the Hibs youth academy. But he had his troubles – most of them well documented in the media – although I am delighted to have since read that he has come through it all and is in a far better place. I wish him well.

Derek Riordan was another local lad who had to be watched away from the ground. I would get fans calling me about Deeks, as he was known, but I never had a problem with him. He was a hard-working lad with bags of talent. He had fantastic ability, decent pace and was blessed with two good feet – as strong on his left as he was with his right. He was a joy to work with.

We had a midweek game at home to Celtic in what, I think, might have been the League Cup quarter-final and Deeks turned up for training with his hand all bandaged up. He had got caught up in a fracas in some pub, which didn't please me, as it was too close to a game. He trained well and was truly sorry for what had happened, so I named him in the squad. He was too good and too important to leave out. I was told that Deeks's relatives were a bit of a crowd and were always getting into trouble and he would get dragged into it. He was another who we had to drag off the training field. He would go on to have a good career – but it could have been better.

Ian Murray was such a superb talent with the great ability of being able to play almost anywhere. He endeared himself to me almost immediately in that opening game against St Johnstone when he scored two goals! Nid, as he was known, was playing at left-back but had such an engine on him that he scored one of those goals coming in from our right! He had such an enthusiasm for the game and could get around the park, which is brilliant for a manager, because it gives you so many options. He'd eventually move on to Rangers and have a spell down south with Norwich. I must admit, I didn't expect him to go into management, because I found Nid to be a quiet, unassuming guy. But he was a manager's dream – such a superb professional and an example to others.

Steven Whittaker was an excellent player who was developing when we arrived. It was clear that Whitty had the potential to reach the top and he would go on to sign for Rangers and play for Scotland. He was very like Nid, quiet and unassuming and another player who could get around the park. We didn't really know his best position; he could play anywhere on the left. We felt he would be better at left-back so that he had a lot of grass in front of him to run into and, boy, could he run! Interestingly, I didn't see him going into coaching either but he has, alongside that young lad who so impressed me that day on the Arthur's Seat run.

Scott Brown and Kevin Thompson have to be mentioned together, as they were inseparable. Both very talented – Kevin left-sided, Scott predominantly right-sided. I remember Rod Petrie telling me he was fixing them up with a flat in Edinburgh to save them travelling day in, day out, as Scott was in Kirkcaldy and Thommo was somewhere near the borders, I think. I didn't think it was a good idea – two young lads left to their own devices in the capital! But I had no need to worry. They both became great players and good professionals. They scored great goals for Hibs. Thommo scored a free kick against Celtic that got us to Hampden to face Rangers in the League Cup semi-finals and Broony scored a fantastic goal against Dundee United from around 20-odd yards with his left foot into the top corner. Scott had started wide right in that United game and then played up front, which will surprise many, given he would be known for his management of the midfield engine room. With Thommo, there was no questioning his position – central midfield. They both brought enthusiasm and energy into the team, which was just what we needed. The fans took to all these young guns, because they played with such heart, such energy and such ability. They gave the impression that if they weren't on the field playing for Hibs, they would be in the stands cheering them on. Broony was a winner and gave everything in every game.

Tam McManus was the joker of the dressing room but he was also packed with ability. The problem was that, for some reason, we could never get him fit enough for a full game and he would signal to the bench that he was done and we would sub him. He might have been playing well and the fans would be wondering why he was coming off. Tam never helped by always looking surprised when his number went up! We just couldn't get him fit enough to last a full 90 minutes and each time we had a physical day in training, usually a Tuesday, Tam would break down after a while, sink to his knees and start throwing up, meaning he had to stop the session. Tam had great ability. I remember him scoring two fantastic goals – one at Ibrox, one at Parkhead – and he was a great lad in the dressing room, always trying to wind people up. We played Celtic at Easter Road in the League Cup quarter-final and Tam started the game but, as usual, had to be subbed. He put on his tracksuit and sat there on the bench, kicking every ball. We were winning 2-1 and, as the clock ticked down, I noticed Tam removing his tracksuit bottoms. When the final whistle blew, he had the top off and ran on to the park to celebrate with the rest of the players. I immediately sussed out why. The fans who had not made the game would think he played the whole match when they saw the pictures in the papers the next day. He was a clever wee sod! Such a good player as well – just a pity his fitness levels were so much of a problem.

With this core of talented young players, we had the makings of a good unit but it was going to be too much to ask them to perform for the entire campaign. They had all the skill in the world but they were still raw and inexperienced.

Working on the tightest of budgets, we had to bring in some old hands. We brought in Colin Murdock from Preston. I had spoken at length to Craig Brown, who was the boss at Deepdale at that time, and he felt Colin would be a good addition. He was an intelligent lad, a qualified lawyer and a good pro. He didn't start well but found his feet. He was left-sided, which was a real asset.

We also brought in a number of Bosman signings. That was John Parks's department. John would find the players and we would have a look and work out if they could fit into the way we wanted to play.

I told John that we needed full-backs, so he looked around and brought in three for us to have a look at – Roland Edge, Craig James and Hungarian international Janos Matyus. That was always the way I worked. I'd get three or four players to have a look at, put them in order of preference and let the CEO or whoever sort it out. I would be honest with the CEO and say that if he couldn't agree with the first choice over wages or whatever but could strike a deal with the third choice, then I would be happy with that if it was the best financial outcome for the club. Likewise, I would be honest with the players. I would tell them that we were talking to a number of options, so if they wanted to join us, they would have to fit in with our wage structure and should be sure their agent was aware of that.

On this occasion, the three of them went into the discussions with Rod. When all the talks were completed, Rod came to see me. He doesn't smile often but, under his moustache, I could see he was pleased with himself.

'Which one did you want?' he asked me, still trying to stifle his smile.

'I'm happy with whatever best fits the club – they are all good players,' I replied.

Rod then nearly knocked me off my feet when he told me he'd signed all three! I couldn't believe it. I know Rod probably thought he'd worked a great deal – getting three for the price of one – but it was only going to give me an enormous headache. From then on, I was going to have two unhappy players kicking their feet around training and sitting in the stand because they weren't getting a game. Instead of just one player being paid a good wage, Rod was paying three players a lesser wage. It didn't make sense but, with time running out and the transfer window closing, the players didn't have much option.

That first full season was one of ups and downs but, with such a young squad, it was always going to be the case. In the end, we finished seventh – so, top of the bottom half of the table, never threatening the leaders but never fearing relegation in the rearview mirror either. We had too much to do to get into the top six but I thought our league finish was a good achievement when you think that, when we took over, we found a team lacking in confidence and belief. We lifted them and got a great response from the players.

In saying that, when we faced Hearts at Tynecastle for the New Year derby game, we knew that if we won, we would leapfrog our city rivals into third place. We hadn't started the season well and had some poor results but I felt we were heading in the right direction. I knew what young gems we had coming through. The fans didn't. They only want results today and aren't bothered about tomorrow and, to be fair, I understood that.

But no matter how hard I tried, I couldn't get the fans onside. I would hear it all the time. 'You're just a Weegie Hun! You're just a Weegie Hun!' I mean, I hardly played for Rangers really, my broken leg saw to that. I thought to myself, 'Alex Miller had been a previous boss at Hibs and was something of a Rangers legend and he didn't have to cope with this!'

It might all have been different had that New Year derby gone our way.

It must have been a great game for neutrals. It finished 4-4 but, to us, it felt like a defeat. We had gone 4-2 up in the 90th minute and that should have been that but two mistakes cost us the win – one from the referee Stuart Dougal and one from our most experienced player! I don't know how much time the ref had added on but we should have been able to see it out. There was a long ball played up from their half and Grant Brebner went up to head it. The Hearts lad up against him got a bit of leverage by putting his boot into Grant's thigh and won the header. From the flick-on, the ball broke to Graham Weir and he scored. Grant needed treatment for his knock, which was a clear foul. I knew the referee worked in Edinburgh and wondered if he favoured the boys in maroons, but that's enough of my paranoia! From the kick-off, we had a rehearsed move for this type of thing. Restart the match, get the ball to big Mixu wide left and let him keep possession, flick it on, anything to run the clock down. To my utter astonishment, Mixu was taking the restart! He was out of position, so our plan was doomed. We lost possession, Hearts raced up the field and Weir slotted in his second for the equaliser.

I was raging. As I started to walk down to their dugout to shake Hearts manager Craig Levein's hand, he was already running on to the park to celebrate. He checked and headed back towards me. There was a previous game when Hearts had beaten us – a 5-1 defeat but let's not talk about that – and I walked towards their technical area and Craig had taken off to celebrate with his fans and players. I waited for him to finish and when I shook his hand, I said: 'Could you not have done this first instead of me standing here watching you?' I've always made a point of not over-celebrating in front of the other manager. I know how bad he's feeling; I've been there plenty of times. To be fair to Craig, he did realise and shook my hand and let me go back to the dressing room.

We lost our way after that game and slipped down the league into the bottom six and a poor end to the season. If we had won the Hearts game, who knows? Football is a game of 'what ifs'.

That summer was to bring another crisis – well, two, in fact.

I was shocked when I got a tax bill for a tidy sum of money. I just couldn't understand it and, when I investigated further, I discovered that the agent's fee that had been paid by the club for doing my deal had been declared as a benefit in kind to me, meaning I was liable. It turned out Rod had declared all the players' agent fees, meaning the players were liable, too. Hibs were the only club I ever experienced who did this and the players were rather disgruntled, to say the least – as was I. I never agreed a fee with the agent. He agreed the fee with the club, as he was working mostly for the club. I went to the agent's office and asked him why I was paying the tax for the money he had received? Why had he not informed me that this was the case? The agent, who I won't name, simply shrugged his shoulders and said it was my bill and, therefore, my liability. I was fuming. I wasn't even his client. I didn't have a contract with him. He was working for the club, who had headhunted me! It was a shocking situation but my financial adviser, John Roberts, got it sorted. Even though I had to pay the taxman something, it wasn't the full whack.

The next problem came when I discovered that, unbeknown to me, a clause had been written into my contract stating that the club could serve me a year's notice at any time – effectively making my five-year contract a one-year contract. The first I knew about it was driving to training one morning when Lorraine phoned to say I had received a registered letter to the house from Edinburgh and did she want me to open it? It was from Rod, giving me a year's notice. I'll never forget it. It was 13 August 2003, my 42nd birthday, and days before the first Edinburgh derby of the season. Talk about great motivation! I phoned the chairman, Ken Lewandowski, who said he was totally unaware of the situation and that Rod hadn't said anything to him.

In hindsight, I know why that clause was inserted in my contract. The club, or Rod, didn't want to or couldn't afford to pay me the money that was agreed and we would have to renegotiate. So, it was back to that agent's office, where he tried to tell me that the clause had been added on the Monday, the day I had signed it. I knew that was nonsense. I knew that I had signed on the Saturday, because the club were so anxious to get the deal done to prepare for the St Johnstone game. I had, at Rod's insistence, signed the contract and the resignation letter for Killie on the Saturday and the agent had been there at the time.

It was not a nice situation. Another call to John Roberts, my financial adviser, and a new contract was negotiated on less money. There were reports all over the place that Hibs were already looking for someone to replace me and the new contract made me vulnerable, on less money and on a year's rolling deal.

The club released a statement which read: 'The board confirmed that discussions over contractual issues are taking place with Bobby Williamson and that it is hoped to resolve these issues as speedily as possible.

'These talks – dealing with personal and confidential matters between the club and its employee – are properly conducted in private. The club has no intention of breaking that confidence.'

The board also stated that I remained the manager and 'dismissed out of hand mischievous speculation that the on-going discussions were designed to end the manager's tenure'.

Even though I loved working for the club and was desperate to see the job through, the writing was on the wall. My relationship with Rod had been damaged. I didn't appreciate the fact that, even before I joined the club, Rod hadn't been up front with me. I had an office with a secretary, over beside Rod's office, which I used every morning. After that, I never went back. I did all my business from the staff dressing room. For Rod, it was just business and for the better of the club. For me, I felt cheated and decided that if another club approached me, I would go.

Rod only had the club at heart and did his best to control the finances – which he did very well, especially when you look at the young players he sold on for millions. He did a good job in that respect but I don't think the team, or football for that matter, was high up in his priorities. It was all about the money, whereas, for me and the fans, it was about the team. We wanted to see the money on the park, not in the bank!

On the park, we had picked up a few injuries and we had a few guys accumulating yellow cards and heading for suspension. I spoke to Rod on the phone and made him aware of our predicament and asked him if we could bring in a midfield player, as we would be struggling in that area in a month or two. There was a lad at St Johnstone who I felt would fit the bill and, as we had a surplus of centre-backs, I was willing to offer Paul Fenwick as a swap. I could have done the deal without any money changing hands. Rod told me in no uncertain terms that I couldn't do it, but I wasn't going to leave it there, so I phoned the chairman, Ken Lewandowski – a straight shooter and a good guy to work with. He was understanding of my problem but said Rod was right and it couldn't be done. I don't know if there was a clause in Paul's contract that meant he would be due money and that was why I was being denied. But I knew it would come back and bite us – and it did.

I tried to sign Andy McLaren, whose contract had expired at Killie. He came and trained with us for two weeks but Rod wouldn't sign him. I was so frustrated. I knew Andy could do a job for us, as we were short of wide players. He was really disappointed but, thankfully, he managed to get a contract at Dundee United and came back and scored against us at Easter Road. Andy hadn't forgotten and ran to the stand as he celebrated and shouted towards Rod. He never got paid for the two weeks he trained with us. We were both disappointed and again I never got a reason why Rod wouldn't sign him.

While our league form had not been great, we had performed brilliantly in the League Cup – putting out Celtic in the quarter-finals and Rangers in the semis at Hampden after a penalty shoot-out. It meant we were in the final against Livingston and 37,000 Hibs fans were going to the national stadium. For some reason, the media, pundits and bookies had us down as favourites. I couldn't understand why we had earned the tag. Livingston were in serious financial trouble, meaning they were having a squad clear-out, but they were hanging on to all their big names until after the game. They had a good manager in Davie Hay, and Jim Leishman was in there as well. They were packed with experience and I knew we were going to have a tough time.

Our lack of midfield options – which I had highlighted to Petrie weeks before – meant I played young Alan Reid which, in hindsight, was a mistake. I should have started with Tam McManus and brought on Alan when Tam had run his course.

In the game itself, we had two good chances. In the first half, Scott Brown was through one-on-one. It wasn't a great angle and the keeper blocked his shot and Marvin Andrews was able to clear Garry O'Connor's follow-up off the line. Broony also had a good chance at a corner. When Livi scored through David Lilley, it came against the run of play and their second, from Jamie McAllister, came when we were short at the back as we chased an equaliser. The dream of taking silverware back to Easter Road was over.

I knew my time at the club was coming to an end. No matter how hard I tried, I couldn't get the fans onside. In all honesty, I don't think they ever took to me and I was fighting a losing battle from day one. I was always a 'Weegie Hun'. I did one interview with a Scottish journalist and the headline read: 'If you want to be entertained go to the cinema.' To this day, I maintain I never said it and when I confronted the journalist about it, all he said was that he wasn't responsible for writing the headlines. But it has stuck and is thrown back at me to this day.

Despite all that, I loved my time at Easter Road. It was great to be involved with such a fantastic club with such a great history. I felt I was the right appointment at the time, along with Clarky and Cabey, as the money had fallen out of the game and clubs had to look to their kids and develop them. We had a great bunch coming through and we took a great interest in moulding them into first-team players. We weren't afraid to give them their opportunity and a handful of them grabbed it, taking their first steps in what would be incredibly successful careers.

It was a difficult decision to leave Hibs. I knew what we had coming through and that, with the right experience around them, they would be some team. I wanted to be a part of that but I knew my salary was a big concern for Rod and I felt the axe was hanging over my head if we really struggled. No one is indispensable and the contract row had really soured it for me. I never had a problem with contracts at Kilmarnock, where the club and directors kept improving the terms and conditions.

I was contacted by an agent to say that Paul Sturrock was leaving Plymouth for Southampton and would I be interested? I felt the opportunity to work in England was too good to turn down – it was something I had always wanted to try. I went down to speak to them, only to find that the same agent was also putting Terry Butcher in for the job. I wasn't happy and phoned the agent but he said not to worry – the Plymouth job was mine if I wanted it.

It was not any easy decision. I knew what I was leaving behind, on and off the park, at Hibs. Plus, I was dropping £25,000 in salary. The agent told me that, to sugar the pill, Rod would pay me the £25,000 but I never saw it. I was told Rod had taken offence to an interview I had done with Iain King in the *Scottish Sun*. I hadn't said anything derogatory about the club. Jock Wallace had always told me never to say anything bad about a club, even if it ended bitterly. I stuck to that advice but never saw the money.

There were great people at Hibs and although the fans never took to me, I took to them. They backed their team to the hilt. I met so many great Hibs fans and when I look at their results, I am always happy to see them doing well. Through the club, I met some fantastic people. The chairmen I worked with, Malcolm McPherson and Ken Lewandowski, the unsung heroes like the groundsman, Tam McCourt, and his team, the office staff. I even mixed with celebrity Hibs fans like actor Dougray Scott, who introduced me to American star Jennifer Love Hewitt. I met The Proclaimers, although I still don't know which one is which!

I wish I could have given them the success the club deserved but I will always maintain I left the team in a better place. Every time I watch and hear the Hibs fans singing 'Sunshine on Leith', be it at Hampden or Easter Road, I get a lump in my throat and a tear in my eye.

CHAPTER 16

PILGRIMS PROGRESS

I LEFT Hibs knowing it was a job unfinished and that, had that clause in my contract not been imposed, I am sure I would have stayed and could have brought success to Easter Road. I knew the club had to sell their promising young players but I also knew there was another stream of talented players coming through, led by the likes of Lewis Stevenson. But it was not to be and my future lay 500 miles away in Plymouth.

The Pilgrims had been languishing at the very bottom of the English leagues until Paul Sturrock took charge in the year 2000 and led them into the third tier, where they were pushing for another promotion into the almost unheard-of reaches, certainly for Plymouth at that time, of the Championship. But that success meant there were envious eyes watching them and, especially, their manager. Just along the coast, Premier League Southampton had announced that Gordon Strachan was leaving and they quickly appointed Sturrock in his place. He had put in a good word for me when the Plymouth post became vacant and the recruitment process, for what it was, was extremely straightforward.

As I have said, I didn't want to leave Hibs but I had always wanted to try my hand at management in England and this seemed a perfect opportunity. It all meant that I was joining a Plymouth side that was in buoyant mood and pushing for another promotion.

In the days and weeks before I joined, I was being kept up to speed by their assistant manager, John Blackley. Sloop, as he was known to everyone after the Beach Boys' song 'Sloop John B', was, ironically, a Hibs legend. He was No.2 to Sturrock and was holding the fort at Home Park, alongside Kevin Summerfield, until my arrival. Both were top coaches but neither wanted to be the main man. They were going to be joining Sturrock, and Sloop was imploring me to get down there as soon as possible. They had taken nine matches in temporary charge, had just lost back-to-back games against Bristol City and Oldham and I think things were getting a bit nervy.

I arrived at Plymouth with three games remaining. We only had to win one to be guaranteed promotion. It was odd going into such a positive set-up, knowing I had absolutely nothing to do with that success. More often than not, you start your job as a new manager when things have not been going well for the previous incumbent. There is usually a squad needing to be lifted or, indeed, cleared out, angry fans upset at the way the club are doing and a hell of a lot of work to be done to turn around results. This was totally different. Plymouth were a team who were used to winning. The first game was against QPR at home and they just happened to be one of our rivals for the title. I arrived just a few days before the game and thought it best to take a backseat and let them get on with it – watching and assessing from afar.

On game day, I had planned to take a seat in the stand and let Sloop and Kevin deal with the team. But David Friio,

Plymouth's talented, goalscoring French midfielder, came to me to say the players would appreciate my presence in the dressing room and technical area. I was happy to do that but I didn't think it was right to pick the team. I had, of course, done all my research on the squad but I had no idea who was on form, off form or carrying an injury.

I had a quiet word beforehand with Kevin, asking him if his team selection was leaving out anyone who would feel they should be starting. He told me that he was not going to be playing club captain Paul Wotton – I can't remember the reason for his decision – and, while I wasn't going to interfere, I felt a bit of my managerial experience would be valuable to Kevin. I suggested that it would be best to have a quiet word with Paul, so that he could digest the disappointment in his own space without it dominating the dressing room. Kevin chose not to take my advice and, when he named the team just an hour before kick-off, I watched Paul for his reaction. He was distraught. Being named on the bench for such an important game was no consolation for the guy. He stormed into the shower room and the rest of the team couldn't help but notice. I followed Paul in. Remember, I hardly knew the guy at this point, but I told him he still had a huge role to play in the day, that he was the captain and he could still show leadership for this vital game, even though he wasn't playing. I think Paul understood and, to his credit, he returned, hid his disappointment and gave the team all the encouragement they needed.

I think such a situation is a critical point in management and I have learned from my mistakes – such as that League Cup Final with Kilmarnock, when I left out Paul Wright and Martin Baker. The way you handle a player can be crucial. It can be a crushing disappointment to them when they are not named in the team. They have worked all week for game day and are being told to sit it out. It can be embarrassing, as the rest of the players look for a reaction. As a manager, if I had to make changes to the team who started the previous game, I would tell the player before I named the team so that he was prepared and didn't show his disappointment to the rest. If he wasn't happy, he could come and see me on Monday. The dressing room before a game is neither the time nor the place for such a discussion.

In all my time in management, I don't remember a player ever coming to see me on a Monday morning.

I gave the lads a bit of a team talk, which was more like a pep talk really. I told them to be powered by their desire to win and their desire to secure promotion.

Plymouth's Home Park was bathed in sunshine for the visit of QPR and nearly 20,000 fans packed into the place. In a tense encounter, we left it late before goals from Mickey Evans and David Friio, scored in the last ten minutes, wrapped up the points. The place was absolutely bouncing. One game in and I'd already won a title! But, as much as I was delighted for them, I didn't think this was my triumph at all. I was just happy to share in the party atmosphere.

I got presented with a medal for winning the league but I gave it to Jacko (the late Ian Pearce), the kitman at the time. He was a lovely man and a good part of the dressing room. The players used to take the mickey out of him and he used to give as good as he got. I'm sure he is sadly missed.

The season had finished and Clarky and Cabey, who were still in Scotland, were to join me for pre-season. I got a phone call from Paul Sturrock asking me for a favour and, as he was instrumental in getting me the post, I thought I owed him one. What he was asking left me with a heavy heart – he wanted me to keep Sloop on as one of my assistants. I had absolutely no problem at all with Sloop. I liked him and had a lot of time for him but I always worked with just two assistants, so it left me with a very difficult decision to make. It was good having Sloop around. He knew the place, the players, the lay of the land, as it were, so he was very useful to me. But keeping him on was a big mistake, because it meant I would have to be giving Cabey or Clarky some bad news. I had known Cabey for such a long time but I also loved working with Clarky. I knew his wife, Anne, and his family. We were good pals but, if I was going to have a difficult conversation with him, I had to do it face to face. I drove to his house, all the time trying to convince myself that taking him all the way down to Plymouth was not a good move. I told him that the travelling from the south-west of England was a killer, that every away game meant overnight stays and that it would be detrimental to his health. Even now, when I think about it, I am saddened. It was the biggest mistake of my career and one I regret to this day. Clarky had been key to everything we had achieved. He was a rock who had helped me tremendously and I had let him down. It says everything about the guy that we remain good friends to this day. He could easily have binned me – I wouldn't have blamed him – but he didn't and I will always be grateful to him for that.

At the end of the season, the club had fixed up a trip to Magaluf for the players and directors. I loved these trips and I thought I should go along and get to know everybody better. It was a good trip, incident-free; just a lot of drunkenness, which is what these trips are all about. They call it team bonding. It's frowned upon nowadays. These days, everybody has a mobile phone, and a video of players can quickly be on social media and in the press. Nobodies taking pictures of somebodies for a few quid. Back then, it was a bit more innocent and I soon found out that Plymouth was a very sociable club. That is good to a point but I don't think it's healthy when players make friendships with directors and members of the board. I know for a fact that when these friendships are struck up and a player becomes disgruntled for one reason or another – and it will happen – he will fabricate crap about the manager, and the director will share these gripes with his peers. It doesn't happen too much in Scotland but it is prevalent in England and it's cost many a manager his job. In the press, they tend to say, 'He's lost the dressing room.'

The club organised a pre-season trip to Austria. It was a training camp I had been to with Kilmarnock, so I knew my way around. It was a good trip and one that allowed me to build my relationship with the chairman, Paul Singleton. One night, we let the lads off the leash, as there was a festival going on, with drinking and food tents all around. It wasn't unusual for the directors and players to be together. I don't know who talked me into it but the locals thought it would be a good idea if I put on a pair off lederhosen and pranced about on the stage. The local beers were kicking in, so I agreed.

The players were killing themselves laughing. We worked hard on these trips but I felt I was building a rapport with the players, which is very important.

To get home, the chairman and I found a couple of bikes, which we borrowed, and tried to negotiate our way back to where we were staying but, through a combination of the booze, the darkness and the strange surroundings, poor Paul came a cropper.

It was a laugh and the whole club were bonding. We had a few games arranged and wherever games are, fans will always follow. I remember one night we found ourselves in a pub with a lot of Plymouth supporters, who were mingling with players and directors. The chairman had brought his son and daughter with him and his son had heard a fan say something derogatory about his sister. He confronted the lad and then Paul piled in and threw a punch at the offending fan. Okay, drink may have been taken but I won't blame any father for defending his daughter's name. There were press guys with us and I did worry whether this incident would get out. But we had a meeting with them and it never came into the public domain. I've had my issues with newspaper guys before but the Plymouth crew were very supportive and positive about the club.

I had a meeting with Paul before the season started and asked him what he expected from me and what he would consider a successful season would be. He said all he wanted was for me to ensure we stayed in the Championship. It didn't matter if it was by a single point or even goal difference – survival was key.

I had bigger ambitions than that. I wasn't fazed at all with mixing it with some big clubs in England – it inspired me.

I inherited a good bunch of players. I had good competition in goal, with a young Luke McCormick pushing Romain Larrieu. There was Tony Capaldi, a Welsh international on the left, and David 'Chuck' Norris on the right. At centre-back, we had Paul Wotton and Graham 'Coco' Coughlan. Hasney Aljofree could play there as well and at left-back, which gave Peter Gilbert a challenge at right-back. We had David Worrell and Paul Connelly, Mickey 'Trigger' Evans and Marino Keith. Nathan Lowndes and Scott Taylor gave us competition up front. David Friio played in midfield, with competition from Stevie Adams and Lee Hodges. I felt these guys deserved an opportunity, after winning back-to-back titles, to play in the Championship.

We started the season well and Friio found himself out of the team through suspension. When he was available again, he couldn't find a way back into the team and had to settle for a place on the bench. He wasn't happy and came to see me, looking for a transfer. I had heard that Nottingham Forest were keen on him.

I was honest with him. I said: 'David, if you were playing and the team was winning, would you be happy if I took you out? I've got a squad of players, which we need, and I'm not changing a winning team. You'll just have to be patient.'

He still wasn't happy and was in and out of the starting line-up, although he did score twice in injury time to get us a win against Gillingham in October, when we had been a goal down going into the 90th minute!

Leaving players out is the hard part of a manager's job but it is also difficult to get the directors to understand. They always want the best XI to start but my best XI was the team that won the previous week. If my best players were sitting in the stand and we were still winning, it would hold us in good stead when they got back in. If I took a player out because a supposedly better player was available and we lost, what next? The player I take out is going to be disgruntled and his head will go down. You've got to look after the whole squad and it is difficult to keep them all happy. You can't be telling them one thing, then be doing another. If a player got injured or suspended and the team were winning, they would have to earn the right to get back in. That's what directors, fans and journalists can't understand. They will say: 'The manager doesn't know his best XI.'

Bollocks! It's not just about the XI on the park, it's a squad. Have managers got to state their best XI and tell the other 20-odd players they will only be playing if one of those XI is unavailable? And then, that when they do play, they will automatically drop when the rival for their place is available again? No way in hell would that work. You have to create competition in your squad and be honest with them. No player is happy if not selected but there were very few times when a player came to me to tell me he should be playing – although one or two directors did!

Our first game was the visit of Millwall to Home Park and we fought out a goalless draw. Then it was Brighton away, Cardiff away and Sunderland at home. Three tough games but wc won them all. We lost at Watford but then won when Nottingham Forest came to our place. What a start to the season it was – I think we were top of the league at one point. But it is often the case that the newly promoted team in a league starts the season like a train. Opposition clubs don't know you that well and haven't worked you out. They soon get the measure of you, though, and that season certainly got tougher. As the team had earned back-to-back promotions, there was a great spirit in the squad and that can carry you a long way. I didn't want to change much but I did add a few to strengthen the squad, mostly from a market I knew. We brought Stevie Crawford, then a regular in the Scotland squad, Lee Makel, Matt Doumbe, Steven Milne and Keith Lasley, all down from Scotland, and, even though Stevie had to return home for family reasons in the January window, they all did really well for me.

Despite results beginning to turn, we were still very much batting above our average. We were never in any relegation trouble. In the FA Cup, we held our own against Premier League Everton before eventually losing 3-1.

I always looked on the Championship as three leagues of eight. The top eight were pushing for promotion and the play-offs, the middle eight were always safe and the bottom eight were the ones for whom relegation was a concern.

But I was also finding out a lot about the players in my squad – what they were capable of and, more importantly, what they were not. The Championship is an incredibly tough and competitive league and the quality is very high. You are aware that some players who have performed so well in League One and League Two struggle when they make the next step up, because they are coming up against teams and players who have performed in the Premier League and are desperate to get back there. It all becomes too much for them, the gulf proving too big.

We played a game at West Ham, who had been relegated from the top flight a couple of seasons before, and were really pushing to get back up. They had Teddy Sheringham playing up front – a real class act of a striker. Our defender Graham Coughlan, or Coco as he was known, had been outstanding for the previous two seasons and he was a huge fans' favourite who always gave everything in every game. But he had not faced someone like Sheringham and we were 3-0 down when the Hammers launched another attack. The ball was played out wide but I kept my eye on the box to see how we would defend the cross. Coco followed Sheringham all the way and was touch tight on him. Then the striker took two steps back and Coco followed but, by then, Sheringham was making three steps forward. By the time the cross came in, he was five yards clear of Coco and scored with a free header at the near post.

That was the difference and it was hurting us.

We had a run of three away defeats – 5-0 at West Ham, 5-1 at Sunderland and 3-0 at Millwall. I had a meeting with the chairman, Paul Stapleton, and he was not happy. He said he was concerned, because he had never lost three in a row in all his time at the club.

'With all due respect, Mr Chairman,' I said, 'you've been used to playing the likes of Rochdale, Hartlepool and Stockport. Sunderland and West Ham are still getting their parachute payments from when they were in the Premier league. Millwall were in the FA Cup Final last season.'

I really felt the criticism was unfair and, eventually, Paul agreed with me. But it was a warning sign.

Paul Sturrock's tenure at Southampton lasted less than six months. Appointed in March 2004, he was out by the August – leaving the club by 'mutual consent'. You would wonder why that would affect me at all but life at Plymouth got harder once Sturrock was appointed to Sheffield Wednesday in September. At Southampton, in the Premier League, none of our players interested him. But at Sheffield Wednesday, who were in League One, he knew our players could do a job for him. He also took John Blackley to Wednesday, which disappointed me greatly. When John spoke to me about joining Luggy, I felt he had let me down. I had left a good man back in Scotland to keep Sloop on and he had left to go to a guy who had left him behind when he got a job in the top flight. I had to find another assistant and I persuaded Jocky Scott to come to us from Sunderland. It was another big mistake. Cabey wanted us to go it alone, as his wages would have increased, but I wasn't comfortable working with one assistant. In my time as a manager, Jim Clark and Cabey had worked brilliantly together, so, too, did Sloop and Cabey but Jocky and Cabey never worked. Jocky wanted to do everything. He wouldn't include Cabey and the relationship and the atmosphere just deteriorated. It got to the stage that Cabey was so unhappy he became homesick and hankered after a trip back to Scotland. He desperately wanted to go back at Christmas but that is a really heavy fixture programme for clubs in England and we had a game at Elland Road against Leeds around Boxing Day. Cabey called me and asked if he could miss it, go home to Scotland and come back after. I told him I couldn't give him permission for that and tried to explain that we all suffer in football around the festive period. I said I would ask the chairman, who said 'no', but Cabey went anyway and was fined when he got back. We lost the game to Leeds 2-1 in what was also Stevie Crawford's last game for us. He scored but the ref, under pressure from the Leeds fans, ignored a foul on Matt Doumbe, which led to a Leeds winner.

I thought we had a decent season, we played some very good football and finished top of the bottom eight, despite having the lowest wage bill in the division. We were never in a relegation battle. The previous summer, the chairman had said he would be happy if we escaped the drop on goal difference but I think he must have changed his mind as the season went on. Nevertheless, I was delighted with our season and thought we had really done well.

I thought I had a good relationship with Paul Stapleton. We socialised a lot together and he would invite me and my wife over to his house. I liked both him and his family. He was a great guy and we would dine together most weekends. But things changed when Sturrock went to Wednesday. Luggy was never one to burn his bridges and always kept in touch with his former chairmen – something I never did, because I always felt it was unfair to the current manager. Luggy's friendship with Paul certainly affected my own.

I had lunch with the chairman one day and we got round to talking football. I felt we needed a creative midfielder player who could play off the front in the No.10 role. I told him I had had a conversation with Terry Cooper, who I never met, but had a great working relationship with. He was always available to me at the end of a phone but sadly passed away a couple of years ago. He was always a font of knowledge when it came to talent and he mentioned a player at Southampton who could do a job for us. We had already taken Jason Dodd and Dexter Blackstock from them and both were good acquisitions, especially Doddsy. He brought great experience as a good professional and a good organiser. Dexter was with us for experience but had huge potential.

I mentioned Terry's player recommendation to the chairman, who couldn't have appeared less excited. I dropped it there and then – if I don't get encouragement from a chairman about a player, there is no point pursuing it.

Later that night, Paul phoned me and said he had been speaking to Luggy, had mentioned we were looking for a creative midfielder and Luggy had told him about the lad from Southampton who I had mentioned at lunchtime!

I was raging.

'Paul, that's the lad I mentioned to you at lunch!' I said.

'I thought I'd heard his name before,' Paul replied.

'Are you telling me we've to get Luggy's say-so before we can sign a player?'

Paul didn't answer but I was fuming. When I told Jocky Scott about it the next day, he joked that Luggy must be some manager if he could manage two teams!

It was also starting to affect my relationship with the players and it was with Coco Coughlan that things really started to concern me. He was looking for a pay rise, because he had seen the club skipper, Paul Wotton, get a rise when he signed his new deal. Coco felt he deserved the same. I explained to him that Wotty could play at the back and also in midfield, scored goals from dead-ball situations, penalties and free kicks and that was why he got an improved contract. I told Coco he would be getting a new deal but not on as much as Wotty.

I spoke to the chairman, who told me Sturrock wanted Coco at Wednesday. I said I wanted him to stay but the chairman questioned my decision, given he was aware I wanted to bring in other centre-backs. I argued that I wanted four in the squad competing for two places and that Coco – even though I had concerns about him at Championship level – was certainly one of them.

But I believe the chairman was revealing all this to Sturrock, that he wanted him to get the player and that Sturrock, in turn, was telling Coco. So, when I was telling him I wanted him to stay, Sturrock was telling Coco that the chairman had told him otherwise. For that reason, I don't think Coco believed anything I was telling him.

He eventually got his move to Wednesday. Coco is a good guy and a strong family man. I wish him all the best.

That summer, after one season in the Championship when we finished top of that bottom eight that I talked about, I knew I had to get more experience into the squad. I brought in Anthony Barness from Bolton and Rufus Brevett from West Ham. I also signed Hungarian international midfielder Ákos Buzsáky from Porto and Bojan Djordjic from Rangers, having already brought in striker Bjarni Guðjónsson in an earlier window.

I was then made aware that Taribo West was available. He was out in Italy, where he was managing to stay fit, even though he was without a club after a short spell in Qatar. He was a legendary figure who had starred for Inter Milan and had 42 caps for Nigeria and it was a transfer I thought might catch the fans' imagination. It took a while to get him to Plymouth but I'm not sure he was totally honest about his age. He told me he was 34 but he looked 44!

He came over and did pre-season and travelled to Sweden with us to play a few games. On the way back, we landed at Heathrow and I was standing at the carousel when I got a phone call from immigration. They had detained Taribo and I had to come up to sort it. When I got there, they told me he hadn't got the necessary papers! Taribo had told me he qualified as an Italian citizen but immigration could not find that in his passport and were refusing him entry. Somehow, I talked them into letting him enter. We had a couple of friendlies lined up but he assured me he would return to Italy the following week and sort out his paperwork.

Taribo was true to his word but when he got back, his fitness had dropped off and, even after we got him back to a decent level, he was not the same player. When players get to a certain age, they can still run and look very fit but it's a different story in a game. Taribo only played two games under my tenure. His first was a 1-0 defeat to Hull in which he got booked and was at fault for their goal. But there was so much more to Taribo – he was a God-fearing guy who worked – and still, I think, works – as a pastor. All the time he was with us, he was sending money back to people and good causes in his native Nigeria.

At the end of the season, the players headed off for a well-deserved break. I had a meeting with my backroom staff to schedule everything for pre-season and then headed back to Scotland and a family holiday. Before I left, the chairman pulled me in for a word and asked when the coaching staff would be coming back. I told him the pre-season was sorted and they would be back with me a few days before the players. Paul was adamant that wasn't good enough, demanding myself and my coaches come back far earlier than that and insisting that the break was too long. I told him it was the same break as the previous close season and he fired back that that had been too long as well. I explained to him that, once the season started, it's an end to any breaks – no public holidays, having to work over Christmas and New Year – and that my staff and their families made significant sacrifices to do the job. Paul wasn't having it but I told him I wasn't changing the timings and that if he wanted the staff back early, he would have to tell them himself.

'They're your staff, you deal with it,' he said.

'Well, if they're my staff, leave it to me to decide when they come back after their break,' I answered.

Again, I was feeling this undercurrent within the club that some people on the board were not happy. We ended up with too many board members. I believe that, for a club to function successfully, you need one man calling the shots, not everything being decided by a committee, when there are too many differences of opinion.

Then I got a warning call from Sloop. He told me I would do well to watch my back where one director was concerned, because he had it in for me. I was shocked, because this guy, who I won't name, was a friend – or so I thought. At the time, I was also hearing from people that social media rumours were spreading alleging I was barred from pubs and getting into fights with taxi drivers. It was all bollocks. I don't deny I enjoy a drink – I've never hidden that – but I always ensure I represent myself and my club correctly. And I loved my time in Plymouth, I loved the place and the people. It's a beautiful part of the world and I would often go deep into Devon and Cornwall, touring the countryside. The fans are fantastic. They have a supporters' club in Cornwall St Dennis and it takes these guys three hours to get to a home match. It's incredible. But to hear that these rumours were circulating about me – and to know or suspect who was driving it from within the club – made life very difficult.

Pre-season was tough, trying to get players' fitness and contracts sorted out. We had a friendly at Torquay and, when I was walking up the touchline, I heard a fan say I would be out after six games. He was clearly saying it loud enough for me to hear. Our first game of the season was away to Reading – not an easy game but we managed to win 2-1. On the long journey back, the bus driver turned on the radio to listen to the usual fan phone-in and normally I would have asked him to switch the station. I don't normally listen to or read media stuff, because it is always so negative. But this time, after a good away win, I thought the fans would be happy, so I listened in. A Plymouth punter came on to say he was happy with the result but that I would be out of a job in six games. The same specific number of games I had heard before! As I said, I loved Plymouth but it is like a village and everyone knows the gossip. I worked on regardless.

Our next game was Watford at home in midweek. We were 3-1 up at half-time and looking good for another three points. Then Watford scored two free kicks from a young Ashley Young to clinch a draw. We played Derby away on the Saturday and lost 2-0. The following week, we lost 1-0 at Palace and then 1-0 at home to Hull. We had an international weekend coming up, so it was a free weekend. A former player, who I knew from Scotland and now lived in the area, asked me if he could come in and watch us train. He watched the players in a small-sided game before some serious running and then he asked me where Jocky was. I told him that, because there was no game at the weekend, I had agreed he could go home to Scotland. Just like that, the visitor made his excuses and left. He was a right gossip and, before long, the chairman found out that Jocky wasn't there. I should have told him. I wasn't hiding anything but it was my decision to let Jocky go home. It wasn't helped by the fact that Cabey had already left the club. He hadn't been happy for some time. The partnership with Jocky wasn't working for him and it was beginning to affect his health. Cabey is one of my best mates and to see him like that was difficult. When he agreed his settlement to go, I think it was a relief but allowing Jocky a short break was another nail in my coffin.

We had a long two weeks until we faced Brighton away but I was on the lookout for a striker. Our games were tight. We weren't conceding a lot of goals but we weren't scoring many. I was made aware of a boy at Blackburn I could get on loan – Matt Derbyshire – and I had travelled up to Lancashire to watch him in a reserve game. I knew he could do a job for us, and put the wheels in motion.

We lost 2-0 at Brighton and the chairman collared me and asked me to assemble the players on the Monday for what he called a 'clear the air' meeting. It was strange listening to the players have their say, opening up with criticism of formations and tactics – even the injured players and those on the fringes were having their say! It all became clearer 24 hours later. We had a reserve game at Home Park the following evening and, when I turned up for the game, there was a press photographer snapping away, which I thought was unusual. At half-time, someone said I was to pop into the boardroom after the game. Matt Derbyshire scored a hat-trick, which was positive, but when I went into the boardroom, it was a full house. I sat down and the chairman told me I was sacked. I stood up, shook all of their hands, even the snakes, and wished them all the best. That was all I said. We had beaten Reading away and drawn at home with Watford – both of whom had been promoted that season. I knew that if I had been given time and the new players were allowed to find their feet, we would have done well. I really enjoyed Plymouth but I believe that, financially, the club made a huge mistake. They brought in Tony Pulis – a big name in management down south and one who would appease some of those on the board who felt I wasn't a 'name' – and would have been paying him far more than they ever paid me. With me on gardening leave, they were effectively paying for two managers.

Everybody in Plymouth seemed to know I was getting sacked – apart from me, that is. Well, I did have a good idea my departure was imminent. Everybody in the office heard Michael Dunford, our CEO, talking on the phone to my successor. He was a bit deaf and didn't realise he was talking so loudly.

And the phone-in punter on the radio and that fan in the stand were both right – the sacking did come after six games!

More importantly, the players knew, and when the players know the coach is on his way out, standards drop. I don't know if this is deliberate but it happens. I don't know when they knew but they certainly knew when we had the clear-the-air meeting the chairman suggested. I'm positive one or two were told to ask certain questions. Some players were asking questions I don't think they would have asked if I wasn't getting sacked. I never took any calls from the press, which was a mistake. I should have taken that opportunity to thank the staff and the fans for their support, so I'm doing it now. They were great and the fans were superb – the most loyal and supportive in England. I'm glad they are back in the Championship and hope some Middle East prince comes in, throws money at them and takes the club to the Premier League. I had bought an apartment in Plymouth, on the Barbican. I really enjoyed the place and would have loved to have finished my contract but I believe the directors were over-ambitious.

Jock Wallace's advice from all those years before was going through my head again. When you leave a club and can't say anything nice, don't say anything at all. But the whole episode set my career back. I was on gardening leave and couldn't do anything – no TV work, punditry, coaching, nothing. I feared that I would be forgotten about if I didn't get back in the game.

I headed back to Scotland, regrouped, recharged my batteries and prepared to go again. I thought I wouldn't be out of work for long – aye, right!

I took a call from my old club, Rotherham. I really enjoyed my time there as a player and thought long and hard about going back as manager but the way it was put to me, I thought it was too much of a risk. The money was a lot less than what Plymouth were paying me for doing nothing and my old assistant manager at Rotherham, Phil Henson, was honest and upfront with me. He told me I would be putting out a lot of fires. So, with a heavy heart, I declined the offer, thinking there would be another opportunity further down the line.

I spoke to the Livingston chairman, Pearse Flynn, about the manager's position but I obviously didn't impress. I thought I had done a decent job at both Kilmarnock and

Hibs but now I couldn't get a job back in Scotland. The Dunfermline job was vacant and I spoke to Jim Leishman, who told me I had been badly represented by a young agent. I asked him if the job was still vacant and whether I could apply but I was taken aback by his response. He said that the club had just let Davie Hay go and that they thought I was too similar. Now, Davie Hay was a great manager and Jim had just given me a great compliment but we were from different eras as players. Davie is a legend at Celtic but is about 13 years older than me. When Jim said 'something different', I was thinking, 'Yeah, the First Division will be different.' They brought in Stephen Kenny. His CV stacked up in Ireland but, unfortunately, Dunfermline got relegated.

When the phone stopped ringing, I began to look back at my career. When I took over at Kilmarnock, we flirted with relegation but by the time I left, we were an established top-six team who were fighting for Europe. When I went to Hibs, they were in danger of being relegated but, thankfully, that never happened. Many coaches have come in and done very well. Tony Mowbray had them playing good football, which I think I could have produced if I hadn't left for Plymouth. John Collins won the League Cup and Alan Stubbs won the Scottish Cup to end more than a century of misery. At Plymouth, I had kept them in the Championship, which is no easy feat.

But after more than a year, I was still on the outside looking in. Then I got a call from an agent called Kofi, who asked if I fancied speaking to Chester City, who were in League Two. I had been out for so long that I thought I'd listen to what they had to say.

Kofi was also a boxing agent and had got my number from Tommy Gilmour, a Glasgow promoter. We had been pals for years. In fact, one time, when I was driving up from Kilmarnock, he had phoned and asked what I was doing for my 40th birthday. When I told him I hadn't planned anything, he said it would be wrong to let such a milestone pass. I was driving over the Kingston Bridge and I took a right into the city, parked up and went into the Corinthian nightclub, where I booked a private room which seated about 22 people. It was actually a good night, one of these occasions you invite the people who are in your life at that moment in time. I had even done the seating arrangements and made it guy-girl-guy-girl and, as the night went on, the women would move two places to the left around the table so that it gave everybody a chance to get to know everybody at the table. I thought it went well and the next time I was at Tommy's St Andrews boxing club, I noticed that when he had a big table, he did the same – only it was the guys who moved round. Tommy invited me to St Andrews a lot of times. I'm not a big boxing fan but it was always a good social night. After putting so much pressure on me to have a 40th, I felt sure I would get an invite to Tommy's 50th – the bugger took his wife on a cruise!

I drove down to Chester and met the chairman, Stephen Vaughan, the secretary and CEO. The meeting obviously went well, as I was hardly out of Chester on the way home when I got a call saying the job was mine. I confirmed the wages, which were acceptable, and said I'd be back down on the Monday to sort out the bits and pieces – car, mobile phone, etc.

'No, it's just wages. You can use the phone at the club to make your calls and there's no car,' the secretary informed me.

How was I supposed to do the job without a car? The wife had her own and needed it. I was car-less! And how was I supposed to operate on landlines at the club or at my home? It was like going back in time!

I also had to think long and hard about who my assistant would be. When I had been at Hibs, I had replaced Alex McLeish and, at the time, he had asked me to keep on one of the coaches, Malky Thomson. Big Eck and I had talked often and I remember him asking me to give Malky a job if I got one, so I gave him a call. I told him the plans I had for Chester and he was delighted to come and join me. The added bonus, other than Malky being a very good coach, was that he had a car!

During that close season, we battered Malky's car, driving up and down the M6. It doesn't matter what league you are in, the job is just the same and the pressure is just the same. It doesn't matter how many supporters a club have, you have to please them. Players at all levels have a consistency level – the higher the league, the better the consistency. All players who are playing professional football are good players; it's their consistency that will determine what league they will play in. That's why I'm never surprised when a team from a lower level beats a team from a higher level. At the top level, you don't have to work so hard with the players. These guys know the game and know how to play. At the top level, it's all about man-management. At a lower level, it's still about man-management but you have to structure and organise more and spend more time trying to improve players. How do you improve the Ronaldos of this world? You can't. Show them respect and communicate with them and they will give their best. With lower-level players, you need to do the same but players at the age of 27 upwards are very seldom going to get a move to a top club but they still have to play well to support their families and their careers. We keep hearing about managers who have 'lost the dressing room'. I don't believe that. When teams are struggling, the confidence goes and, when that goes, it does look like players are not trying. Players will always try but, when the confidence has gone, some will hide. That's when a manager has got to manage and recognise that and take the player out of that situation to protect them.

Pre-season at Chester was fine, as the players were mostly running and working on their aerobic systems. We really didn't have a decent training area. There were decent parks we could choose from but we had to get a training area sorted quickly. There was a good Chester fan, called Mark, who helped us a lot. He got us an area which was fine but any rain at all and it was waterlogged. Mark even managed to get me a car, which was a huge relief, as it gave Malky's a bit of a break!

But I hadn't had any time to assess the players individually, so any who were to be shown the door were decided by the chairman, Stephen Vaughan. Our experienced defender, Sean Hessey, was not happy. I had signed him previously at Kilmarnock and he came to me and demanded to know if it was the chairman's decision. I lied to him and told him it was mine. We were letting some good players go. I would have liked to have kept centre-back David Artell, because I thought he could do a job for us.

I had to get players in. I wanted a couple of wide players who had pace and could create and I identified Richie Partridge, who had started out at Liverpool, as a good pro, and the chairman identified Kevin Ellison, who could play on the left and was a big strong lad who could score a goal. I remember a game at Stockport when I changed them over – Richie on the left and Kev on the right. Both scored when cutting in on to their stronger foot and we won 3-2 against a County side who were up there challenging. I also wanted to bring another striker, John Murphy, from Macclesfield but I only wanted to work with a squad of 23 or 24 players. The chairman said not to worry and go and get him but I didn't want to work with too many players. The chairman assured me he would move out the surplus numbers in the squad.

I had a decent squad and had brought in the former Sunderland, Wolves and Leeds defender Paul Butler, a seasoned pro who had good experience. Tony Dinning was a good, experienced midfielder we picked up from Stockport, Mark Hughes a midfielder pushing into the Northern Ireland squad and we had Nathan Lowndes, who I had found at Plymouth.

We started the season well and we were in the top five or six by the time Christmas approached. With a January transfer window ahead of us, I was making plans for strengthening the squad to make a push for the play-off spots at the least. I had a list of players who could help us kick on and get promoted.

I had a meeting with the chairman and wanted to talk him through my list of targets but he hit me with a bombshell – telling me that there was no money and players had to go. In England, the FA come and assess your finances in mid-season and they had obviously picked up a problem. To be honest, I was worried, because I was aware that this time of year was when Chester usually got rid of their managers!

All of a sudden, I had gone from a squad of players in optimistic mood, pushing for promotion, to a squad that was bring pushed out the door. As if that wasn't bad enough, wages stopped getting paid. The mood about the place was terrible. I had a lot of disgruntled players hammering on my door, looking for answers. I couldn't tell them anything; I was as much in the dark as them and I, too, wasn't getting paid. They wanted to know if their name was on the transfer list. I didn't know what to tell them, because it was the chairman who was calling all the shots.

It was a really difficult time and it was not helped when Malky, my assistant, took a job back in Scotland with a manager he had worked with previously. I remember the phone call I got from an agent. We had been at a function in Manchester and Malky was driving us back. The agent told me that Malky was leaving to go back to work with Craig Brewster – a guy I knew very well from my Hibs days. I told him that I didn't think that could be right. Malky was very disappointed with Craig when they had lost a previous job and had told me he wouldn't work with him again. I said it loud enough so that Malky, sitting beside me, could hear it but he never acknowledged anything. The next day, I got a phone call from Craig telling me he was making an approach for Malky. I wished him all the best but that I didn't think Malky would go. The next day was a Friday and we were training. We had no game on the Saturday but were playing Monday. Malky was going back to Scotland and asked me if he could shoot away early. I told him that was not a problem and that I would finish everything up.

The next day, the Saturday, I kept hearing rumours that Malky had left. Now, the curious thing was that we were sharing an apartment, so I went into his room and opened his wardrobe. All his clothes had gone! He never even told me! I called him and wished him all the best and asked him to come down for the game on Monday but he refused. It was disappointing but I could see his point – he wasn't getting paid and he had a family back in Scotland to look after.

I had to get another assistant and I knew Jimmy Bone was available, so I gave him a call and he came down to help me out. Jimmy was a great guy and a very good coach who I knew well from our time down at Largs. But I quickly found out he wasn't rated by the hangers-on in the boardroom. I remember that, after a game at home against Rochdale, I went up to the boardroom and there were a few of the chairman's pals, who would come in for a few beers. They were telling me Jimmy's warm-up was old hat and that the Rochdale coach was 'new school', just because he had cones and markers all over their half of the pitch. I tried to tell them that what Jimmy was doing got the job done just as well. But the chairman was listening to these young guys and told me Jimmy would have to go. He had a lad in mind who could come in and help me but I was greatly disappointed to lose Jimmy and I wasn't too keen on a chairman's pick. Steve Mungall, who I knew from his Tranmere days when I was at Rotherham, came in to assist me. I got on all right with him and wasn't bothered that he knew the chairman well. I had nothing to hide – and, anyway, the chairman's two sons were part of the playing squad and his mate was the kitman!

I felt I had a good relationship with the chairman but there were a few guys around about him I never trusted and I was proved right after Jimmy left. He put a guy, who I never liked, into the apartment. He would float around the club and and I never saw him do anything helpful. He had told the chairman I was out drinking every night! I was out every night but just to get away from him. I wasn't drinking every night. It was very unsettling.

As well as all the problems on and off the park at the club, I was having troubles at home and it was clear that my marriage with Lorraine was breaking down. It was not an easy time and I felt we had grown apart. I felt we weren't right for each other and I couldn't imagine me seeing out my life like that. I take full responsibility for the break-up. I was being selfish and wanted more from life. Lorraine was a very good mother and the children agreed it would be better for both if we separated. My biggest regret was not seeing my children becoming adults. I wasn't really around when they were children, with football being so all-consuming. I was too busy trying to establish myself as a coach and manager and I thought I was doing the right thing, giving them a comfortable lifestyle, with a nice home, instead of giving them more of my time. But I felt I had no option. I remember Lorraine blaming me for the children getting verbal abuse at school when I was at Killie and we lost a game. I told her that it would be character building for them! I said we had a mortgage to pay so I couldn't give it up.

We all have regrets in life and that is one of mine.

At Chester, the form fell off a cliff and I couldn't blame the players. They had totally lost belief. I wanted to tell them, 'Stuff the chairman, do it for yourselves, your family, show him that you deserved to be paid', but I had to watch what I said. The chairman's two sons were part of the squad – they were good players – and I'm sure that whatever I said would be reported back.

We went on a run of 12 games without a win and the CEO, Bob Gray, spoke to me and asked if Stephen, the chairman's eldest son, would be playing in the next game. I explained to him that Stephen wasn't fit enough and wouldn't be playing. Bob then told me it would be in my best interests to play him! That was a first. I had never been told to play a player. I think I squeezed him on to the bench. Stephen was a decent player but had a serious injury that he was struggling with. His brother, James, was in the team – not because of his dad but because I thought he was a good player and could maybe play at a higher level. Both the boys were good lads. I also liked their father and I enjoyed his company and was disappointed the way it ended.

The players' desire had gone and it was difficult to motivate them. We lost my last game, away to Milton Keynes Dons, and I got a phone call on Sunday morning from the chairman, who said he was letting me go. I couldn't get up the road quick enough. I called the PFA and asked them if they could help me get the money the chairman owed me. It took a few months but I did get it.

I really enjoyed Chester, especially at the start, but the wheels came off when the wages weren't coming. I would like to think the chairman paid everyone eventually – he did tell me that he always paid, just not on time, which is not good for the players, who had mortgages and bills to pay. Sadly, chairman Stephen Vaughan passed away in the summer of 2025. He was an interesting character, to say the least, but I will always be grateful to him for giving me the opportunity to manage Chester.

But now it was back to Scotland – and the spare room in the family home. Lorraine and I did speak but it wasn't an easy situation for any of us. I knew I had to move on.

CHAPTER 17

AFRICAN ADVENTURE

I STOOD in the doctor's surgery, looking at a map of the world he had framed on the wall and tried to pinpoint exactly where Uganda was. The prospect of managing in a foreign land had always intrigued me and it was certainly something I wanted to do. But I never, even in my wildest dreams, imagined that my ambition would take me all the way to central Africa.

It was July 2008 and I had been out of football and living in my own spare room since the Chester job had ended a few months earlier. I knew I had to get back in the game as soon as possible and was keeping an eye out for any possibilities. Hearts had brought in Csaba László and it meant that his previous job as coach of the Uganda national team – the Cranes – was vacant. My brain kicked into gear and I contacted an agent I knew called Kofi to see if he had any contacts and could make a call for me. Whether Kofi had any contacts in Ugandan football at all, I don't know, but, like most agents, he said he did and I left him to it. Fair play to him, within a few days he contacted me to say that the president of FUFA – the Federation of Uganda Football Associations – and some colleagues would travel to London to meet me. I didn't see the point in that. If I was going to take the job, I needed to see what Uganda was like and if the set-up and the facilities were any good. They agreed and, pretty soon, Kofi was fixing up flights for us both to go out there. It meant I quickly had to get my inoculations – hence the reason I was standing in the surgery of Rangers doctor Paul Jackson, who is a great guy and had helped accelerate the process. Studying the map on his wall, I realised just what a journey I was about to go on.

The day before we left, I met some pals for a few farewell drinks. We were standing outside a pub in Pollok when a football came over the fence and bounced in front of us. I slipped my sandal off to kick the ball back, only to kick the concrete instead. The guys were all laughing but it was agony. I was picking tarmac out of my busted toes and cleaning it with whisky, which I don't drink, in a basic attempt to avoid any infection. One of the toes was definitely broken, while another had the skin ripped from it. The next day, as we set off on our 4,500-mile journey to Entebbe, I struggled to get my shoe on. I hoped it wasn't an omen.

We touched down and headed to the hotel that the Uganda Football Associations had booked for us. The weather was beautiful and the hotel excellent but to say Uganda was a culture shock was an understatement. It was obviously my first time in Africa and I quickly realised just how poor some of the people were. Some of their accommodation was barely adequate but they all had smiles on their faces. They were so happy and so kind when all they seemed to have was sunshine.

The FUFA delegation were due at the hotel at noon the next day for our meeting. They arrived at 2pm and I quickly discovered this was par for the course for Africans. I sat there sweating as I waited for them to arrive.

We had organised a private room and, over an hour or two, I made my pitch to them. My plans for the future, tactics, targets, the usual kind of thing. I obviously made an impression and when it came to talking money, I decided to exit and leave that up to Kofi, as I'm always happy for the financial arguments to be handled by the agent. The terms were agreeable – it wasn't as if I had a job back home – but I said that, before I accepted, I wanted to see the stadium, the training facilities and offices. I was told that I would be picked up at 7pm.

In Africa, I quickly discovered, at 7pm on the dot it goes black – pitch black – as if someone has just flicked a switch. So, by the time I was picked up you couldn't see anything and when we reached the Mandela National Stadium on the northern outskirts of the capital city, Kampala, it was total darkness. Peering through the blackness, I was aware that there seemed to be people walking around the stadium – even on the pitch itself. I found out later it was a recruitment drive for the police force and these guys were sleeping on the concourse.

They showed me the training pitch, which I couldn't see in any detail in the dark but would later discover was terrible. The offices were very sparse and most of the rooms were empty. After the tour, I was taken into Kampala. There were no streetlights on the way and all I could see were small fires burning on both sides of the road. We went to a Chinese restaurant – which was very nice – and then back to the hotel, arranging to meet for one final time the next day. I had so much going through my head – the logistics of doing the job, the infrastructure, being so far from home. The challenges just looked too much. I told Kofi that I wouldn't be signing. He made the calls to the FUFA chairman and that was it.

To his credit, the next day, our day of departure, the FUFA technical director, Asuman Lubowa, arrived at our hotel to see us off, which I really appreciated. We arrived at the airport, only to find that we had been bumped off our flight to Heathrow. It meant we would be staying another night and, unwilling to impose on the FUFA delegation again to pay for a fancy hotel, we found a really basic bed and breakfast close to the airport. For the first time, though not the last, I was to sleep under a mosquito net. I kept all my clothes on and the sweat was lashing off me. Not that it mattered. I hardly slept a wink all night and was up at the crack of dawn. The sun was already burning brightly and I sat in my shorts, reading my book as I waited for Kofi to wake. When he did, we took a walk, as we had time to kill, and found ourselves on a beach on the shores of Lake Victoria. It was stunning. The water stretched out into the distance and disappeared over the horizon. The place was beautiful, the sky a vivid blue and all around me were friendly, smiling people. Everything was amazing. It was like I was in another world. I turned to Kofi and told him to get the FUFA president back on the phone. A meeting was hastily arranged, at which I suggested that, if they were in agreement, I would take the national team for their two remaining Africa Cup of Nations matches. We shook hands on the deal, there and then – and when we got on the flight back to the UK, I knew I was only going back to pack my stuff and return on my new African adventure.

On 1 March 2008, I had taken Chester for the last time in a 1-0 defeat away to MK Dons. By 8 September, I was standing trackside at the Stade Général Seyni Kountché in Niger's capital city, Niamey, in charge of the Uganda national team. It's funny how life works, isn't it?

The build-up to the game had been interesting, to say the least – getting used to new people, new players and new ways of working. I was living at the Hotel Africana, which was a decent place, and I would be picked up by our bus driver, Kalanzi, in a banged-up old Toyota. I couldn't believe a national coach was being issued with this heap but, as it happens, I don't care too much for cars. As long as it got me to where I was going, I didn't care. Kalanzi was a great guy, everybody liked him and we got on really well. Sadly, he suffered from poor health and it was to take him at a very young age. I remember him texting me, asking for money for some unconventional medication, but it never helped him. Towards the end, he asked for me to visit him in hospital. I had always planned to do it but never realised just how ill he was. When I did eventually go, I sat down with his family and, within a minute, Kalanzi passed away. It was terrible. I still miss the guy.

We had established a great rapport, the two of us, but after a few weeks of him driving me around, I felt confident enough to do it myself. The traffic in East-Central Africa is crazy and extremely busy. Rush hour is the worst but the thing about Kampala – and, I found, also Nairobi – is that you just don't know when rush hour is, because it's so unpredictable. You would head out the door and think the roads would be clear and it would be nose to tail. At other times, you'd think it was going to be busy and there was no traffic at all. And you can forget about the good ol' Highway Code! The rules go out of the window – it's every man or woman for themselves.

Nobody gives way and roundabouts are the worst. Getting on to roundabouts is difficult, even with traffic lights and with police monitoring the flow. In fact, sometimes the police encourage you to go through a red light. A word of advice. If you see an African coming out of a side street, slow down – they're coming out! Whether you let them or not! And if you hit them, it's your fault for driving too fast!

Funnily enough, although there are a multitude of reasons why you could lose your rag, road rage is non-existent. I would be going crazy, shouting out of my window and blasting my horn and people would just stare back and would be thinking, 'What's his problem?' People will cut you up without blinking. If you leave a gap and someone gets their nose in, they are in. The only time you hear a horn is a second after a light has turned green and a car hasn't moved, so the driver gets a blast. Some of the cars are not roadworthy, a lot drive around at night without lights, and cyclists, well, they don't have lights, they don't even have brakes! I had hit three cyclists before I realised I needed to allow for the fact they can't stop. One time, I was going to FUFA House for a press conference. As I was heading down the hill, there was a cyclist in front of me. I had to make a left turn into the car park, so I overtook him and started to slow down to make the turn when I heard the cyclist screaming as he went into the back of me. I made the turn, parked my car and got out, only to be confronted by journalists telling me about the accident. I said I was well aware and suggested the cyclist should get his brakes fixed and I headed into the building.

I was lucky on occasions. One time, I was heading to the team hotel to check everything was okay. It was evening, not very late but pitch black, and there were no lights at the side of the road. On the bypass, as I came over the brow of the hill, I noticed a lorry about 300 yards ahead and it had no lights. It was only when I got closer that I realised it wasn't moving. I was fairly shifting and I knew I would hit it. I looked at the hard shoulder for a bail out but there were pedestrians on it, so that was no good. Then I saw another big truck coming towards me on the other side of the road. The only option was to try and squeeze between them. It was like one of those old cartoons when the character has to breathe in and the car breathes in with him! Well, it doesn't work in real life. My passenger side hit the back end of the truck and slid underneath, pushing my car sideways on to the other side of the road and towards the other truck. He took evasive action but still smashed me at the rear passenger door, spinning the car 360 degrees and leaving me on the other side of the road, facing the right direction. I put the hazard lights on and, when I looked, the truck that had been parked up had driven off. The one which had been travelling on the other side of the road just kept on going. There were a few folk milling around and we managed to push my car to the side of the road. I phoned a guy called George, who would often taxi me around and come to my rescue. He called a cop he knew and told him to get to me as quickly as he could. At night, it could be quite dangerous, as a lot of people were living well below the breadline and were always looking for opportunities. Thankfully, a few recognised me but, when I opened my boot to get my overnight bag, all these heads appeared beside me, peering in my boot. I decided I would leave it there until George came. He and the cop arrived, so I gave the cop the car keys and jumped in George's car. I wasn't bothered about mine. It was a heap of shit and wasn't roadworthy anyway.

It was only later that I realised how lucky I had been. If I had a passenger, they would have lost their legs or maybe their life – that side of the car was totally crushed.

Boda-bodas are a nightmare. These are guys on motorbikes who will pick up passengers and drive all over the road. They go through red lights without blinking. They don't care. They overtake you on the inside and you have to check your wing mirrors to make sure it's clear when turning left. I've seen all sorts on these bikes – I've seen them carrying sofas, livestock, passengers holding windscreens, flatscreen TVs. I've seen as many as five or six people on one bike. I've even seen a woman breastfeeding her baby! It's the only way they can afford to travel. If you hit one, or one hits you, you quickly drive to the nearest cop shop, as you will have as many as 20 bodas around you in minutes, all claiming they are witnesses and that it was your fault. It can turn nasty.

The Matatus are worse. These are privately owned public buses which show no courtesy at all. They will overtake you, then stop to let passengers on and off and pull back out as soon as. They can turn a two-lane road into three lanes, jamming the road and even stopping the traffic coming in the opposite direction by being on their side.

It certainly made life interesting.

In the build-up to the Niger game, we had the local players training with us in the two weeks before the tie, which was great, because it gave me a chance to get to know them. The training ground wasn't great and I was concerned someone would get injured. When I brought up my concerns, I was told the players were used to it, and when I started watching games, they were right.

When I first took training with the Cranes, when players were looking for a pass, they wouldn't shout a name – they would clap their hands or whistle or make a noise for a pass. So, I stopped the training after a while and brought them together in a group. I told them to use names and that, when they passed, to give an instruction – 'hold it … turn', that type of thing. I said: 'How am I going to get your names if you don't use them?' Later, when I had moved to club side Gor Mahia, I knew all the players' names and nicknames by the end of the week.

I didn't take any of the coaches I had worked with over to Uganda with me. I thought I had to get to know the culture and to get to know the people, and the best way to do that was to have local coaches around me. The Ugandan federation gave me a couple of coaches, and they were all right. Obviously, managers take their own backroom team because they trust them and I didn't know these guys or whether they were talking behind my back. But I was confident in my own ability and was happy to work with them. You do need these guys around you to get to know people and to get to know the players. There's a lot of tribalism goes on in Uganda. Players come from different tribes, different villages, and that's why they normally employ foreign coaches, because we're not influenced by that and we've not got the pressure of people from one village saying you have to play this player or that player. I was immune to all that. It's why local coaches don't get those jobs.

I never tried to learn the language – Swahili – either. The way I looked at it, these guys had to learn to understand me, especially if they wanted to go and play in Europe. If they could understand me, they could understand anybody. So, I used to drum it into them; listen to what I am saying, don't worry about my accent, listen to the words I am saying. Some were getting it, some weren't.

The players playing outside of Uganda, we could only summon them five days before the game and, with the travelling, we only really had them for three days. Some wouldn't come straight to camp either. They would go home first and pitch up when it suited them. So, the foreign-based players would roll in and I would have to make room for them and let local-based players leave the camp. I hated doing that, having worked with them and coached them and then having to let them go for a player I'd not had a chance to work with. You can't win. The press want the international players involved and I was told the players would pay the journalists to push for them in the stories they wrote. I don't know if that's true but it was what I was told. Some press guys, however, would push for local players. Truth be told, you could work with local players longer and get them organised and create a togetherness and club atmosphere. But the international players are more professional and are playing at a higher level, so it is a catch-22.

The timekeeping was also really bad – not only from the players but in all aspects of life. I would tell the players to be at training for nine in the morning, knowing I wouldn't be starting until after ten, and players would still be late. I couldn't fine them like you did with British players – a lot of them had no money, so that was a waste of time. So, I would run them hard after training and make sure the other players hung around to watch, hoping that would encourage others not to be late. I told them to set the alarms on their phones – and that if I was always on time, then so should they be.

One player even accused me of being too professional! I told them if they wanted to play in Europe, which they all did, then they had to raise their standards and that timekeeping is important with European coaches. If you were constantly late in Europe, you would be out.

The week of the Niger match was difficult. There were players who were going to be playing who were not even in the country. The likes of defender Timothy Batabaire, who was playing in South Africa for Bloemfontein Celtic, only pitched up at a training camp we were having in Mali before we flew on to Niger for the game. Our captain, Ibrahim Sekagya, actually turned up at the hotel the night before the game after jetting in from Austria, where he played with Red Bull Salzburg. It was the first time I had met these two guys but they were both solid professionals and good players, as well as being good lads.

We trained at the stadium the night before the game and Edgar Watson, who worked with FUFA, had travelled with us. I didn't know Edgar, so I was a bit apprehensive when he asked me if he could take part in the keep-ball session I always did before we started. It didn't take me long to see Edgar was a player – I didn't realise until that moment that he had previously played for the national team – and he certainly wasn't out of place. In fact, I don't think he ever gave the ball away. When we were finishing up, Edgar came over and asked why we hadn't worked on any set pieces. I explained that I didn't want to do them on the training field, as the opposition would undoubtedly have spies watching us.

Instead, I explained, we'd do them on the flip chart. It was a good job I had the chart with me and was able to illustrate what I was talking about, because I don't think the players understood a word I said.

The day of the game was stiflingly hot but we were firmly in control and David Obua, who was playing with Hearts at the time, had put us one up. I was watching from the dugout and was impressed by how good the guys were. We were strong at the back whenever we came under pressure and, when we went in at half-time, I told the players I genuinely could see no way they could hurt us. Usually, I would be able to see where the danger would come from but I had seen nothing. I just told them to keep doing what they were doing. The second half couldn't have been worse. They had made changes and battered us 3-1.

I had no knowledge of the opposition and even if I had, they had made so many changes from the team that played the previous game. I was even told that they all had new passports issued two days before the game and people on the technical bench were questioning their nationality, suggesting they came from surrounding countries.

I sat down with the players and asked them what had happened. I was getting feedback that the heat was too much for them. But they're Africans, I thought, they must be used to it. I was being naïve. The players, certainly the international players, were from clubs in Scotland and Austria. Joseph Nestroy Kizito played for a club in Serbia; Mike Sserumaga in Sweden for Helsingborg.

I was also concerned about their pre-match preparations. What really disturbed me was that the night before the game, they were all drinking sodas and stuff like that. That is no good at all. It gives you a sugar rush, a false energy. It builds up your sugar levels but burns off very quickly and your body doesn't have time to replace it.

I asked David Obua if he drank sodas before games for Hearts. When he said he didn't, I questioned why he felt it was okay to do that before a game with the national team when the heat made even the smallest detail in preparation so important. So, I banned sodas 48 hours before a game – it was fresh juice or water. I believed that sugar rush could have been a factor as to why they ran out of steam in the second half.

When we arrived back in Entebbe, I was told Rogers, the press officer, would drop me home, which was fine. When we detoured off the Entebbe-Kampala road, he explained he had to pop into FUFA House. When we got there, the place was alive with journalists and a press conference had been arranged. I had no idea but I sat down to answer their questions. As you can imagine, the mood wasn't good and when I got back in the car, I told Rogers in no uncertain terms never to do that to me again. I felt I had been railroaded!

Back in the Hotel Africana, I was left to my own devices. I was still pretty apprehensive about going out. It was fine going to training but I was still naïve and didn't want to leave the hotel. I started going to a place just around the corner, an Italian restaurant, which was fine but I always wanted to get back early. I didn't see any white people. Then one day, I got a phone call from a Scottish guy called John Hamilton, who worked for the British Embassy, asking if I wanted to meet up for a beer. He suggested we meet at a sports bar called Just Kicking – JKs, for short – and there were quite a lot of ex-pats there, guys from

Europe, the UK, South Africa. There were even some more Scottish boys, working in the oil industry. JKs became my local, along with an Irish pub called Bubbles. It was run by a couple of Irish lads called Nigel Sutton and Declan, two good guys who were always this side of the bar. They owned the bar but never seemed to work in it. I started to feel a bit more at home but was still unsure about the future. I was sitting by the hotel pool one day – without a game or an office, there was little else to do. It was a large pool but there was no one else there and I could see out on the street where people, all suited and booted, were heading to work and meetings while here was I, lounging around. I made a call to a pal, Jim Docherty, back in Scotland. He asked how I was getting on and what I was doing. I told him I was at the pool reading a book but I was really thinking about chucking it in, that I couldn't see me lasting and that I was probably going to be heading back to Scotland.

'What's the weather like?' Jim asked.

'Oh, it's roasting, there's not a cloud in the sky,' I replied.

'What would you be doing if you were on holiday?' Jim asked.

'I'd be doing this,' I said.

'Well, shut the fuck up then,' Jim fired back. 'I'm in my car going to work, it's freezing, pitch black, raining and the de-mister can't clear the window! Why on earth would you want to come back here?'

He was right. There was nothing for me back there, apart from family and friends. I had no job to go back to. The best decision I ever made was to get on with it.

Before too long, I found myself a flat and really began to settle in. I was getting around watching matches but there were never any team sheets, so I had to write down shirt numbers and positions and a general description of the player. When I got back to the office, I would ask around to see if anyone knew who the player I was interested in was. However, pretty soon, I got to know the players and during one of these games I identified Vincent Kayizzi for the first time. I asked my assistant, Sam Timbe, why he wasn't invited into training before the Niger game and he told me he was injured. I remember after the Niger game getting a phone call from a Scottish journalist saying the Hearts manager, Csaba László, who had been in the Uganda job before me, had criticised me for not selecting Vincent for the Niger game and wasting all his good work. I called Csaba and he said he was misquoted. If a reporter tells me a manager had said this or that about me, I will always phone the manager up to ask if it was true and usually they have been misquoted. I would rather do that than have a war of words in the tabloids. I've never criticised anyone in the press – player or manager.

The last game of our Afcon group was against Benin at home. Two weeks before the game, I got a phone call from my sister, Donna, to say our father had passed away. I knew he had been struggling. I had seen him just before I had left for Uganda and he was in a hospice struggling with cancer. I was sorry I wasn't there for him, just as I was for Donna, who had organised the funeral and everything by herself. It was the weekend before the game but I jetted back to Scotland and as soon as the funeral was over, I was back on a flight to Uganda.

It wasn't that different with our mother, who passed away a few years later. She had cancer as well and passed away in the hospice. Once again, I wasn't there. I got back for the funeral and it wasn't a case of hanging around; it was the funeral and then back to Africa. Looking back, if you asked me if I regret not being there for those last weeks and days, in one respect I have to say I don't think I can regret it. As I say to my own children, they have their own lives, they have to go and live them, they have their own families. But I do have a big regret at not being with my parents in their old age. Donna was there for them, doing everything – shopping, medication, making sure they got the benefits they deserved after working all their days. My dad was easy but my mother was a difficult one. Donna was on the phone to me most weeks telling me I was my mum's favourite and all she kept saying was what a great son I was. I assured Donna that Mum was on the phone telling me what a great daughter she was. Donna had told me Mum was in the hospice and she didn't have long to go. I got on the earliest flight back to the UK but I was too late. She had passed away before I boarded the flight to London. Donna said she was skin and bones at the end and that I would have hated to see her like that, which is true.

But it would have been good to have been able to say goodbye. Life is full of regrets and not being there to help Donna or being with Mum and Dad at the end still hurts.

The Mandela National Stadium holds 50,000 but I was blown away by the passion and numbers for that game with Benin. The fans were squeezed in everywhere; in the passageways, on the running track around the pitch, even sitting around the dugout. The preparations for the game, my first at home with Uganda, had gone well but the game started badly for us and we were 1-0 down at half-time. The nation had never qualified for the Afcon finals before and this was a great chance to write a piece of history. The crowd took my breath away and I addressed the players at half-time.

'Listen to those fans,' I told them. 'Listen to the support they are giving you. You can't let them down.'

The second half was immense and we scored two goals through Geofrey Massa to win 2-1. Heartbreakingly, it was not to be enough and we missed out on qualification on goal difference. But I realised one thing – I had fallen in love with the country. The fans were very passionate and supportive and the people so warm and friendly. My deal was up, however, and I desperately wanted to stay. I was hoping the president would keep me in place for the Cecafa tournament, which was coming up in December – a tournament for nations in East and Central Africa and a great opportunity to identify and blood new, talented young players.

As it turned out, I would be with the Cranes for five years that were as fulfilling as they were challenging.

I had a month to get a squad together and work with them ahead of the Cecafa tournament, which Uganda were hosting. I watched a lot of football in that time and got to work on that. In Uganda, most clubs were playing with a defensive midfielder and an attacking midfielder. I think it's easy to play against a team set up like that. I want my midfield players to be able to defend and attack. When the ball's on our right, I want the left-sided midfielder getting into the box and vice versa. We got a lot of goals in the tournament by perfecting just that system.

The squad was made up mostly of local players but if there was a foreign-based player who wanted to make himself available, I would use them. The defender Andrew

Mwesigwa was always one to step forward, even though he played in Iceland. He was a good guy and a good player. Midfielder Dan Wagaluka came in from his club in Tanzania and Geofrey Massa gave us options up front after coming in from his club in Egypt. We had young home-based players like Habib Kavuma. He actually had a younger brother who was also a player, although not yet part of the national set-up. When his passport was checked, it suggested he was older than we thought – in fact, Habib's younger brother was actually older than him!

We would go on to win the tournament, beating Kenya in the final, with Brian Umony getting the only goal. Uganda hadn't won the tournament for five years and in my first Cecafa we never lost a game. In fact, in the five years I was in charge, we would win the tournament four times. The only time we didn't win it was in 2011, losing to the hosts, Tanzania. It was a real sore one, because I still feel we were hard done-by. In the semi-final against Tanzania, the Kenyan referee refused to send off one of their players. We would go on to lose the game and I do believe the tournament organisers needed to have the hosts in the final, because, without them, the crowds would have disappeared. They won the final in their own country and we finished third.

I'm not sure how many games I was involved in at Mandela Stadium in all my time as Uganda coach but I only had one defeat and it was on penalties to Zambia in the Afcon qualifiers. Zambia had won the previous tournament, so there was no shame whatsoever, but it was a major disappointment. We had lost 1-0 in Zambia from a goal scored following a long throw and, if the assistant referee had been doing his job, the goal wouldn't have stood, as the thrower's foot was on the park when he released the ball. We beat them 1-0 back in Uganda and, instead of playing extra time, we went straight to penalties. When I queried it, I was told it wouldn't be fair for the away team! What utter nonsense! It finished 9-8 and our sub missed the last penalty – we had scored all the rest. Uganda had never qualified for Afcon and we were so close that day. History was there to be written!

Despite the disappointment, I was loving life. I loved it on matchday at the Mandela Stadium. Hours before the game, the fans would be out on the street. The colours and the noise were fantastic. The horns would be blasting and people would be making their way to the stadium. The Mandela held 50,000 but at some games there were thousands more crammed in, sitting on the track yards away from the technical area. It was electric and made the hairs on the back of your neck stand up. The fans began to call me Mr Bobby and because we were successful, the smiles on their faces lit up the place. I was loving it. I'd do all the tourist stuff. Like Murchison Falls – they are actually named after some Scottish geologist – which really has to be seen to be believed. It's where the River Nile forces its way through this narrow gap in the rocks. It's amazing – you can feel the ground shaking. And in the national park, elephants and lions roam freely. We would head up to Jinja, which is the leisure capital of Uganda, and there you can go white-water rafting, bungee jumping, kayaking, jet boating or enjoy Lake Victoria's beaches.

My life was also changing closer to home, as I met Michelle – the woman who would go on to become my wife after my divorce from Lorraine. We would live together for some time before Michelle discovered she was pregnant. We hadn't planned on having children – Michelle had a very good job with Amnesty International and was focused on her career. We talked it through and decided we would tie the knot as soon as my divorce was finalised. Our baby daughter was born and we called her Saoirse, since Michelle is half Irish. It took me long enough to pronounce it right! I had chosen her middle name, Tia, as it's a lot easier for everyone and she tells children on holiday it's her name. Michelle would be on maternity leave and on most days she and Saoirse would be in the garden, splashing around in a paddling pool, with the sun shining overhead.

This was my home now and I was settled. I know some African coaches – like Nigeria coach Stephen Keshi – have complained about the number of white coaches who come to work in Africa from Europe for the money. He has a point. When Berti Vogts was with Nigeria, he never lived in the country. Some people think they can come in for a game, do their job and fly away again. But I was living in Uganda. I had come for the experience and for the job; I never came for the money.

On the football front, it was all about tournaments and we had entered the CHAN competition. It's the African Nations Championship featuring only players in domestic leagues and not to be confused with the Afcon, which includes all players, even those in foreign leagues.

My first experience of it was a major disappointment. Our preparations were fine but a few days before we were due to fly out to Sudan, where it was being held, players were disappearing and leaving the country for trials elsewhere. We were frantically looking around for replacements and organising travel and plane tickets for them. After the tournament, I put forward a proposal that the tournament should not be played when the transfer window was open. I was all for players looking to get employment but it would have been better if they had played the tournament and put themselves in the shop window. We lost more than half our team as they all went on trials. Our strikeforce had gone and two of our better left-sided players were missing. We patched it up as best we could and the players who were left gave a good account of themselves but it was always going to be a struggle.

It was in Sudan, while I was watching the group games, that I was first introduced to Milutin 'Micho' Sredojević, a Serbian coach who had been knocking about in African football for some time. He seemed pleasant enough but later would give an interview to Ugandan journalists and criticise me for not bringing enough experienced players to the tournament. I was disappointed in him. I would rather play young players who have the potential to play in the national team, rather than a senior pro who wouldn't be selected. As it happened, Sredojević would replace me in the Uganda job and, when he took the team to the CHAN tournament, he did exactly the same thing I had.

The most disappointing thing about the tournament – along with the results – was a dispute which arose because the players had their names on the back of their shirts and wanted to keep them. The team manager said he had been told to return them. What use would they be for FUFA with the names on the back? I wouldn't wear a shirt with someone else's name on the back.

That was certainly something I was aware of – the equipment was not the best. It is all down to finance. There is a shortage of balls, a shortage of pitches. Even with the national team, we didn't have a sponsor. We had to buy our own adidas strips. Once, we wore fake adidas strips and we were caught out and reprimanded! These things happen in Africa. But it is disappointing. You would have thought somebody, either Puma or adidas, could supply these guys with shirts, because I know what it is like with Scotland when I have been with the national team. They get all the stuff they need and, because they get two strips each, they can each take a strip home.

So, we had this standoff with the Uganda players wanting the strips and FUFA not allowing it.

It's a bit crazy. The Cranes should be a big marketing brand. You see millions of people wearing the Uganda football strip now. When I first arrived, it was all Chelsea, Manchester United and Arsenal. Now you see a lot of Uganda strips, because we have done well at home.

I suggested a compromise to the team manager that they should be allowed to keep one, with the other set returned to FUFA. The players decided on the set they wanted and we could finally move on.

With Uganda, it was all about tournaments. We tried to qualify for the Olympics, which involved players under the age of 23. We narrowly beat Tanzania at home in the first round and our press were saying we would struggle to go through. We had Kenya up next and, again, our press dismissed us but we won through to the group stages in Mozambique. With it being for younger players, I let other coaches take the team, as they were very capable and I was involved with the senior team in an Afcon qualifier. I went to Mozambique to support them but the tournament came a bit early for the hosts to organise the facilities. They had built an entire village but there was no furniture in the rooms, nothing but a mattress, which was fine, and all the teams ate in the same canteen. But the standard on the pitch was high and we never got past the group stage.

In 2011, I took the nation to the final of the Nile Basin tournament, which was hosted by Egypt. We were in the same group as the hosts, plus Burundi and Tanzania. We beat Burundi, draw with Tanzania and it was between us and Egypt to see who finished top of the group. I watched Egypt hammer Tanzania. They dominated the game down the wide areas, had two good wingers and their full-backs overlapped all the time. I thought about it and didn't want to suffer a heavy defeat, so I played with four full-backs – two on each side, with one of each pair more or less playing as a midfielder. The guys did really well and, although we lost the game in injury time, we still made it into the knockout stages. We played the Democratic Republic of Congo in the semi-final. They were a really good team who had just returned from a competition which pitched together the champions of all the continents. Nobody gave us a chance but our defender, Habib Kavuma, scored the only goal midway through the first half.

The final saw us up against the hosts once again and the Cairo International Stadium was rammed. I was astonished – there were 74,000 fans in there. I didn't want to play as defensively as we had done when we met them in the group stages and I thought that, if we could keep it tight, we could have a chance. But Egypt were a very good team. Their players were playing all over Europe and we just had the home-based players. We gave a good account of ourselves but lost 3-1.

Ahead of the game, I was aware just how poor the eating habits of the players were. It was chips and all sorts but I reckoned they had made the final, so there was little point in changing it. These were our home-based players. Our foreign-based players were different; they lived well and ate well. The local boys, some of whom were living in poverty, just ate what they could get. You can't educate them to eat the proper stuff that gives you fuel and energy, so I didn't change anything.

The Afcon was very much the Holy Grail and, after coming so close in the penalty heartache against Zambia, I was determined to get Uganda to a tournament they had never qualified for.

The 2013 Afcon qualifiers started ever so well. We had beaten Guinea-Bissau home and away, drawn with Kenya away and beaten Angola at home. We lost away to Angola, which left us one point ahead with one game to go and we had Kenya at home, while Angola had Guinea-Bissau away. It was in our hands – we had to beat Kenya at home to qualify. A game against our near neighbours was never going to be easy. The day before the game, I was summoned to see FUFA president Lawrence Mulindwa. I had a lot of respect for him and whenever we came back from trips after doing well, he rewarded the players with a meal and cash, which the players appreciated. He was a very clever man who, in 2001, had started a secondary school in Kitende called St Mary's Boarding Secondary School, which was designed to give kids a top-class education, as well as promoting sports in the country. It was hugely successful.

We met at his school early on the Friday morning. I made sure I was there on time but waited while the president cleared his waiting room, which was busy. When I got in, he suggested I leave a couple of players out, as one of them had travelled via Nairobi and the president thought he would have been 'compromised' by the Kenyans. Indeed, he felt another player had been 'compromised' as well. He was certain that both of them should be left out but I didn't share his paranoia. Kenya had only the slimmest of chances of qualifying – they would have to beat us by a few goals and hope that Angola lost away to Guinea-Bissau. But Kenya didn't come to win the game, they came to ensure we didn't win. In Jose Mourinho's words, they 'parked the bus'. It was one of the most one-sided games I've been involved in. We battered them but, unfortunately, we came up against a goalkeeper who was on top form. We hit the woodwork so many times, missed good chances and the game finished 0-0. Angola won their game and we were out. The Kenyans celebrated as if they had qualified! We only lost one game in that qualifying campaign and scored more than anyone else and conceded less and still could not qualify. The conspiracy theorists were in their element and there were suggestions that Angola had given Kenyans incentives and paid off Guinea-Bissau, who had nothing to play for. It was more paranoia and I didn't believe any of it.

There had been drama in the build-up to the game. We were honoured to be visited by Ugandan president Yoweri Museveni, who had been in charge of the country since 1986 and – as far as I know – still is. We waited and waited for his arrival into our training camp – all the players hanging about – but one player, David Obua, had had enough and left to go back to the hotel. Lawrence Mulindwa wasn't happy and neither was I. Forget about politics, it was hugely disrespectful. The president and I ruled that the only course of action was to send Obua home. It was not an easy decision, although it was made somewhat easier by the fact Obua hadn't trained all week and was very unlikely to feature. He was a good player and a very good servant to his country, scoring lots of goals. Even though Obua wasn't playing regularly with Hearts, I had always called him up and he had always started. I told Obua the decision and said that, if he wanted, he could say that he recognised he wasn't fit, wouldn't play in the game and that he was so disappointed he had left to go back to the hotel.

But there were no winners in the situation, only losers. I know now that many of the players felt we would have beaten Kenya had Obua not been banished from the squad. But I knew for a fact he wasn't fit, although I underestimated Obua's influence around the squad. He was a popular individual and, with the benefit of hindsight, we should have kept him with us. The backlash after the game certainly suggested that but, as a manager, you have to set a precedent. All the players knew David had left before president Museveni turned up. I know that, if I had been a player, I wouldn't have been happy as I waited. I'm sure there must have been a few disgruntled players. The press would have found out and complained and the management would have been portrayed as weak for not taking action.

Obua would later say that FUFA boss Mulindwa had told the squad they could not ask the president any questions so he didn't see any reason to stay. I don't believe that reason either. The president of the country took the time to come to wish us well. It's about respect.

Obua was such a key player and a bit of a target for the fans. In one previous qualifier, I subbed him and, as he came off, he walked past me and threw down his shirt. He then proceeded to walk to the dressing room on the opposite side of the pitch and, as he was walking round, it was like a Mexican wave of booing. When we got on the bus, the fans were trying to get to him. I was disappointed in his attitude; we had won the game and that was all that mattered. The next day, he arranged a press conference, along with a couple of senior players, to apologise to the fans. Obua was well respected by his peers and myself but I don't think our relationship was ever the same, even though I would regularly select him.

I was beginning to get some criticism for not travelling around the country looking for talent in outlying villages. I tried to explain, arguing how could I cap a player playing for a village team with two men and a dog watching? Put them out in front of 50,000 fans or more at the Mandela Stadium and they wouldn't cope. It was up to clubs to find this talent and put them in their teams, as every club would have games in Kampala and I would see every player in the country. If there was talent out there, it would be discovered and brought to my notice. As it happened, towards the end of my tenure I didn't go to as many games as I previously had. I knew the players who were capable of being in the national team. I didn't go abroad to check on the international players, as FUFA couldn't afford it. But I did go to South Africa at my own expense to touch base with striker Brian Umony and keeper Denis Onyango. I went to watch Denis in a reserve game for Mamelodi Sundowns but he didn't play – they played their third-choice keeper! Denis was a very talented keeper who went on to be one of the best in Africa, and Brian was a talented striker who had everything a good striker needed.

The backroom team FUFA had assembled for me was also working well. David Otti was a legend of Ugandan football – he had a great a knowledge of football, was always there for players to confide in and was a gentleman to boot. He advised and helped me tremendously. I was devasted when David passed away after complications from diabetes. It was a huge loss to the game in Uganda and a massive loss to me, personally.

Jackson Mayanja – a legendary former Cranes player – also assisted me very well. I remember saying to him one day that he should take training but he refused, saying it wouldn't be right, as the players expected me to take the training and I would lose respect. A load of nonsense! I don't know why he or Sam Simbwa didn't want to take a session. If it had been me, I would have dived in. I think they thought I would have judged them – which I would have – but these guys were head coaches at their respective clubs, and been successful and had great football careers behind them before FUFA had employed them. Jackson was a good guy and a friend and we still keep in touch. Sam Simbwa left the team; in fact, he was removed and it wasn't my decision. He told me he had learned a lot from me but then, after Sam left, he was doing a lot of media work and was criticising me at every opportunity! I thought he was very two-faced, so, when I met him at a match, I pulled him aside and asked him what his problem was with me. Sam had been hired to coach Victoria

University after leaving the national set-up and I knew the chairman there, who I thought was a friend. Sam had been told I was involved in getting him the sack. I got the chairman on the phone there and then and demanded he told Sam I had nothing to do with it. But this didn't appease Sam – the criticism kept coming.

As my time with the team was coming to the end, we were involved in the qualifying campaign for the 2014 World Cup finals in Brazil. We were drawn in a qualifying group with Senegal, Angola and Liberia. We opened up with a 1-1 draw in front of 40,000 away to Angola, with Emmanuel Okwi getting a late leveller for us. Then we hosted Senegal, who had the likes of Sadio Mane, Papiss Cisse and Souleymane Camara playing for them. Cisse gave them an early lead but Godfrey Walusimbi levelled late on for us with a penalty.

Our next game was away to Liberia and, in the lead-up to it, a guy who I thought was a friend invited me out for lunch. We were just chatting away and he asked me how much I was earning. I didn't think anything of it, as I had known him for a few years – plus, anybody could have found out my wages by asking a few questions. About a week later, my old Serbian 'pal' Milutin 'Micho' Sredojević was in Kampala and I was told he wanted to meet up. I agreed. We chatted about football and he blew smoke up my ass about how good a job I was doing and all that nonsense. But I knew he was digging, trying to find out things and I was very suspicious.

I met the FUFA president to discuss the travel arrangements for the Liberia game and he suggested we get there a few days earlier so that we could get settled. I thought it was a great idea, as we usually scrambled to games. Our travelling arrangements were always two or three flights, never direct, with a lot of time spent in airports, with players trying to get comfortable, laying around concourses in their tracksuits. True to form, the new travel plans never occurred. Once again, we got there the day before the game and some of our training kit was left back at our last connection as we went via Ethiopia, then Ghana and into Liberia. We nearly missed the Ghana connection, as we were detained in Ethiopia waiting for a flight to come in with passengers who were connecting on our flight to Ghana. It was madness, scrambling to get our flight to Liberia, which certainly wasn't going to wait for us. It was why some of our training gear and luggage was left behind.

It was hardly surprising that the game didn't go well. We lost 2-0. Back in the hotel, one of the senior players was having a go at one of our younger lads, Emmanuel Okwi, for missing an opportunity when he could have set up someone in a better position! Our goalkeeper coach was also complaining about the fitness of one of our centre-backs. This guy hardly spoke to me but had plenty to say behind my back. But he knew I was being replaced and even knew my replacement – Sredojević.

I had heard his name mentioned a few times by different people in my backroom team who had been conversing with him. I never thought he would get the job, as I didn't think his CV stacked up, but he was friendly with our vice-president, Mujib Kasule.

After the defeat, there was the usual post-mortem or a reason to have a go at me. There was no need; they knew they were sacking me and so did 'their' backroom team. The president never questioned me but he had loaded the gun for all the other committee members to ask his questions. He would just sit there and smile as I batted all their questions out of the park. I did resent the interrogation – even the press officer asked a question and he knew nothing about football. One guy who I had a lot of respect for, Edgar Watson, piped up that it looked like I had all my substitutes planned before the game. I'm sure the president had put him up to asking the question – he looked embarrassed. I told him I had to have a plan B but, hopefully, wouldn't need to use it. I had a lot of respect for Edgar and I even encouraged him to go for the CEO position when FUFA started looking. He puts a lot back into grassroots with his academy and his development of young aspiring players.

Some days later, I got a phone call from the office to come and pick up a letter. I knew what the letter was and told them to bring it to me. We had agreed to meet in the car park of the Silver Springs Hotel down the road from the house. I was met by a wee guy from FUFA, who I referred to as 'Blatter', as he appeared to do everything. He was the one who would get my wages to me. He was a good guy and I really liked him. He asked me to sign for the letter, which I declined to do until my lawyer had seen it. The problem was, I didn't have a lawyer. A friend, Ivan Kakembo, introduced me to someone who dealt with the settlement. I was due a six-figure sum but settled for a lot less. I only wanted money to see me into another job, which it duly did.

I've got to thank FUFA for the way they handled the situation. It was really amicable, no squabbling in courts, as I would experience a few years later. Ivan is a good pal and very helpful. He has actually relocated to Glasgow and I try and see him and his family most years when I'm back.

I can only thank the then president of FUFA, Lawrence Mulindwa, for giving me a fantastic opportunity and it was an honour and privilege to manage and coach Uganda. The players, especially the local players, were very respectful and wanted to learn. The international players were also great to work with. My only gripe was the fact I believed that they could have got to camp sooner than they did. I would like to thank all the staff at FUFA for their help. As for the fans, their support was as good as I've witnessed anywhere.

The most disappointing thing, and something I think about to this day, is that I don't think I was far away from achieving that all-elusive qualification to a major tournament, and I do know that the squad was in better shape when I left than when I arrived. I've no regrets – just one defeat at home, on penalties, in five years wasn't bad. Any team turning up at Mandela Stadium must have been overwhelmed by our home support. Talk about a 12th man!

Uganda is a passionate footballing nation. The talent is there and I'm sure that, if they can get everything right, they can be a top team. Even now, when you look at teams like Uganda, they have brilliant players who are scattered across the continents. Many of them are playing in France but also there is a large contingent of African footballers in places like Japan and Asia. In terms of their actual footballing ability, some of these guys are top-quality players.

They can run with the ball, pass the ball and strike the ball as well as most professionals in the UK but what they lack is that tactical awareness and footballing knowledge. So, when I went in, my job was to help give them that. A lot of players in England and Scotland take for granted that they know where their players are making runs and when they are going to make them.

In African football, that awareness must be taught but, once they have it, they do have the ability to do great things. Above all, that is the passion of the African people and the players. They are so willing to learn and want to be the best player they can be. That attitude, especially in recent times, is sadly missing in many players.

I got to experience so much with them. We even played in a tournament in Morocco, with Sudan and Cameroon, in which Samuel Eto'o, the Cameroon captain and legend, turned up for the press conference wearing a pair of those slippers hotels supply for guests. I remember thinking that he was a multi-millionaire and, surely, he had a pair of shoes! Still, as a multi-millionaire, I suppose he can wear what he wants!

I really felt I had achieved a lot with Uganda and was proud of the job I had done. When I took over, we had an experienced team with a core nucleus of the squad coming to the end of their international careers. It was up to me to find and then introduce new talent and I did that. There were a number for whom I gave them their international debuts. I've no doubt that if I had been allowed to see out my contract, we would have qualified for Afcon. Goal difference and penalty shoot-outs had stopped us but we were getting there. My record of four Cecafas is going to be hard for any coach to surpass. I also took the team to the final of the Nile Basin tournament and achieved success in the four-team tournament at Morocco. Whoever followed me was going to be in a far better situation than I was when I took on the job.

But my time with Uganda was at an end. I remember getting a call from the journalist Alan Pattullo back in Scotland. He asked me what I was going to do.

I said: 'Alan, at this moment in time, it's ten in the morning, I have my shorts on, my flip-flops on, I am walking around the garden, the sun is beating down. I don't want to leave all this just yet.'

So, I just sat back and enjoyed the weather with Michelle and Saoirse and waited for the phone to ring.

CHAPTER 18
GOR BLIMEY

I WAS enjoying being able to devote all my time to Michelle and Saoirse, watching them play in the sunshine and be a family, but I was always hopeful I would get that tap on the shoulder and another chance to get back into the game. I wasn't going to rush my next move. I believed it was important it was the right job and not just any job.

Uganda is a country that is full of poverty and problems but, as for so many people around the world, football acts as a release and an escape. In African countries, it can mean so much more, and to be a part of that, and to feel that responsibility is something special.

Out of the blue, I received a call from an agent telling me that there was a job vacancy he reckoned I might be interested in. We met up in my local and he told me a club side in Kenya were looking for a coach. I wasn't really that enthusiastic. I was wanting a return to a national team, not a club job, and I explained that to him but said I would go away and think about it. The club were called Gor Mahia.

Gor Mahia are a huge club in Kenya, alongside their fiercest rivals AFC Leopards. Their supporter base is rooted in the Luo, which is the fourth-largest ethnic group native to western Kenya. The club can trace their roots back to the 1920s and the name comes from that of a legendary Luo warrior. Like many things concerned with football in Africa, there is a political element to everything. The former Kenyan prime minister Raila Odinga was a prominent supporter of the club.

But they were in the doldrums and, for some inexplicable reason, had not won their national title for 18 years. They were, therefore, very much a sleeping giant and the job was an opportunity to wake them up. But I still wasn't sure. I went home and spoke to Michelle. I assumed, being Kenyan, that the chance of a move home would be attractive to her. But I was wrong. She was less enthralled about the situation than I was. She was enjoying being on maternity leave, spending all her time with Saoirse and enjoying the life we were building in Uganda. But she agreed that it was something to be considered, so I arranged to meet officials from the club to hear what they had to say.

We met in a hotel in Nairobi and I was immediately impressed by the club president, Ambrose Rachier. His love and passion for the club was infectious. He spoke about the grand plans he and others had to take Gor Mahia back to the top of the domestic game. It was fantastic listening to him; he was so positive and enthusiastic and the more he talked, the more I wanted to be a part of it. I was to be taking over from Croatian coach Zdravko Logarušić, who had apparently refused to return to the club after going away on holiday. The money was not a motivation – to be honest, it never has been – I just asked the agent to get me what they could afford. I said to Ambrose I would join on one proviso

– that if a national job came up, he would not stand in my way. He agreed.

I suppose, as had happened previously in my football career, I was being selfish again, but when I told Michelle I had accepted the job she understood. I set off to Nairobi and left her and Saoirse in Kampala, where her mum had come over from Ireland to help. Fortunately for me, the governor of Nairobi at the time was a Gor fan and had a flat set aside for whoever the head coach was. It was empty, so I moved straight in and I would be on my own for a few weeks before Michelle and Saoirse joined me. On and off the park, it was a smooth transition.

Gor Mahia were sitting second or third in the table when I joined and had become the great underachievers.

I was introduced to Bobby Ogolla – a bit of a club legend, who had been a defender for Gor until hanging up his boots in the late 80s. He was to be my assistant and he was a really experienced, capable and likeable guy.

Frank Ouna was also to be part of the backroom team. There was Iddi the goalkeeping coach, Fred Nyawaka was a cracking young physio and there were also a couple of fitness coaches called Geoff and Nduta. Bonge was our kitman and helped out with the equipment, while running the office were Judy and Celestine. They were all great people, a great team and it was a surprise to me, therefore, that, with everything operating so well off the park, the team were underperforming on it. We played our games at the Nairobi City Stadium, to the east of the city centre. It was in urgent need of repair and renovation – something that has happened subsequently – and was a ramshackle home.

Much to my relief, I found we had a very good team. Their skill levels were high and they just needed to be properly coached. They needed a system, they needed to be organised to give them better game awareness. And they needed someone to believe in them. From day one, the players responded brilliantly to my demands. I found the players, like the Ugandans, had a hunger to learn and showed a lot of respect towards the coaches. I knew I was going to enjoy working with these guys.

The fans were extremely passionate as well and, with the political aspect to the support – the AFC Leopards, for example, are associated with the rival Luhya ethnic group – things could get rowdy. I remember early in the season playing a game away at Kasarani, which is in the north-east of Nairobi. We drew and actually played well, passing up a number of chances to score the winning goal. We hadn't been helped by two of our best players leaving to go on trial with clubs elsewhere! Danny Sserunkuma was one of them. He was a Ugandan striker and, in the end, his move fell through. Rama Salim would move on loan to Qatari club Al-Markhiya Sports Club. It was crazy that, during the season, the players could move on but the fans were more frustrated at the dropped points and were throwing plastic bottles, which rained down on the technical area.

I turned to Bob Ogolla and asked: 'What do they do when we lose?'

He looked at me and replied: 'You don't want to know, Boss!'

Off the field, I was getting settled. Michelle and Saoirse had joined me and we rented a house in Lavington, an upmarket suburb in Nairobi. It was a great place to live, with great schools, shops and restaurants. It was really fantastic, with beautiful houses and smart, tree-lined streets. I had run into a couple of guys I knew from Kampala – Mathew Keoch, who is Kenyan, and his mate and work colleague, Johnny Evans, a Welshman with not a hint of a Welsh accent. I would also socialise twice a week with the club president, Ambrose Rachier, with whom I would drink and chat to into the early hours. It was a friendship more than a working relationship. These guys helped me find my feet in Nairobi and before long we were settled into our new life. This was definitely home for us now.

The mood around the club helped. We were playing well, winning games and the possibility of ending Gor's long wait for the title looked a distinct possibility as we climbed to the top of the league. Then came a twist. Tuzo, a major dairy in Kenya and one of the club's main sponsors, had decided not to renew its contract and, therefore, its money was no longer coming into the club. In African football, you are never too far away from a crisis and this was ours. If the club wasn't getting paid, neither were the staff – it meant that, for the last six months of my time there, I wasn't getting wages. My players could barely survive and it was a very difficult situation.

Even after I left Gor, I was still having to hound their vice-treasurer for the money I was owed. He was a good guy, another one who was a drinking buddy, and he did his best. It went on for more than a year, with a little bit dribbling in here and there. In the end, they would owe me thousands.

Kenya, like so many African countries, is one of contrasts. Some people live very well, others in poverty. We had a driver at the club, Patrick. He was a lovely fellow and was always inviting me to his house – an invitation I didn't take up until, one day, I decided to go. He lived in a district called Kibera, which is statistically the largest housing slum in all of Africa. I Googled it. In 2009, a census reported that Kibera's population was 170,000. Other sources suggest the population might be as high as anything from 500,000 to well over a million. On my experience, I would go with the higher number.

It was incredibly humbling. The houses, if you could call them that, were built with corrugated iron. There was no running water and the open sewers flowed right past Patrick's door. The house was one single room, with a curtain splitting it in two. On one side, there was a bed where Patrick, his wife and children slept, and the other side was a sitting area, with a small television. The guy had nothing but I was shocked when he presented me a gift of a teapot and cup. I reluctantly accepted it. I had had the presence of mind to ensure I hadn't arrived empty-handed. I had asked Michelle what I should take with me and she suggested flour, milk and other groceries. As I say, it was a humbling experience and one I have never forgotten. Patrick and his family may have been poor but they were proud people who opened up their home to me. After that, I would give him a little bit of money – not much – Patrick never asked for much anyway. Sometime later, I was stunned to be told Patrick had passed away. I felt so much for his family and what they were now facing. I suggested that the money I was owed by the club be redirected to Patrick's family to fund funeral costs and such like. I don't know if they ever received it but, as I think about it now, I wish I had given him more.

The season was going better than even I could have hoped for and we were rarely out of the top spot but it was not without its tensions. There was one game away to Sony Sugar, a team based in the western town of Awendo, which is close to the border with Uganda, and their stadium is called the Awendo Green Stadium. The city is the base of a huge sugar company, hence the team name. We were trailing 2-1 in the 84th minute when our defender David Owino, who was nicknamed Calabar, rifled this shot from about 40 yards and it cannoned in off the underside of the bar. The referee and assistant both deemed the ball to have crossed the line. All of a sudden, all hell broke loose. The Sony players went crazy and were confronting the match officials and they were soon followed by some of their fans, who joined them in lambasting the poor referee, a guy called Nassur Doka. The protests went on for a full 20 minutes before Doka abandoned it. The trouble continued outside the stadium and there was a press report in the aftermath that described the Awendo-Migori road as 'a no-go zone for the faint-hearted'.

In the days that followed, the Football Kenya Federation carried out an investigation. Doka's report stated that the match had been abandoned because a Sony player and official had assaulted one of the assistant referees. Their initial ruling was that the match would need to be replayed but we felt that was unfair. Our players were very much innocent onlookers to the chaos and we argued it would not be right to punish them. In the end, the FKF changed their mind and awarded us the points but it rumbled on and Sony were unhappy.

We won the league by ten points from arch rivals AFC Leopards and I was just delighted we had achieved what we had set out to do. I had said at the outset that Gor wouldn't have to wait 18 years to win another title and I was proved right. Our striker, Danny Ssernkuma, the guy who had wanted away earlier in the season, had stayed and he scored in something like each of the last ten games. Winning the title and ending Gor's long wait was fantastic. I was so proud of the players and all my staff and I can't thank them enough for all they did for me. To win the title, despite all the financial problems off the field, is testament to the character of everybody involved.

Our title win put the team – and myself – back into the spotlight and, midway through the next season, Sam Nyamweya, the president of the FKF, approached Gor for permission to talk to me, with a view to offering me the national team job. He had said Kenya 'needed a coach who understood our game and Bobby Williamson is that kind of coach'. I had made clear when I was offered the Gor job that if any national association approached me, I would be released from my contract. Ambrose Rachier agreed to that and was true to his word but I wanted to stay in the job for one last tournament – the Cecafa Club Cup, which was being played in Rwanda. We didn't have a good tournament and failed to get out of our group. We hadn't played badly, we were just very unlucky. In the last game, we were winning with minutes to go, a result which would have taken us through. Danny Ssernkuma was clearly fouled just inside our own half but the referee waved play on and the opposition ran on and scored. I was livid and, afterwards, the referee was severely reprimanded by his bosses. He was that bad that the tournament organisers even apologised to me! It didn't matter; we were heading home and I was worried the result would tarnish my good work. But in my last game at the City Ground, against Sony Sugar, the players hoisted me on to their shoulders.

Frank Nuttall, a fellow Scot, took over from me at Gor. We had a mutual friend in Alex McLeish – who recommended him to replace me. Eck's recommendation was good enough for me and I approached Ambrose Rachier on Frank's behalf. Ambrose joked, sort of, that he hoped Frank was like me and didn't hassle him for money. In the end, Frank had to do just that and I don't blame him – he had family and responsibilities back in Scotland. But he did a great job and would lead Gor to another title, going undefeated in the league. He would win it again the next season before he left to team up with Big Eck at Egypt, and a former Killie player of mine, Dylan Kerr, took on the job. Football is, indeed, a small world!

I had transformed Gor and left Frank with a team that was more than good enough and far stronger mentally than the one I had inherited. For that, I have to thank Ambrose Rachier for giving me the opportunity to manage Gor Mahia. I don't use these words flippantly when I say it was a privilege and an honour. I had such a good relationship with Ambrose. We used to have a few beers once or twice a week but after I left, I sent him a text saying I would not be comfortable socialising with him so much, as I didn't want Frank thinking I was undermining him. I think Ambrose took it literally, because he has never spoken to me since!

I took over the Kenya team, who are known as the Harambee Stars, from Adel Amrouche, a Moroccan coach. I didn't find out until afterwards that, technically, he hadn't been released from his contract. If I had known that, I'm not sure I would have signed. The team were in a bad place, having just been beaten by African minnows Lesotho in an Afcon qualifier.

Nyamweya had said, 'This is the beginning of a fresh start for our football,' and I felt it was vital to be involved at all levels of the national set-up, just as I had been in Uganda.

Our first game was away to Egypt but as it was played outside the official international window, it meant clubs were under no obligation to release their players. None of the Gor Mahia players were involved – for Egypt, Chelsea refused to allow Mo Salah to play. The game was played in front of 30,000 at the Aswan Stadium and we did well to only go down 1-0.

Being a manager of an international team is always filled with challenges. I would scour the leagues in Europe and the Far East to try to uncover a gem of a player we could add to our squad. I brought in Johanna Omolo, who was playing in Belgium with Lommel. We had a home and away tie with the Under-21 team in Botswana and I knew it was the perfect chance to bring Omolo into the set-up. He was such a strong prospect and he trained all week in camp with us. The game was on the Friday and we were due to leave on the Thursday. On the Wednesday, Omolo came to me asking for a chat. He then proceeded to tell me that he couldn't travel for the game, explaining that he had to go and meet his future wife's parents to discuss their wedding. I wasn't best pleased. He had got the federation to pay for all his flights, knowing he had no intention of travelling with us. To compound the problem, Michael Olunga was also unavailable – he was sitting exams to qualify as an engineer!

As it happened, our travel arrangements were not the best. We arrived in Gaborone, the capital city of Botswana, at three in the morning. We got to the hotel, had breakfast and sent the players to bed. I hadn't slept long when I was awoken by a brass band on parade just outside the hotel! I stuck my head outside my window to see what was going on, only to discover all the players were doing the same. The game wasn't being played in Gaborone but at a stadium some two hours' drive away. When we spoke to the organisers, they decided we should leave the hotel at ten o'clock but, with the game kicking off at 3pm, I told them that was too early. Well, I lost the argument, so we were forced to have our pre-match meal at 9.30am, sit on a bus for hours and arrive at the stadium at noon. The players were knackered, laying around the dressing room, trying to get some rest. The game went entirely as you would expect. The players dug in for the first half but their energy levels were shot and we went down 3-0.

The second leg was a week later, back at Nyayo. We got our revenge! We conceded an early goal but the outstanding Michael Olunga would go on and score four goals. I knew he was a great talent.

If I thought that, by joining the national team, I was leaving my money problems behind me at Gor, I couldn't have been more mistaken. Gor hadn't been paying me for the last six months but, when I left the club, the president assured me I would get the money. They tried and a bit dribbled in here and there. But the national team was different – and I wasn't the only one suffering.

We were to play a World Cup qualifier against Mauritius. The first leg was away, and Victor Wanyama, Johanna Omolo and Ayub Timbe only arrived on the day of the match. There were no training sessions – nothing! The three of them played brilliantly, with Johanna and Ayub scoring for us in a 5-2 win which set us up nicely for the return match at Kasarani on the Sunday. We arrived back in Nairobi on the Friday, trained on the Saturday and went into camp for the game on Sunday. I rarely stayed in the camp. I felt the players would be more relaxed without me hovering about but I would always join them for breakfast before training or before the game to speak to them individually. Victor Wanyama, the team captain, called me on the Saturday night and told me the players were leaving, because they had not been paid their allowances. Such a situation is unheard of in Europe but the players' circumstances in Africa are hugely different. Players in Europe are well paid and I know I would have played for Scotland for nothing, as it would have been a huge honour. But here in Africa, especially central and east Africa, players are not well paid. Most of them are living hand to mouth, so I understood their concern. I spoke to Victor and pleaded with him to persuade the players to stay. We had already qualified for the next round, so I told him we would get the game out of the way and then get the money side of things sorted. I called the federation president, Sam Nyamweya, to tell him the players weren't happy and were ready to leave.

'Let them!' Sam said. I couldn't believe it! I certainly wouldn't want to play poker with him!

Thankfully, the players stayed but their hearts were never in it. The game was a non-event. Mauritius just defended and didn't want to concede, while our guys were demotivated and there was no hunger about them. In the end, a 0-0 draw was the best we could have hoped for.

The next round was against Cape Verde. In the first leg, at the Nyayo Stadium, we won 1-0 after Michael Olunga put us a goal up inside the first ten minutes. Ahead of the second leg in Praia, the capital of Cape Verde, I was summoned to a meeting with Sam Nyamweya at his house. There were a few other people from the Kenyan Football Federation there and it was to discuss travel arrangements for the away leg. It was going to be tricky. Cape Verde is a collection of islands off the west coast of Africa. It's a stunning place, with beautiful beaches and crystal-blue water, but not the easiest for us to get to. The distance is about 4,000 miles and there were no direct flights.

I was asked my opinion and suggested we leave Sunday, train Monday and be ready for the game on the Tuesday. To my surprise, given how tight finances were, the president said we were going to charter a plane for the long journey and this would get us in on the Monday, we'd train at the venue at kick-off time in the evening and then rest up all of Tuesday ahead of the big game. I thought that would be tremendous.

I arrived at the airport on the Monday morning – we were told to be there at nine but I arrived at eight. I waited and waited. Nine o'clock came and went and there was still no sign of the players. Then I got a call to say the players were refusing to leave their hotel as, once again, their allowances had not been paid. It only really applied to the local-based players, who needed to give the money to their families before they left, but there seemed to be solidarity among the group. The vice-president of the federation turned up to assure me all would be fine. He suggested we head to a hotel around the corner from the airport for lunch. As we left the terminal building, I looked out on the tarmac and saw this two-engine propeller plane and there was a team of guys sticking HARAMBEE STARS in huge letters down the side of it. I was told that, once they had finished, we would leave. But, at this point, there was still not a sign of a single player. I was really anxious. At least when we returned from lunch, the players had arrived. But the painters out at the plane still hadn't finished. So, it was back into the lounge to wait. We eventually left at 9pm! A full 12 hours after we had been told we would leave.

The plane was a nightmare. There was no food on board, only one toilet, which was overflowing and, therefore, out of commission, and you couldn't even recline the seats. The players had no chance to get some shut-eye, which was a waste of time anyway, because, after just an hour, we were landing in Entebbe to refuel! We had to stop twice more for fuel before we reached Praia. We touched down at Nelson Mandela Praia International Airport two hours before kick-off!

The players were knackered and starving. I told them to put their luggage in their rooms at the hotel, that we would grab something light to eat and then we would have to head to the stadium. Remember, this is a World Cup qualifier – the most important football tournament on the planet and we're pitching up two hours before kick-off. The FIFA rules are that you have to be in situ a minimum of 24 hours before the game. I honestly thought we were going to be disqualified. Amazingly, though, the game went ahead.

Despite everything, we competed very well, only to concede just before half-time from a wickedly deflected free kick. We conceded again in the second half and the goal we needed to go through never came. It was such a shame. Cape Verde were one of the top four teams in Africa and beating them would have been a great achievement. Hell, they qualified for the World Cup in 2026.

As we got to the airport to await our 'glider' home, one of the fans who had bravely travelled with us handed me his mobile phone. He said it was the president and I assumed it was Sam Nyamweya, president of the Kenyan Football Federation. Pretty soon into the conversation, my back bolted straight as I realised it was Uhuru Kenyatta, the president of Kenya! Once I realised who it was, I didn't say a word; I just listened. He told me there would be repercussions and that whoever had organised the ludicrous travel arrangements was going to be held responsible.

That was all well and good but what was the point? We were out when we had had a great chance to progress and no inquest was going to change that.

Despite his determined words, I don't think anyone was ever held responsible.

The 2015 Cecafa tournament was being held in Ethiopia and we had been drawn in the same group as Uganda, Zanzibar and Burundi. It meant that, in the opening game, I was going to be coming up against Milutin Sredojević, the Serbian coach who had manipulated my exit from the job so that he could replace me. I messaged the Ugandan doctor, a guy I still knew, and told him to tell Sredojević not to come near me before, during or after the game. I had no respect for him. He was so blatantly two-faced about it and I didn't want to speak to him. We won the game 2-0 and the coaches were supposed to do a joint interview afterwards but I refused.

Sredojević was bleating on about how his team was young and the Kenyan team had nearly their whole first-team squad. I always picked the best players available for the Cecafa, as I felt you were undermining the tournament and the sponsors if you didn't – it's a sign of respect.

I was back in our hotel when a contingent of Cecafa guys came to speak to me and asked me why I'd refused to do the joint interview with the Ugandan coach. I told them the story and said that anyone else would have done the same in the circumstances. I think it's a terrible idea anyway. Who knows how the game is going to go? It might be a battle and there may have been arguments between the technical teams. Plus, both the coaches probably won't have seen the game the same way.

It's another example of idiots running the game.

In the second match, we got a point against Burundi, which was enough for us to qualify unless something crazy happened in our final game against Zanzibar, which was being played a few hours outside Addis Ababa. I decided to do something I never usually do and I changed a winning team, playing all the players who hadn't featured so far. We were all but sure of qualification and it would have taken a disaster for us to miss out.

An hour into the game and we were 3-0 down! In the end, we scored very late on. Although we were already through, to say I was relieved would be an understatement.

We had been drawn against Rwanda in the quarter-finals. I had scheduled a training session in the morning, just to run through a few set pieces and to freshen things up. The players went into the shade to put on their boots, while myself and the coaching team got set up. I was waiting for them to join me in the centre of the pitch but the lot of them were sitting in the shade and showing no sign of moving. I sent my assistant, Moses Otieno, to get them and he returned to say they were refusing to train. Yup, you guessed it, they hadn't been paid – no allowances, no bonuses, nothing.

Although the players were probably unaware of it, I was in the same boat as they were. I wasn't getting paid either.

I went over and told them the vice-president was back at the hotel and that, when we were finished, they should have a meeting with him. It seemed to remedy the situation and, at the end of the training session, we practised penalties. They were fighting over who's turn it was next.

We got back to the hotel and they had their meeting. I wasn't involved, although, truth be told, I probably should have been, as I wasn't getting my money either. It was a huge distraction ahead of such an important game and something I felt should have been sorted before the tournament, not during it.

In the game itself, we played well but just couldn't score a goal. Their keeper played a blinder, we hit the bar, we hit the post and had so many corners but we couldn't get the ball in the net. Rwanda never had a shot at our goal, no corners even. In fact, they had set up for penalties and it worked for them. With no extra time, it was straight to spot kicks.

Before the game had ended, I was thinking about substituting our goalkeeper to play mind games with their players, hoping they would think the goalkeeper was good at saving penalties. As it happened, when I turned round to talk with our goalkeeper coach, Matthew Ottomax, he wasn't there – he had disappeared to the toilet.

With the shoot-out upon us, I turned to the players to look for volunteers. I got four! They had been fighting it out in training the day before and now they weren't interested. I would never force players to take the penalties; they have to be confident and step forward. One of our young players, Johanna Omondi, did just that. I was reluctant but had no option. The only penalty missed in the shoot-out was his and it was enough to put us out. Thankfully, the disappointment didn't hold Johanna back and he has gone on to have a good career at club and international level.

It was just another example of the fine lines that exist in football.

We played a qualifier for the CHAN tournament against Ethiopia and missed a penalty in both legs. Kevin Kimani missed our penalty in Ethiopia and Ali Abondo missed the penalty at the Nyayo Stadium. If we had scored both, we would have gone through. Ali was not even our designated penalty taker and we were surprised when he grabbed the ball. He hit the post!

We played Zambia in an Afcon qualifier in 2015 at the Nyayo Stadium. We started very well and went one up, with a goal from Michael Olunga, but we eventually lost 2-1. It was so frustrating. We were so close but couldn't find an equaliser. Looking back, I think it was the only game we lost at home in my time as the Kenyan boss.

Fine lines indeed.

By this point, I still wasn't getting paid – in fact, I would go for about a year without my money. It is not unusual in African football for a club who want to get rid of a manager to just stop paying him. Eventually, the manager gets fed up and leaves. But this was the Kenyan national team – and Kenya was my home. I wasn't considering leaving the country at all. The family were all settled and I loved where we lived and the people, who were all so friendly and welcoming. Managing the national team here is the pinnacle and I love this country and the people. It's the reason I'm still here, even though I'm not working. I was honoured to coach the Harambee Stars. People go on about loyalty in football and here in Kenya it is no different. Kenya is my home and, even though I hadn't been paid for a year, I wasn't walking away.

The elections for president of the Kenyan Football Federation were about to happen in mid-2015. Sam Nyamweya was up against my old chairman at Gor Mahia, Ambrose Rachier, and a young guy called Nick Mwendwa, who I didn't know at all. Mwendwa won the vote, so there was a new president and I had a new boss. I waited for the phone call to find out my future. Would I be kept on or was I out? The call duly came and it was arranged for us to meet at the Four Points Hotel in Hurlingham. He asked me, given all the financial problems, why I had never walked away from the job. I told him it was the job I wanted and that Kenya was my home. I had no idea if I was being kept on or not but there was a lawyer there from the association, which wasn't a good sign. Nick said he hadn't made a decision yet but revealed he had once been on a flight with me when I was Uganda boss and he had been impressed by the discipline the team had shown.

I took that as a positive but I was wrong.

Nick told me he was going to Switzerland for a FIFA meeting and we would speak again when he got back. I felt I had to be given an opportunity to see if we could work together. I still had a contract after all. Nick returned from his FIFA trip and I awaited his call. It never came. Instead, through his lawyer, I tried to find out my position but he just kept fobbing me off and never returned a call or a text, which disappointed me.

I was in limbo until, one day, I went into my local and one of the regulars came up to me and said he was sorry I'd lost my job. I looked at him as if he was mad and asked what he was talking about. He showed me the newspaper and there was a picture of Mwendwa with his new technical staff.

That's how my loyalty was rewarded – the thanks I got for going so long without pay. I'd still done the job, turned up every day, still taking the team while having to deal with all the problems of players not getting paid when I hadn't received a penny either.

It was so disrespectful. No thank you from them. Nothing.

I was still under contract and felt they could have arranged a settlement but that wasn't forthcoming. I wasn't happy. If we had sat down, we could have settled things. I wouldn't have been looking for my contract to be paid in full, the same as with the Ugandans. But the sit-down never happened, so I decided to fight.

I only had two options. I could go to FIFA or take the federation to an employment tribunal. If I had gone to FIFA, the country would have had sanctions imposed on them until it was resolved and they might have been banned from tournaments. That was not an option I could consider. The only ones being punished would have been the players and the fans. Football is a short career and players, even if they are lucky, might only play in four top tournaments. Plus, Kenyan players need the exposure of Afcon and World Cup qualifiers to better their careers. I was not prepared to risk the players being penalised, so I took the employment tribunal route, which is not a quick process.

I fought for five long years before the court decided in my favour. I was awarded a sum that covered the remainder of my contract – a substantial amount of money that the FKF claimed they didn't have. It could have been settled for a lot less but the new president didn't show me any respect to settle it amicably. I asked my lawyer if she could come up with a payment plan that was manageable for the FKF. It was agreed by both parties that I would be paid a sum of money every four months for three years. It started off fine and I was getting paid but then it would stop and my lawyer would have to go to court every time we were due a payment. I was trying to help out the federation by agreeing to the payment plan but even then they wouldn't honour it.

As I'm writing this, it is now April 2025 and I've still not been paid what we agreed. I worked for two years and got paid six months' wages. They were supposed to pay my accommodation as well. I was prepared to settle out of court but they wouldn't answer calls or speak to my lawyers.

The two coaches before me didn't get paid either, so it's nothing new.

This could all have been avoided if the president had let me see out my contract and then replaced me or, if that was not workable, then sack me, but he didn't give me a chance. He actually said when he replaced me that he was going down the local coaches route, which is fine. But he brought in a guy called Stanley Okumbi, who is a nice bloke, but if the stories are to be believed, he had left his previous job because he couldn't handle the pressure. He lasted a year.

Jacob 'Ghost' Mulee and Francis Kimanzi have also held the post. Both are capable but, again, they didn't receive the backing to do the job. Ghost has held the post five times! I don't know of any other club or country who have hired a coach five times.

I would argue strongly that getting rid of me was a mistake and I shouldn't have been replaced. It cost the FKF a lot of money. I was introducing a lot of new young players into the squad and, given time, I know we would have been successful. Since I left, there have been ten coaches – that's one a year. If you look at the successful teams in the world, they have continuity with their coaches.

But I certainly wasn't wanting to leave Kenya and return to Scotland. I find the family values in Scotland and Africa totally different. In Scotland, it is every man for himself. Here in Kenya, they are very much family-orientated. And they have respect for their family. I know men here in their 40s and 50s who wouldn't swear in front of their parents. They just have so much respect for the older generation. The majority don't have a wealthy lifestyle but they look after each other.

For example, it's expensive here for medical treatment. There are no hospices or anything like that and it costs you a fortune to go into hospital for a couple of days. It's a lot of money but the whole family will chip in to get the hospital bill paid, because, if you don't pay the bill, you don't get out.

It's different here – and I wasn't going to leave.

Little did I know that the fight I was having with the Kenyan Football Federation would pale into insignificance when compared with the battle I was about to face.

CHAPTER 19
CANCER

'STAGE 3,' renowned oncologist Dr Ganesh Jadhav said as he discussed what had been diagnosed as an undifferentiated nasopharyngeal carcinoma.

He was responding to a question my wife, Michelle, had asked about what stage my cancer was at and, for the first time, it was sinking in just how serious the situation was. Without Michelle, I wouldn't have made it. It's as simple as that. But I'll never forget the look on her face. All the treatment back in Nairobi – the suspected polyp, the biopsy, the colonoscopy and the endoscopy, the cholera diagnosis, the operation on my nose and then the cancer confirmation from Professor Isaac Macharia – had led to this moment at the Delhi's Indraprastha Apollo Hospital and the capable hands of Dr Jadhav. All the nose bleeds, the trouble breathing, the refusal to consider it was anything serious. The dismissal that it could be anything to worry about, because, other than the blockage in my left nostril, I felt absolutely fine. In fact, I felt perfectly healthy and, until that moment, I didn't have any feelings that this was life-threatening in any way at all.

I hadn't been afraid in the slightest.

All of a sudden, I was beginning to question my own mortality. I was 56 years old and beginning to understand that I was not, after all, indestructible. If you're in good health, you don't pay much attention. You think, 'It won't be me', but it could be. People die for no apparent reason.

Fortunately, the cancer was localised, meaning it hadn't found a way to travel through my lymph nodes or into my blood. But it had started spreading into my head. I was getting headaches and my left eye was swollen. The treatment was to consist of seven rounds of chemo and 35 sessions of radiation therapy.

It is, perhaps, worth recapping what had brought me to this situation in more detail.

Around August 2017, I was aware that I was having difficulties breathing through my nose. I didn't think too much about it and put it down to having my nose broken a few times when I was a player. It felt like there was a blockage in it – something that, if you could only get to it, you could pull out.

It was annoying more than anything else, because I didn't feel ill in any way. I had a blocked nose but I wasn't feeling bad.

I was due to meet a fellow Scot for a couple of pints but I was early, so stopped in at one of my locals before we were due to meet up. Chris Harley was from Greenock and had moved to Nairobi through his job with a major betting company. I was with another lad called Joe – you know what, I've known him for ten years and couldn't tell you his second name – when I felt a gentle tap, tap, tap. I put my hand out and the blood was landing in my palm. I rushed off into the toilet to deal with it, the blood now flowing from my nose. It was bleeding heavily and I was in a right mess but I had to clean myself up as best I could. I was worried someone was going to come in and see me, so I stuffed toilet paper in to stem the flow and made for the door, grabbing Joe as we went out and telling him that he had to drive, because I couldn't get the blood to stop. All the way to Chris's hotel, I was dealing with this blood and when we reached him, I told him I would have to come up to his room to borrow a shirt. Both Chris and Joe were concerned about it but I wasn't going to let such a stupid thing as a bleeding nose spoil a good night out, although I was bleeding non-stop for more than an hour.

By the time we went out, things had stopped and I never gave it a second thought. The next morning, I was driving Saoirse and the twins who lived next door to nursery and, as I drove through the gates, the blood started again. I grabbed anything I could find, some old paper or something, and managed to block it up enough that the kids were unaware of what was going on.

I'd never suffered from nose bleeds before but it was my left nostril that was giving me all the bother, causing the breathing difficulties. Not once did I consider it was anything serious.

Things went quiet for the next few days – nose bleed-wise – until the following Thursday night into Friday morning, when it happened again. There was no way I could hide it from Michelle. She asked me what was going on and if I had been picking at my nose. I told her about the terrible nose bleeds I had been getting for the last few weeks and, while I was ready to dismiss it as something unimportant, Michelle insisted we get it checked out and made an appointment at the Agha Khan Clinic, one of the main hospitals in Nairobi. They cauterised my nose to stop the bleeding and said I should get it checked out.

We made appointments at the Anderson Clinic, which is part of Nairobi Hospital, and were booked in for a full check-up. It took a whole day, getting one test after another. Eventually, I was sent up to the ENT Clinic. I was looked at by a Dr Caroline Muturi. She thought it was a polyp but was confused, because, according to her, polyps didn't bleed. She said she would take a piece away for analysis and get back to me.

After the examinations, it was decided I should come in for a colonoscopy and an endoscopy, so I had to arrange a date to return to the hospital.

I got word back from the ENT Clinic and was told the biopsy wasn't conclusive and they would have to do it again. I said they had to take it out, the blockage, because I couldn't breathe. I was booked in for the op anyway and it made sense to do it when I returned for the colonoscopy and endoscopy.

It was when they took it out that they discovered it was cancerous. The tumour had been removed by Professor Macharia and, while he had been confident he had removed all the cancer, I would still have to undergo radiotherapy and chemotherapy. The professor had gone through all the details and the course of treatment but Michelle decided that the best course of action was to go to India, where they had certain equipment that was, at the time, unavailable in East Africa, let alone Kenya.

Michelle organised flights to Delhi, via Dubai, and we were booked into the Radisson Blu Hotel, which wasn't far from the Apollo Hospital, for a week. We had taken Saoirse out of school and brought her with us and Michelle had to take time off work. She had arranged everything, all the appointments, the whole lot. She would go to reception check-in with the insurance documents while I just sat down and waited for her to call me and follow her. We were only supposed to be there for ten days but the PET scan showed there were still roots of the cancer in place and I had to be fitted with a mask for the radiation. We were going to be there a while.

We had to find accommodation, because staying in a hotel for three months wasn't viable.

The hospital staff were remarkable and extremely helpful, every step of the way. They helped us find an Airbnb not far from where I would be having my treatment and we hired a tutor for Saoirse so she wouldn't fall behind with her schoolwork. Michelle even managed to get her mother over from Ireland to help her, as I was not a good patient. Her mother had been a nurse in a psychiatric hospital, so I wasn't a problem!

The programme was radiation every week day and chemo on the Mondays. Radiation was at 10.30pm each day. The hospital would send me a taxi to bring me in and they would strap the mask on for 15 minutes. Then it was out, back in the taxi and back to my bed.

Everyone would be asleep by the time I got back, so I would go into my own room and watch Indian football until I dropped off. I watched John Gregory, who was managing at Chennaiyin FC, and Steve Coppell, who was at Kerala Blasters FC, both in the Indian Super League, and think: 'I could do that.'

But I was kidding myself. What I really needed to do was concentrate on my recovery.

I don't know if they started the treatment gently or not but, in the initial stages, I thought, 'I can handle this.' I really wasn't finding it too bad. My appearance was changing, though. I had a full beard when the radiotherapy first began but it was gradually falling out and I had to become creative when grooming. I was trying to make the facial hair passable but ended up with a moustache, which had to come off. All these many months later, I still haven't got full growth on the left side of my face. The moustache is a mess and my face is numb in parts. I also lost my sense of smell and my sense of taste had gone as well. In addition, I was having a problem with my left eye, due to the radiation, but at least I was breathing through my nose again.

The first few weeks in Delhi were manageable. We could go out for a walk, go for food with the family and, apart from the smog, could enjoy the city. I was taking tablets because of the treatment but was also on pills for the cholera recovery and, to cap it all, I had been recently diagnosed with diabetes. I was popping about 20 a day. I discovered the hard way that my mouth was having a reaction to the combined medication. I developed a mouthful of ulcers and I mean FULL! My tongue was white, the roof of my mouth was white, they were everywhere and the pain was excruciating. I couldn't swallow anything and eating any food was torture. After a couple of days of suffering, I had to be admitted to hospital, where I was put on a drip and a course of painkillers for the ulcers. The doctor changed the medication and it settled down slightly but I still couldn't eat. Michelle was giving me protein shakes that were also difficult to take. I got home and was all but bedridden. The only time I could get out of bed was to go into the hospital each evening for my treatment. Michelle would bring me my medication and a milk shake and leave me there to try and swallow three pills at a time every hour. It took me an hour to take the tablets; it was agony. I used to dread the bedroom door opening if it was Michelle with more shakes or tablets. It was a blessing when it was Saoirse. She was only four, yet she was having to witness all this. She would come in and keep me company until I dropped off again, which was frequently.

I lost 20kg in three weeks but the doctors had probably seen it all before and everything they told me would happen did happen.

Lying in my bed, dealing with the pain from the ulcers, the impact of the surgery and the effects of the chemotherapy and radiotherapy, I began to look back on my life. It is often said that when people go through something like I had, a near-death experience I suppose, you begin to re-evaluate what you have done. Does your life flash in front of you? I don't know the answer to that one but I did begin to think about friends from the past and my life, those early days growing up in Easterhouse. I would be drowsy but I would be thinking about people I hadn't seen or heard from since childhood. Former classmates and old teachers – people I hadn't thought of for more than 40 years. It was strange.

I also began to think of the friends and former team-mates I had lost. Guys like Colin McAdam, my great pal from those days at Ibrox. A gentleman. I missed his funeral, because I was in Africa. There was Ian Redford and Davie Cooper. Gone before their time. I would have tears in my eyes as I reminisced.

I began to look at my life away from football and how determined I was to get back to my wonderful world in Nairobi with Michelle and Saoirse. I suppose I knew then, and I definitely do now, that my career in football was over. All I wanted was to be there for Michelle, to support her in her own career and to watch her succeed. Michelle is a great wife and mother and I love her so much. She will get to where she wants to go career-wise – I'm just hanging on to her coat tails and hoping I'm not holding her back.

It's the same with Saoirse. Thank God she has developed her mother's intelligence. I know she will go on to university and be a success at whatever she chooses to do. I was determined to be around to see it. She is a pleasure to be around, always happy, although she is a pre-teen and I'm sure there will be difficult times ahead. It was the same with my first two – Emma and Steven. I'm so proud of them. They have developed into wonderful human beings, who have carved out their own careers as a nurse and a firefighter. I reflected on how I wasn't there for them when they were kids, how I put building my own career in football front and centre of everything. Their mum, Lorraine, deserves the credit – she did a great job. I've always felt that, as a parent, you've got to let your children grow and be independent and just be there to pick up the pieces when there's a hitch.

And I looked back on my career in football. Could I have done better? I suppose I could have but I realised that, around my late 20s, I had found my level. I wasn't going to get any better and having a few beers, sometimes more than a few, at the right time wasn't going to make me any worse. As a coach and manager, I always tried to be positive and make sure the players enjoyed the training every day – as I did. I've worked with some great footballers and met a lot of great people through football; the folk who worked behind the scenes who don't get the recognition they deserve.

As I lay there, I played through the highs and lows of my life. The people I had met and the impact they made on me – whether they were aware of it or not.

Each time I went in for the chemo treatment, I had to fill in a form. There was one section where one of the questions would be: 'State of the patient?'

At the beginning, I wrote: 'Alive!'

The following week I wrote: 'Still alive!'

By the end, I was writing: 'Barely alive!'

I don't think the medical staff got my sense of humour but, as the treatment went on, my determination to put black humour into everything I did disappeared. I was miserable and it was really taking a toll, not only on me but on Michelle. I was becoming a major pain in the arse to her but, thankfully, her mum was there to help her through it. She would tell Michelle I wasn't being rational, that it was the treatment and that my reaction to it was to be expected. I just longed to be home, to be back in Nairobi. To be well.

We were in India for three months. It felt like three years but I have only got gratitude for all the people there who helped me. People like Dr Jadhav and all the staff at the Indraprastha Apollo Hospital and the medical team in the hospital in Nairobi, led by Professor Isaac Macharia. I don't know where I would have been without them. Actually, I do and it doesn't bear thinking about.

We were due to leave Delhi around Christmastime. Michelle had worked in India before and thought it would be a good idea to spend a week in Goa, on the coast. I had no idea where Goa was and discovered it was south of Delhi, about two hours away. But when we were returning, we would have to fly back to Delhi to get a connection to Dubai before we could go on to Nairobi. The thought of that drained me, so, thankfully, I talked her into having a week's holiday in Dubai. By God, did she deserve it. She had put so much into looking after me, making sure I made all my appointments, taking my course of drugs. She did everything.

We reached the airport and I couldn't walk. I desperately needed to rest, so we managed to get me into one of those little single sleeping compartments while Michelle looked after the flight details. By the time we were to board, Michelle had managed to commandeer a wheelchair and someone to push it. It's the best way to travel – you are first on and first off – but the flight itself was a test of character. I was uncomfortable and struggling. They had a wheelchair waiting for me when we landed and it was straight to the car and the hotel. When we got to the reception desk, there was a problem with Michelle's bank. A payment hadn't been sent and, with the time difference, it was taking a while to get sorted. I wasn't stressed. I knew Michelle would do it.

This break, the week in Dubai, was for Michelle and Saoirse. They had been put through the mill in Delhi, away from home, stressing about me and my treatment. I can't remember what was said but I had Michelle in tears one day in the room. I think everything she had handled had caught up with her and I wasn't myself. I still feel bad about that. I wanted them to have a good time but I wasn't going to be able to join them. While they did the tourist stuff – SeaWorld and that type of thing – I was barely able to make it out of my room. I would make an effort, as I knew I had to eat, but I would make it down for breakfast, be unable to get anything down and head back to bed. Michelle would force me to drink the protein shake and take the medication. The two of them would go out for the day and see the sights while I lay in bed and drifted in and out of sleep – again thinking about players and pals from the past.

There was a friend in Nairobi, Christine, who knew I was in Delhi and had asked me if I could source some jam jars for her, as she was wanting to start up a honey business! I know it sounds mad but it's true. She obviously wasn't aware how ill I was. At the time, she had travelled to Dubai and she came to my hotel. I managed to get down to the lobby and waited for her to arrive. As she entered the hotel, I saw her and got up to greet her. She looked at me, looked ahead and then walked on past me. I called out her name.

'Christine,' I said. 'Where you going?'

She turned around and looked straight at me. It took her a good few seconds to realise it was me. The treatment had certainly changed me. The hair had gone and I had lost more than 22kg. She was shocked looking at me and I was shocked by her reaction. We went to the pool area. She had a couple of beers – I couldn't even finish a glass of water.

Michelle and Saoirse did all the tourist stuff while I lay in bed with my medication and protein shakes lined up. I think, apart from an episode at the butterfly sanctuary, they had a good time. Saoirse swam with dolphins, getting some fabulous photographs. As for butterflies, she now has an eternal fear. Unbeknown to her, one of the keepers put one on her shoulder, one of those big ones. She was only four and, when she noticed it, she freaked out. She screamed the place down and they had to leave.

At last, we were heading back to Nairobi. I have to be honest, I don't feel I've ever been to Dubai, even though I stayed there for a week. Thanks to the wheelchair, we were first on the plane again but, just as before, the flight was uncomfortable. Then, as we went through immigration, my passport was flagged and we were detained. It was around 10pm at night, I was in a wheelchair, with four-year-old Saoirse on my lap, and they kept us for two hours. While I worked for Gor Mahia and the Kenyan national team, neither team had ever obtained a work permit for me, which was something that had been agreed in the contract. I usually had to pay for a visiting visa and get reimbursed. As I was not working, immigration was proving difficult. I tried to explain my predicament but I was not getting any sympathy, even with my little girl trying to sleep on the chair. Eventually, it got sorted. They checked the computer and had identified that I had applied when I was with the national team. The problem was they never paid for it. No shock there.

Back in Kenya, I didn't leave the house for a month, apart from going to the doctor. Michelle was pretty positive but I know I disappointed her on a number of occasions, because I was complaining about stuff. I know people will laugh at that, because I've a reputation as a moaner, but I was definitely unfair on her. I stopped responding to text messages, because I was on 20 tablets a day and I didn't know if I was coming or going.

And I was hallucinating. Stupid things. Like I'd be watching TV and be having a conversation with someone laying beside me and there was no one there. I'd think I was hearing a conversation but it was solely the medication.

I still had a few months before I could step out of the house. The post-treatment consisted of check-ups every fortnight and I had to have further surgery after six months, as my nostrils had fused shut. As time went on, the check-ups got less frequent. Eventually, as it is now, it's twice a year. But I had also developed chronic sinusitis and tinnitus. Given what the alternative was, I can live with that.

A few people I drank with in Roadhouse, my local at the time, popped in to see me. Christine, who I had seen in Dubai, came with two of her sisters, Lynette and Linda. I could see the tears in Linda's eyes when she saw how much I had deteriorated. I assured her that this was me getting better.

Martin and Marsden pitched in as well. They sound like a double act – but they're not funny! Marsden's wife, Gladys, a lovely lady, came along too. They couldn't stay long, as I was so tired, but I appreciated them making the effort. Chris Harley, who had been there when this cancer story began, also paid me a visit. Chris was doing his best to get Dafabet up and running but was struggling and really needed an intelligent Kenyan on board who knew the culture and the way things worked in the country. Michelle had left her job to look after me full-time but I wondered if this was, perhaps, an opportunity for her. She had been a deputy director with Amnesty International and was well qualified – probably too qualified. They spoke but it was well below her pay grade. But it wasn't about the money. We both realised I didn't need the 24/7 attention, so Michelle said she would help them out. They made an agreement that she could leave when a new job came along – which it did but not before she had restructured the company and moved them into a better office. It was so different for her, working with a betting company, not human rights, but she saw a different way of getting a job done.

Eventually, things began to go back to normal – or as close to normal as possible. I began to think about getting back into work again.

I hadn't worked since I was replaced as the Kenyan coach – my treatment had seen to that – but I only received one offer, from Bob Munro, who ran Mathare United. He was an interesting character – a Canadian who had settled in Kenya in the 80s and built up the club and a youth association aimed at developing young people. Bob, who sadly died early in 2025, impressed me but I thought it over and decided I didn't want to work in the country when neither the national team nor Gor Mahia could fulfil their obligations to me. I didn't want the hassle. I did recommend Frank Ouna, who I had worked with at Gor, and Bob hired him. He did a good job, kept them in the top division and then left to take up a post in Tanzania.

I couldn't understand why no one wanted my services, not just in Kenya but in East Africa. I'm the most successful national coach in East Africa and won the Cecafa Cup – the big East African tournament – four times, which no one else has done. I felt I had proven myself as a decent coach by helping Gor to their first title in 18 years. I had won a trophy in all the countries I worked in – Scotland, England, Uganda and Kenya. My record stands up pretty well but still I couldn't seem to get a job.

Funnily enough, my illness hasn't been publicised a lot in Africa. People didn't know I had been ill – they had just thought I'd left the country. But Kenya is my home. I'm happy and content living here. It's home and I enjoy the lifestyle.

So, now it's about supporting Saoirse and Michelle. If a job came up, we would think about it, but it's over. A career that has given me more highs than lows – and a barrel load of laughs.

Regrets? I have a few.

I never played for Scotland but I did work with the national team. I was invited by the SFA to go along to a game in Belarus, which was great. Craig Brown was in charge, so he would have been the one who arranged for me to be there. I liked Craig and had been in his company plenty of times down at Largs and at games and found that he always had time for younger managers and was more than willing to share his experiences and wisdom. It wasn't a great game; I think Scotland won 1-0, with Gary McAllister scoring the goal. After the game, I found myself in the pub with a few journalists – not unusual, I know. We had a few beers and headed back to the hotel, which had about 20 floors and one of those lifts that was extremely fast and had you at your floor in no time. I entered the lift, pressed the button and … zoom! Within seconds, the doors were opening again and I got out of the lift. I knew it was left, then left again to get to my room but, as I looked around, it was unfamiliar. There was a room, mostly with glass walls, with scantily dressed women sitting around smoking and drinking. I thought to myself, 'This is odd, I didn't notice this before.' Then it dawned on me. I was on the wrong floor and I had to get out of there quick. I hastily got back to my room, wondering if the SFA blazers knew there was a brothel in their hotel? I've never been in a brothel but I'm convinced there was one on that floor.

I was so proud to be involved with the national team – no matter what the level. There was a time I was actually in charge of the Under-21s in Poland. Craig Brown had called me, because Alex Smith – who normally took the team – was unavailable. It was an honour and privilege to take the team. The trip itself went well and there were no hiccups. The senior team was also playing, so it was good to spend time with the coaches. Jim Sinclair assisted me and big Jim Stewart was the goalkeeping coach. We were on the bus after the game, heading back to the hotel, when Mark Burchill came down and asked me if the players could head into town, as it was the last game of the season. I said I'd think about it. I turned to Jim Stewart and asked him for advice, as I was unsure what the lads were allowed to do while on international duty. He said they were not allowed out but we could get them a crate of beer to share at the hotel, so that's what we did. The night was going well until we were made aware that there was a load of noise coming from the players' rooms. As I stood up, Jim Sinclair got to his feet and said they would go and sort it, as they were staff and I didn't need to get involved. Pretty soon, they were back and it was all okay.

When Walter Smith was in charge, he asked me if I could go to Rome and watch Italy play Ukraine, who were in our World Cup qualifying group. I was between clubs at the time, so I jumped at the chance. It was my first time in Italy and Rome is a fantastic, historical city. All the tourist sites are within walking distance – the Colosseum, the Trevi Fountain, the Spanish Steps and, of course, the Vatican. I was walking around and bumped into a few Scottish journalists who were over for the game. We had lunch, then we did the sights. I was in the Vatican when Watty, as Walter was known, called me and asked me what I was up to. I told him I'd tell him when I got back!

The game was later that night and I was there to report on Ukraine, as Scotland were playing them in the next couple of days. After the game, I met up with the journalists and we went looking for a drinking hole and, to our dismay, all the pubs were closed. We jumped in a taxi and found a place that was open. We went in and were told it was a darts club, members only, and we had to join to gain entry, so we did. My membership card was in my wallet for years. We all had early flights in the morning but my bag was already packed and I decided to drink through and sleep on the plane.

Watty was picking me up at the airport, so I did my report on the flight. I'm not sure it was comprehensive, or even comprehensible, but I talked Watty through it over a couple of beers in a pub he and his business partner, Paul Burns, had.

Watty was a great guy with a lovely family; Ethel and the boys were great company. I remember we stopped in the Moodiesburn hotel for a couple of beers after coming back from a game in Dundee when a guy walking past noticed Watty and called him an 'Orange bastard!' or something else derogatory. I was getting up to confront the idiot when Watty said to let it go, as it happened all the time. I was furious. A nicer guy you couldn't meet.

We only worked together for a few months at Rangers but came up against each other as managers and worked together down at Largs on coaching courses. I had so much respect for the man. I remembered a game Killie had won at Ibrox, and we were passing each other on the way to and from the press conference. He shook my hand and said, 'Well done.' I had responded by saying we had defended for the entire game and had managed to get a goal and hang on, so there was no need for a 'well done'. Walter looked at me and said: 'I paid millions for these guys, you paid nothing for yours, that's why it's a well done.' That was the measure of the man – so extremely humble.

They were great days and, as I reflected on my career, I was proud of what I had achieved and so grateful for what football had given me. When I joined Rangers at 23, I never even had a passport. Now, when I reflect on the years gone by, I've managed to visit just under 70 countries worldwide. If, way back, you had said that, it would have been hard to believe. If there are any aspiring footballers growing up in Easterhouse and reading this book, don't give up on your dreams. Easterhouse won't hold you back. Many footballers have come out of Easterhouse. But don't do what I did, by putting all your eggs in the one basket. Study hard and get an education – football isn't easy.

My life has been one of ups and downs. I would like to thank my first wife, Lorraine, for producing two great kids and helping me throughout my career up until our split. Lorraine's a great woman. Unfortunately, my feelings changed over time and I believed it would be better, for us both, to separate. I know I let her down after being together for all those years but there were plenty of good times. Our two children, Emma and Steven, are a credit to her. They have grown up to be two great people and I'm so proud of them. Emma was the first person in our family to attend university. She's a nurse and, when I called her to tell her I had been diagnosed with cancer in my naval cavity, she told me that was the department she worked in! Emma got married young to Alistair. He's a good lad, likes the occasional beer and his music, and between them they gave us two grandchildren, Callum and Sofia. I don't get to see them very often and, when I do, they have changed so much. I'm sure they see a huge change in me! They are great kids.

Steven is a firefighter; not an easy occupation. I'm glad he's found a job he's passionate about. He married a lovely lady called Leanne, who had a child from a previous marriage, little Rosie, who is a little smiler! I was thrilled when they added to their family with the arrival of little Hannah. She is a wee gem and they make a great team.

It would be remiss of me not to mention my parents. They gave me and my sister, Donna, the best childhood they could afford. When my mates were cycling about on their Raleigh Choppers, I still had a bike, just not as good as theirs, but I kept up. They made sure I always had a ball at my feet – a little plastic one, not expensive, but still a ball. I used to drive Mum crazy because I would ruin my shoes very quickly, as I was predominantly right-footed and the left shoe would get dragged on the ground and quickly wear away.

Football has given me a lot in life but it has also cost me. I missed my children growing up, I moved to Africa to continue my career and missed my grandchildren growing up. Another huge regret is not being with my parents in their old age. Donna was there and I have to thank her for all the support she gave them. I'm not usually an emotional person but I'm in tears typing this, as I missed my parents' final days. I wish I had been there to say goodbye. I know I haven't been a great son or a great father but I sacrificed it all for football. The game robs you of your family time – of time with the kids and your partner. I know I'm not the only one in football who's been in that position. All footballers, coaches and managers have had to sacrifice things for the sake of their careers and I know plenty who have had bereavements on a Friday and still played on a Saturday. It's not selfish; it's an escape for a couple of hours from their grieving.

I was a couple of years in Uganda before I met my second wife, Michelle. She is a fantastic individual – intelligent and career-driven. She has a great personality and is well on her way to achieving her goals. That's why I want to be around to support and encourage her and run around after Saoirse. She is 11 years old now and was born in Uganda but raised a Kenyan. We love her and, thankfully, she gets her brains from her mum. Education is really important here – as it is everywhere, I suppose – but I just didn't realise it growing up in Easterhouse. Coming from Easterhouse, I don't think much is expected from you. My parents never pushed me educationally, which I was fine with, as all I was interested in was football. But now, as I get older, and with my cancer experience, I look back and wonder if I couldn't have achieved more.

I was very fortunate to be a footballer. I've got so many people to thank. My playing career was mediocre, my managerial career was not record-breaking but I really enjoyed meeting great players who went on to have great careers and helping to develop them. Managing was a joy. You never knew, when sitting behind your desk in the morning, what problem you had to deal with that day. There was always something!

And I have to make a special mention for Jim Clark and Gerry McCabe. Without them, I would never have been a manager, and without Cabey, I would never have been a player. Two better guys you couldn't meet.

I try to enjoy life now. Football is over for me. I've been out of the game too long. There's lots of things in the game nowadays which I don't agree with. Plus, I'm 64 as I write this, not a spring chicken. There's lots of young pros becoming coaches and looking for jobs and, by all accounts, it's all about algorithms and all sorts of nonsense. That's how people are getting selected as coaches now, so I think I'm well out of it.

In any case, the whole carry-on with the Kenya national team and trying to get my money has been a bit of a nightmare and I've really lost a lot of my enthusiasm for the game and respect for people who are supposed to be running it. And you look at VAR and all that carry-on … I mean, referees have been getting it wrong from day one, they've made huge mistakes and it was never highlighted back then when I was playing – unless it was Rangers or Celtic! Then it would be highlighted in their favour. I took a break from writing this book to watch Celtic playing away to Kilmarnock. Celtic got a penalty after the referee went over to look at the monitor, while Kilmarnock were denied a penalty, with the referee not even being asked to look again at the incident. That's just wrong.

I find football now very boring. It used to be a 100mph game but now it's so slow and pedantic and pass, pass, pass, pass, pass. If I was a striker nowadays, I don't think I could play. Most of the best passes I received were just a hook over the shoulder from a midfield player, played in behind the defence, and I would run through on to it. Nowadays, it's such a slow build-up that the defender can see you, can see the ball, can anticipate the pass, anticipate the run. It's so easy now for defenders. It would have been difficult for me to play in this modern type of game.

That's disappointing. I don't watch a lot of football now. I start watching games and, before long, I think it's boring, there is nothing happening. I don't sit down to watch a game holding my breath that it is going to be exciting end-to-end stuff. If it's that slow build-up, I'll just switch off.

I don't love football as much as I used to love it when I was a kid, that's for sure. When you start playing football and it's your livelihood, you lose a bit of love for it, or I certainly did, because it becomes a job. You've got to be 100 per cent focused and, even as a coach or a manager, you would go to watch a match but you're not watching the game, you're watching defenders, watching the striker's movement. You're trying to look ahead of the ball to anticipate or make sure players are in the right position before they receive it. So, you don't actually watch the game. You watch the rhythm of play and the style of play – you don't watch the game at all. That certainly doesn't help with the love of the game.

But it's a fantastic game to be involved in. I feel fortunate that I had my life in it, and I enjoyed it, I really did, but nowadays it's not on my list of priorities.

I think of all the people I have played with or against who are no longer with us and realise how lucky I am. Guys like Ally Dawson, known to everyone as Dozy, and John Sludden. I was writing this book when my good mate Jimmy Bone passed away. I was very fortunate to have met up with Jimmy when I was on a trip back to Scotland maybe a month before he passed. He was a great guy, a very good footballer and a great coach. We worked together at Chester, when he came down to assist me. It was short and sweet. The chairman had other plans, but we shared a flat, a few beers and enjoyed ourselves as best we could. Jimmy always made time to come to Glasgow to meet me when I was back in the country. I remember joking with him that they had to have a toilet on that bus for his trip home. I had the pleasure of meeting Jimmy's wife, Shiona, a couple of times in Chester. She's a lovely woman and I'm so sorry for her loss. The word 'legend' gets bandied about too frequently but Jimmy was one, that's for sure – loved by the fans at every club he represented.

I've been away from Scotland for 17 years – five in Uganda, the rest in Kenya. It's home and I enjoy the lifestyle. They love football, especially the English football, although Benni McCarthy has come into the national job and they've got behind him. But once results start going against them again, the fans will turn away from it and they will go back to being big Arsenal, Manchester United, Chelsea and Liverpool fans. These teams are hugely supported in Kenya and in Uganda. If you go into a pub, invariably these teams will be on the telly.

I enjoy Kenya, I enjoy the people and living here but, to be honest, I've been here a bit too long. I'm starting to get itchy feet. Michelle works here and Saoirse goes to school here but I'm getting too old to go to the pub all the time, so I am quite limited in what I can do. The good thing is that you've got different climates and countryside. Go down the coast and it will be really hot and sunny and you're on the Indian Ocean. If you go up north, it will be cold, with mountains and forests to explore. So, you have a real diversity in the country.

Would we ever come back to Scotland? I'd never say never.

I look back at my journey and it has been quite remarkable. When you look back to where it started, surviving Easterhouse – because it was a bit of survival of the fittest. If I thought where it began and that I would end up working in Africa, or even being in Africa, I don't think I could have imagined it. I've met some fantastic people and experienced different cultures, so I know I have been fortunate.

Would I have changed anything or done anything differently? That is hard to say. You can't turn back the clock. Obviously, the injuries I sustained, I would have liked to have avoided – and the broken leg in Oz that was self-inflicted, I could have done without that at that stage of my career. But it happened, I dealt with it. I moved on and still managed to make a career in football. I also made some great pals, both in and out of the game. Guys like Gordon McClelland, who invites me to Parkhead when I am ever home, and Glen Huston, who takes me to Ibrox. And I have to mention my old mate Dom Sullivan – who starred for both Celtic and Aberdeen.

A year after my cancer diagnosis, life had improved and my health was strong enough for a trip back to Scotland. Before we left Kenya, I had to give my doctors my email details in case they needed to get in touch. It was while we were in Scotland that they contacted me to say I had been given the all-clear.

When we read it, Michelle was delighted. She was happier than me. I'd felt as though I was clear anyway. I never got too excited about the news, just as I never got too despondent when I was getting treatment. I try to stay on a level, because you don't know what's waiting around the corner. It could come back tomorrow. It was quite an aggressive type of cancer which can come back anytime, anywhere.

I will get check-ups every few months and if it does come back, I will be on top of it and, hopefully, get it resolved quicker.

I'm happy about it, though, because you do question your mortality. You understand you're not indestructible. I never felt like I was at death's door but I felt terrible and I know I looked really bad.

The last medical procedure I had was getting my nose unblocked. The doctors couldn't do anything for six months, because of the amount of scar tissue I had. They were widening my nostrils and draining them. I'll spare you the details but I have made a mess of a lot of pillows, I assure you! But that was when they found the cancer had gone.

It was a period I don't want to go through again and I hope no one else ever has to. I take five tablets a day now.

The cancer medication has stopped but I still take meds for diabetes and test my blood sugar every day. It's hard to get a balance. Some days, it goes up for no reason. They recommend I eat a lot of salads and vegetables, which aren't things I like. I like pasta and pizza. I over-indulge on one thing and don't eat enough of others.

The aftereffects are that the hearing in my left ear has gone. The radiation centred on that side and it now feels like I've got a seashell taped to my ear. The left side of my face is a bit numb and my taste buds have gone. I've spoken to the Kenyan ENT doctors but they have said my symptoms might not improve. So, I'll maybe have to live with that.

But at least I'm living.